MYTHOGEOGRAPHY

A User's Handbook for Walking Out On The Spectacle (E-Spectacle) and an Account of the Search for the H(urst) Oaks

Narratives, commentaries and interpretations by A. J. Salmon, The Crab Man, Comte de Saint Germain, Wigan P. A. and others

Theoretical and practical sections compiled, edited and annotated by The Central Committees from the documents of the radical and philosophical walking movements (confessions, memoirs, pamphlets, ghosts, various)

T0164223

A Guide to Walking Sideways

Compiled from the diaries, manifestos, notes, prospectuses, records and everyday utopias of the Pedestrian Resistance "there's a difference between knowing the path and walking the path"

Morpheus   The Matrix

MYTHOGEOGRAPHY

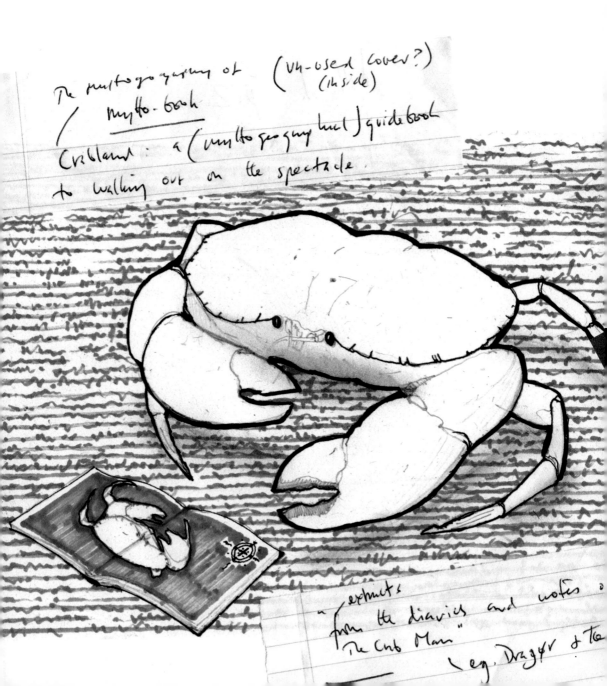

Published in this first edition in 2010 by:
Triarchy Press
Station Offices
Axminster
Devon. EX13 5PF
United Kingdom
+44 (0)1297 631456
info@triarchypress.com
www.triarchypress.com
© Triarchy Press 2010

Design and Art Direction: Anthony Weaver Design
CAD and Pre Press: Terry Weaver

Main text set in Humnst777 Cn BT

Activating Your Book

Before you begin to read your book you will need to activate it. Holding the book in two hands,
lay the spine on a flat surface and then, a few pages at a time, gently open and ease back the
pages from the front and back alternately. This will catalyse the spine. Work through the book
slowly until all the pages have been gently eased. The book is now activated.

CONTENTS

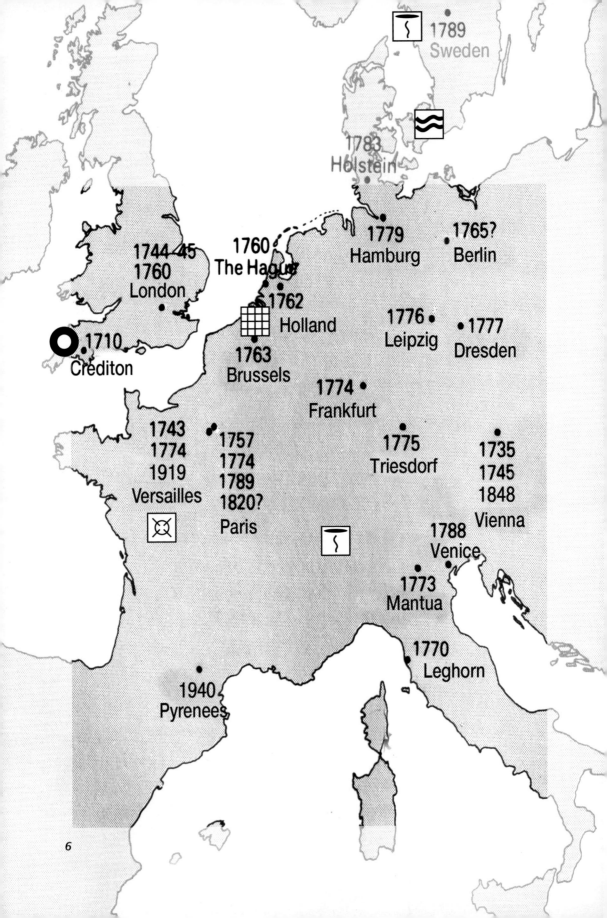

1789
Sweden

1783
Holstein

1779
Hamburg

1765?
Berlin

1760
The Hague

1744-45
1760
London

1762
Holland

1776
Leipzig

1777
Dresden

1710
Crediton

1763
Brussels

1774
Frankfurt

1743
1774
1919
Versailles

1757
1774
1789
1820?
Paris

1775
Triesdorf

1735
1745
1848
Vienna

1788
Venice

1773
Mantua

1770
Leghorn

1940
Pyrenees

6

INTRODUCTION

Why, pray, this nostalgia in everie revolution today? Ancient formes, dustie authorities and demagogges grimed in archaeologie's mukk turn everie effort for Benevolent Futures to sentimental-blistered journies! Democrats clutch mapps of their moderne Home, newe Woman, brave Pavements and Pededucts, while beneath their feet a Constant tangle of briars strangles citie squares!

And do they march like armies on Coming Glory; ranked and mechanic? Nay, these ganggs wander, a zonzo, eyes wide like split fruit, gaping into empty spaces and spidery voids, whispering among themselves about what is Past! What Fort falls to such conspiracyes? Efery Market is encumbered with their pamphlets, charmes, kits, chalks and planchettes! Efery poor-gull is pinned to their pedestrian excursions, when coaches and clippers might speed their Tour, and is strung in the thicket of their obelisks, urnes and Venereal temples! If they wish to begin, let them begin from nought!

Comte de Saint Germain (1790, Salzburg)

(The editors would like to thank The Sisters of Revolutionary Remembrance for permission to print this extract from A Report On Tremors In Europe including the Great Wave at Lisboa of 1755 and The Recent Évènements in Paris.)

Map of sightings of the Comte de Saint Germain

* Publishers' note: The designation 'The Central Committees' is surely a jest? We are confident that the individuals who gave up so much of their time to bring this project almost to completion, before slipping back into the shadows, were not proposing themselves as sole representatives of Mythogeography. Although their only communications with us were indirect ones, in bringing their project to publication we have attempted to follow their intentions wherever possible. As final arbiters, any errors are ours alone.

PREFACE

This book is a guide to thinking and acting through the connected practices of walking, performing and disrupting. Within its covers are many suggestions for organised pleasure-seeking with applications to today's hyper-velocity marketplaces and reconstructive post-politics.

Those familiar with the exhausted history of the arcane will pretty quickly identify the structure of the book (a remnant of previous attempts to secure its publication.) For those who are not; the documents below pretend to be a handbook, but whether their accounts of cells, journeys and tactics are embroidered or unembellished, what is more important is that they are there to be given life by their readers.

Those less than thrilled by literary intrigues are advised to avoid the narratives of A. J. Salmon and The Crab Man. The former is retained for its cautionary value. The latter recounts an often solitary and male affair, whereas the key mythogeographical tool of our ambulatory movement is a group walk (f1), a collective practice of dialogue and anti-wayfinding that can only be realised and theorised on the hoof and in communion with others, and not in any book. Not in any book.

Serious dérivistes should apply themselves only to the notes, toolkits and manifestos that follow.

The Central Committees*, 12.11.07

f:1   The walking group is the cellular model (ffa) for a mass working within the cracks in the pavement. See Martyr, page 203, and The Eye and the Cell, page 163.

f.a   In Second Life one avatar, Muji Zapedzki, has gathered to herself a crowd of account corpses, bodies of abandoned avatars from Help Island.

DISCLAIMER

(The following notes are remnants of previous attempts to collate the documents contained in this book. The editors (see Publishers' note above) decided to retain these notes in order to counter suggestions that they had imposed their own shape on the book's diverse materials.)

Introduction - The various parts of this book are available for reuse and rehashing. All insights and constructions are open to reversal. Despite the "orreries" and "orbits", the contents below are only one approach to the transformation of all things passed through the prism of a vulnerable practice. So be warned: despite its roots in various kinds of gentle resistance, the practice here is susceptible to co-option by adventurous, febrile and risk-taking marketeers as well as by its natural audience among the adrift. The test of its basic patterns will be their success or otherwise under false names, flags, brands and titles.

"If you want to scare someone, leave three snakes in their room. But if you really want to get their attention, put two snakes in their room and leave a note to say that you left three." What follows is a third snake.
(unnamed, 2001)

I wrote all the documents here. The rest is a literary device. But you are the characters.
(unnamed, 7.1.08)

note.

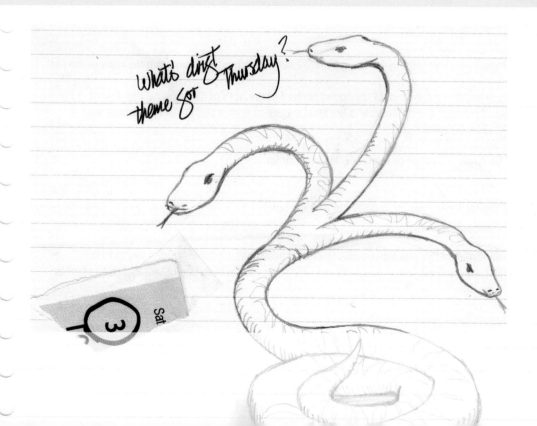

LEGEND

 Crowhurst Computer – when Donald Crowhurst's boat Teignmouth Electron was found abandoned in the Atlantic, rescuers discovered that wires from all the gadgets on the boat ended in a tangle. Crowhurst had never found time to install a computer. This symbol depicts a 'body without organs', a multiplicity without an organising principle.

 Mythogeographical fault-lines – thematic trajectories.

 A McCurdy – a small-time criminal (his final loot was described at the time as "the smallest in the history of train robbery"), Elmer McCurdy was gunned down by a posse in Osage Hills, Oklahoma in 1911, his body embalmed and displayed as "The Bandit Who Wouldn't Give Up". Decades later it was found, under layers of paint, a looming 'dummy' ghoul in a Ghost Train. A McCurdy is something that was one thing, but is now another.

 Pecten - any occult symbol or practice co-opted by business or state (see the Benchmark symbol below, appropriated from pre-Christian worship as the logo of the English state.)

 Plaque Tournante – a junction where decisions change everything, a place of will alone.

 Pylon – a trajectory of ideas or commodities.

 Tripods – an opportunity for reverse archaeology, building the future from the ruins of the past.

 Benchmark – a memorial of the sound emitted at the birth of the universe (the Awen). Benchmarks in the UK indicate a sea level measured from a Datum on the harbour wall at Newlyn, Cornwall.

 Wormhole – a portal to another place, near or far.

 Z worlds – microworlds, a galaxy in a beach hut.

 The Liberated Eye – whenever this symbol appears, allow your viewpoint to slip to the landscape around you. If this is not possible close your eyes for a moment and think of what is ahead.

 Twin Pillars – where god splits.

Grid – a place of homogenisation.

Ik (red & white stick)   Twisting the straight line. "A thing never exists in itself." Daniel Buren

Dragør Ribbons - "I walked down to the Vinterbadere from my hotel in Dragør. These winter bathing huts are accessed from the beach by a narrow wooden walkway. Evening, cold, a spectral blue sky. Suspended above the water, I approached the bone-grey, wooden buildings; utilitarian, unfussy, but tinged with existential menace, like the derelict pier of Carnival of Souls. Overhead a hundred geese flew in articulated ribbons, coherent and chaotic, reaching out and then recoiling, tentacles touching the unfamiliar, a momentous octopus in the sky – with agency, reach and articulation." (From a letter in the records of the C---- P. A., unnamed.)

denotes a footnote.

denotes a footnote to the footnote.

denotes a footnote to the footnote to the footnote.

denotes an endnote, these begin at page 122 after the text of The Crab Man Document, along with various lists, a manifesto, routes and other items. (Reference in the text to these endnotes are indicated as follows: (E-Myth))

'See' denotes a transfer to another section of the text.

All footnotes, glossaries, etc. have been compiled or provided by members of those 'Central Committees' administering the walking cults and ambulatory conspiracies.

All illustrations have been taken from the handbooks and archives of the various cells and their 'tight associations'.

OPENED FILE OF THE DISAPPEARED A. J. SALMON : THE E----- WALKING CULT

note. letter of explanation, please read this note on page 122 before continuing.

In the late 1990s a body was discovered in a courtyard off Cathedral Close in the central part of the city of E----- in the English county of D----. The deceased was dressed in the costume of a stage pirate. It has been suggested that there were parts of two distinct bodies: one of either sex. However, most interested parties understood that the body was complete, the remains of a male, about 60, so I heard. In the double-corpse version the deceased are both much younger (their ages adding up to about 60) and the plot is more romantic. This confusion may have arisen from the site itself: the body was, or the bodies were, found close by an old well, long believed haunted by the ghosts of a nun and priest who leapt into its depths on the public exposure of their private affections. My authority for this (I do not follow the popular mood, being a homebody) is an old "handbook" on the ghosts of the city prefaced by the author's teasing confession that one of its accounts is of her own invention. What I am certain of, however, whether for one body or two, is the coroner's open verdict. This I heard directly from the primary source of all written here; a fellow now sadly departed, both from this city and from my friendship, for a lucrative post in the design department of a vile international commercial organisation. An adventurous and garrulous artist, something silenced him shortly after his telling me this story in the shadows of the afore-mentioned Close and handing over some notes on the subject. The next day I read in the local evening paper of his unexpected change of career.

You must excuse me if I bang on about places (the Close, the well, the courtyard, the old house, the design department, the closed museum, the corner of the square), but place was almost everything to them. And I have come to rather like their sorts of place. Not in a way that they'd approve of, I suspect. But I am now, perhaps, all they have to represent them: a hedonist with few needs.

There are some oblique references in my-friend-the-traitor's notes to the Cathedral Close. But, characteristically, through the prism of another place: the Bishop's Court Quarry on the edge of this city. Here, the strata of the Sandstone in the quarry is laid down in the form of Aeolian dunes, its layers made by the action of the winds, the inclination of their crossbedding azimuths indicating a predominant wind direction, 300 million years ago, of South East to North West. It is a museum of prehistoric wind, hacked out and reappearing in the walls of the Close, alongside bricks of bubbled purple magma ripped from the huge knob on which R----------- Castle once reared proudly, but which is now surrendered to anaemic productions of Shakespeare, hauled out into the open air like tubercular invalids. To build from instability – gale and eruption – is an ideological trick these wandering bishops of the back alleys would have appreciated.

The group had been inspired by an itinerant Professor they heard discourse on migrant mountains passing through at the same rate that their fingernails grew. Although in their notes they interpret this as a sign of both the mutability of place and the potential for a more far-reaching political change, I wonder if the gentle pace was not an equal part of its appeal. They seem to have been, by temperament, conservative, yet somehow circumstances were against them, they were always banging up against the policing of space, provoking anxiety in others by their lack of product and outcome. I am unsure if I would ever have been sympathetic to their project, let alone have ever participated in one of their slow-motion escapades, being, as I am, of an essentially sedentary and reactionary nature, but I do sympathise with them, if only in the luxurious security of hindsight. Even with their miasmic, fabricated existence, if that is all they had. My own reading has led me, unwillingly, into the simpler and more speculative parts of the popular scientific press (an unfortunate necessity nowadays if one is to get anything from the modern gothic novel) and I recognise in their beliefs some of what I have reluctantly read there: of the instability of location, of the behaviour of half-imaginary particles that borrow energy to bring themselves into being and then pay it back (without interest) as they disappear. It is not surprising, then, in a physical world that appeared (if it appeared at all) to them so provisional, that they themselves should be so elusive (perhaps even to themselves).

The hooded statue of Anonymous by Ligeti Miklós in the Városliget City Park, Budapest.

I have learned certain things from their notes: never to take for granted "the site in itself", for example. And, given my predilections, I have rejoiced in their celebration of anomalies: blemishes on their photographs playfully exhibited as swirling spirits or sparkling craft (sadly, none – neither photographs, spirits nor craft, as far as I know – survive), the coincidental linking of their personal lives and the sites they explored, the appearance of simulacra in trees and detritus (the dead lobster that appeared on the path to their landlocked home the day after rehearsals for their performances as underwater characters were abruptly cancelled by the authorities). These sites were always somehow infected by their enthusiasm and wont to wrangle with them.

Indeed, this 'site' that they wrote of in all their documents – if these notes are reliable and not the work of my traitor-friend – is a place that they were not at home in, almost at war with. Its complacency about its own past, blatancy about its appearance, its bathing in visual and extravagant culture, its decoration with secret signs and intervals, its inscription with associations and scenarios, its ordering by urban, agricultural and forestry practice; all these rendered this 'site' a wet battery for driving memories, microscopic wave-formations expressing, in miniscule variations of temperature, fluctuations in the gigantic structures of the cosmos. (*I think the manuscript loses credibility here*). This 'site' they foresaw in the future, flooded with nano-machines, 'smart dust' that would put it under surveillance and report all its movements and temperature signatures, that would capture an existence transferable to maps, memories, advertising, settings for TV dramas, security areas, and their most hated things: identities.

I have been unable to discover their names or appearances.

The only pictorial element among the notes was a postcard of the Városliget City Park in Budapest, prominently featuring the hooded statue by Ligeti Miklós of the monk Anonymous. On the reverse of this card, written in a minute and barely discernible hand, is this:

> *With what justification, if any, can we say: "myths are as present on or stored up in the landscape as in individuals' minds?"*

> *Even in the classical physical world there is action at a distance: gravity, and we may be able to use its variability as a language to communicate with other universes through the multi-dimensional membrane to which our universe precariously adheres.*

> *The borders of the body include these structures. The flow of energy to and from the body, whatever negotiates between the organism and its environment = the body. Our organism's 'border' is not a thing, but a process, "conferring upon the organism a persistence that endures as long as its boundary can adaptively modify the flows of energy and matter."*

I have been unable to find a source (or sources) for these quotations (apologies to the author or authors), but I can confidently say, given extensive knowledge of both, that nothing here has been taken from the works of either H.P. Lovecraft or P.G. Wodehouse. The whole passage may, of course, be an invention, quotations and all. My former friend was quite capable of spending a whole afternoon in a public library. His best porcelain pieces were fired in bile.

Unfortunately, I have been unable to discover the number of people involved. It may simply have been a conspiracy between the two individuals discovered (if two there were); what else is necessary if there is a writer and a reader? Or it may have been an imaginary movement existing only in the older man's mind; a conspiracy between him and his city, eluding them both. Only the walking has meaning (and I do as little of that as possible). All their notes, their examples, their blessed 'tool kits' have come to nothing. Their walking, however, alone of all their activities, ambles on. (Unless there is some secret part of this whole thing. But I must restrain my gothic tendencies.)

I am not impartial. I confess to being affected by the circumstances under which I received these notes. For my former friend had taken me, that afternoon, to the cellar of The Well House pub, with its two voids: a well (not the haunted one) and a mediaeval garde-de-robe, mouth and anus in the same cool, stone enclosure. (f2) Here, my friend, drunk by now, presented me with the notes before the exhibited bones of a woman, to all appearances forced by a subterranean movement of earth from the cathedral burial grounds, under the roadway, through the cellar wall, to be exhibited in a glass case captioned: "Birth Is The First Step Unto Death." I have no idea if I was meant to read into these words an epigram for his scribbled history of the walking cult, or if they were part of his evasive display under cover of which he was departing for lesser work. Perhaps, by then, he no longer knew the difference.

The proximity of anus and mouth mirrors the feedback of 'situation' and 'condition'. See The Significance of Walking, page 198.

To say one is haunted by a memory is to deploy a cliché; but it is the same to regard memories as spectral and insubstantial. A late, but noted photographer of atrocities was unable to "demolish the memory" of a skeletal albino child delicately licking a lozenge of barley sugar. This child reappears in a book I have read recently (in the mistaken belief that it represented a new generation of horror story) as an architectural force; tunnelling an elastic hallway deep into a home, burrowing staircases down miles deep. (f3) The temptation to re-imagine this mutant architecture as 'spectral' persists, as the author's sister sings on her album Haunted, "one look at the ghost before I'm going to make it leave". But it is at our peril that we fail to understand that in "ghost" we are talking not about some human past, but the inanimate present, the concrete locus that we cannot demolish intellectually, exorcise or fictionalise as horror stories.

See also The Museum Vaults by Marc-Antoine Mathieu and Glacial Period by Nicolas De Crécy

So when I say that I am haunted by the circumstances of my receipt of these notes you will understand that I am not referring to a gothic conceit, but rather to the continuing presence all about me of such places as are now no longer themselves, that are beside themselves. As I am, now, beside myself. Ye gods, the hand scratching at the door… yeeek, yeeek….screeeee… (ha ha).

However, it was not the unpleasant consequences of my reading that led me to re-read the notes more closely. Rather, that I heard from a second source, (f4) someone I had not hitherto connected to these affairs, that the corpse or corpses were not only decked in pirate costume, but that forensic evidence suggested they had been forcibly dressed.

A fragment of newsprint from this second source – mutilated by much folding and frotting in a back pocket – part of the report from the coroner's court, documented a submission by a representative of 'The Dental Association' (misprinted as 'The Denial Association'). Searching relentlessly through the thumbed, smudged, snipped and mutilated back copies in the reference section of the public lending library, no doubt (ironically) the vandalous resource of my second source, I may have missed, by dint of fatigue, the article I was looking for, though I did discover some references to the Close as a place of "previous tragic and strange events" at the murder trial of a character with the street name of Aslan; a laundry deliverer to the nearby C------- Hotel told the court that "(at night) there was always something going on" in the Close, but would not give examples. In those daytime hours during which I was familiar with its commerce, the Close had long returned to the character of a desirable tourist destination, the site chosen by the stage manager Bram Stoker for the offices of Count Dracula's property conveyancer.

It now seems certain that this "second source" is the individual who appears in the main body of this book as 'The Crab Man'. In some ways as sedentary as A. J. Salmon, this crustacean underwent a (suspiciously ardent) conversion to the virtues of the ambulant and adventurous. It is clear from his document below that the 'Crab' is rather more than the simple researcher he sometimes represents himself to be, and rather less than the complex exemplary that he hopes he is. By all accounts, the methods and portfolio here have been lifted directly from the records of the unknown walkers described in the Salmon document. However, the Crab Man document that now follows constitutes the main part of this book, with a number of glosses and notes (and a few appendices) at its conclusion. The Salmon document will be concluded as one of these appendices. The justification for this unconventional violence to the organisation of the book rests on this alone: that the Crab Man's manuscript is entirely derivative of the work of others. Like a translucent Ghost Crab he possesses no substance of his own, but only exists in what he displaces. It is thus possible to trace the fluid shape of others, and betters, who went before and came after him: the modesty of his project is entirely authentic. It is to this displacement, most vividly available in the notes and appendices, that we point you now. (Editors' note)

The Opened file of the disappeared A. J. Salmon continues at page 220.

f.4

f.c

THE CRAB MAN DOCUMENT

"I began my journey in the interest of the English oak at about half past nine on the morning of Monday, the 26th of March... I trudged through a maze of mean streets, it began to rain... I made haste to the centre of the city... The street passing L------ Road Station turns to the left, skirts A------- Green and runs southwards ... the most direct from M----------- to the D------------- Hills..."

It begins in that city of M ---------, in a stained room, walls dirtied with tobacco smoke, lit sickly by yellow lamps. The paint on the sills is broken and the rectangular prism of the room's frame (f5) sways to the blows of bass beats from a club somewhere below.

The one remaining decoration in the room is a soiled, cream frame that has lost its print, privileging a rectangle of ribbed, brown cardboard. When the Crab Man stares into this arid expanse, he feels a desert nervousness, an uncertainty trembling somewhere between void and industrial corrugation, and is calmed by the combination of field and abstraction.

f.5

Dérivistes should always walk with the slippery script of a pattern of patterns playing in the Scala of their skulls. By wandering among the diaphanous shadows of such spectral theatres of science, they will see the bumps and grindedness of the everyday spectacle set in dramatic motion.

Such walkers can make meditative ropes from historical and hysterical sands. The resulting personal topologies endure the edge of chaos, and serve as constant companions to their explorations.

An example of such historical/ideological patterning is the Southern coastline of the English county of Devon from Sidmouth to Torbay, where geological, architectural and social features interweave with intellectual narrative.

A sinew of eccentric materialism links the Sidmouth grave of John Fleming, founder of Creationism, inventor of the diode and the right-hand rule used by every electrician in the world, then Lockyer's observatory where the second phase of astro-archaeology begins, the Starcross birthplace of William Kingdon Clifford, discoverer of space's curvature 50 years before Einstein and deviser of 'Clifford Algebra' essential for quantum computations, Babbage at Teignmouth inventing the computer, the laboratory of Henry Forbes Julien, gold refiner and colonialism's alchemist, at the Ness (J.K. Rowling claims in the first of her Harry Potter novels that Nicolas Flamel died, aged 666, in Devon; Julien disappeared with the Titanic), the self-designed and never-enjoyed retirement home of I.K. Brunel at Watcombe (in 2006, the 200th anniversary of Brunel's birth, Devon was flooded with Brunel impersonators - comic Brunels, serious Brunels, Brunels on stilts – and then, like 1989 for Lenin impersonators, it was suddenly all over, where did they go?), in Torquay a tank under the eaves of the home of William Froude, where a model navy on miniature waves was the experimental origin of the dimensionless Froude Number and the Froude Law of Steamship Comparison, resonant for mathematical biologists and the

likes of William D'Arcy Thompson, (here the serpent of sand swallows its own gritty tail) the patterns of patterns (see Patterns of Patterns, page 174) interweaving with the crazed swerves of the paranoid and brakeless cyclist Oliver Heaviside careening through Paignton, second only to Maxwell in electromagnetism, Heaviside of the Layer, sensing science's ever-closer association of animate and inanimate, the living with the dead.

Then other paths interweave with the first; a set of Devil's Footprints, a trail of strangely shaped marks in the snow leading from door to door and over rooftops, appearing on the night of the 8-9th February, 1855, stretching from somewhere around Exmouth, then leaping the Exe and down the coast, Starcross, Dawlish and Teignmouth to Torbay, before cutting inland. At Dawlish a party of armed residents set out to hunt the Devil, while elsewhere folk sought kangaroos and ducks wearing horseshoes. Later, shades of Roswell, 'researchers' speculated on a failing experimental balloon released by the Navy at Devonport, blown off course and bumping through gardens and across roofs. Or did the Devil really skip across Devon that night collecting Victorian science for his 20th Century of bombs, atomic labs, reactors, barbed wire, computed death camps, motors, grinders, optic fibres, gold teeth and mother boards?

These threads are re-woven by Bron Fane (nom de plume of the Fortean and Reverend Lionel Fanthorpe) in one of his trash-erudite novels for pulp publishers Badger Books, UFO 517 (1960):

"Zelby consulted the dials, then shook his head. 'We've come forward very little..... 1855 even.'

... The disc ship spun like a gigantic coin flipped by a gambling gargantuan. The deadly silver streaks continued to flash past. Val and La Noire clung to Elspeth, and hung on to the saucer's rim fittings...... There was a rift in the snow clouds, and as Zelby dived low again to evade the withering fire of his pursuers the South Devon countryside opened out like a great white and silver panorama... Topsham, Lympstone, Exmouth, Dawlish and Teignmouth...

'Oh, I know the story! Of course!' said Elspeth. 'The mysterious trail that appeared overnight!'

'Now we know what caused it,' said Val. 'Those pencil weapons of the Negons...'

There was a thoughtful silence, and La Noire said, 'I'll make some coffee.'"

The Sun newspaper reported the Footprints' reappearance in Devon in March 2009.

The threads are twisted again: police staking out a suicidal British Intelligence Officer in the penultimate house on the Dawlish prom for A Perfect Spy, Arthur Askey chases his hat down the track outside Teignmouth in The Ghost Train (solution to the mystery: West Country Bolsheviks), and Norman Wisdom deconstructing that town for a bus chase in

Press For Time. Echoing C.L.R. James's belief that the artillery fire of the Second World War was first heard in genteel English 'tea shoppes', the ripples of communist revolution and Stalinist reaction are played out as light-hearted seaside tragedies, modernist 'permissiveness' in tawdry, provincial and municipal fragmentation, topless waitresses in Teignmouth, striptease pantos at Exmouth, black magic aboard the Electron. Cultural history is spatialised. And miniaturised.

Knowledgeable groups of drifters or dérivistes, Mobile Machinoeki and Fabulous Walkers, then re-weave the whole thing as they explore and re-explore this coastline and its post-colonial, cultural and Fortean entrepôts, subjecting them to their subjective associations.

The Crab Man (ffa) walks and performs these threads repeatedly, weaving his own autobiography (ffi) into the skein, transforming these unpromising spaces from faded and undignified resorts to cryptic texts, landscapes in the form of treasure maps that identify the affordance of their sites, where $X = m^2(ythogeography)$ then "X" marks the multiplicity of patterns and histories, locating, through a symbolist language, those tipping points and zones of satellite capture, where small cultural interventions can still destabilise existing orbits of meaning, creating fluid stages ('situations') for re-making living. Everything in this book is a toolkit for performing this magic, for raising 'situations' in places of obscurity, for enabling everyone to use their claws; bringing to an end, to his great relief, the burden of the 'Crab Man' and his shell.

The Crab Man is so named for scuttling sideways, off the linear 'a to b'.
See also E-The Crab Man.)
See Walking, Writing and Performance, ed. Roberta Mock, (Bristol: Intellect, 2009) and Autobiography and Performance, Deirdre Heddon, (Basingstoke: Palgrave Macmillan, 2008).

All through the night the crustacean stirs, sleeplessly, under the unremarkable covers, imagining the bodies of the clubbers shifting below. He dreams fitfully of people. Of one he must follow, long dead, and others he must meet who are psychogeographers. The morning approaches sluggishly. He has a journey to complete, an unfamiliarly functional task; some of those he dreams of are relying on his cracked exterior to see it through.

Down the long hours of the dull bass night The Crab is comforted by a causeless fear he feels whenever he looks towards the dread cardboard space (f6) within the empty frame.

In the morning he rises and opens The Book (E-Book), cupping its sellotaped spine in one numb, clawed hand, and reading for the umpteenth time the words of the Engineer (E-H----):

"After long consideration I began my journey in the interest of the English oak (f7) at about half past nine on the morning of Monday, the 26th of March, in the year 19---- ..."

With his other hand The Crab rubs ointment into his knee. (f8) "You should be fine," the Doctor had said, typing out a prescription for tablets and gel: "don't jump, don't run and don't carry a heavy rucksack" – but anxiety is heavier.

f.6 *see Taxonomy of Spaces, page 203.*

f.7 *Government leaflets rant against "alien invaders" like Himalayan Balsam or Japanese Knotweed. National institutions organise "Rhodi-bashing" parties with their sinister echoes of violence against immigrants, but one invader somehow avoids all their attentions: a pernicious incomer that has exceeded all the other invaders in the depth of its infiltration into the British landscape and psyche, landing first in the West Country, then edging north and east, its advance averaging 150 metres per annum, sustaining itself for hundreds of years wherever it puts down roots: the English Oak, quercus robur.*

f.8 *The Crab had injured his leg while walking for a day with He Yun Chang, a Chinese performance artist. Chang was walking around the edges of Britain carrying a considerable rock, collected from the beach at Boulmer in Northumberland in September 2006, returning the same rock to the same beach four months later. There is an exclusiveness in such walking. Other examples are Richard Long's and Hamish Fulton's exceptionalist walks, solo and gargantuan.(ffi) A more democratic model for extreme walking might be Franko B's slow walk I Miss You, where he, movingly, in woozy vulnerability and painted white, walks on a canvas catwalk, blood gently dripping from catheters in his arms, so that no one else need do such a thing again. (See E - The Voyage of Donald Crowhurst and The Significance of Walking, page 198.) Or a young and destitute Norman Wisdom walking from London to South Wales with another boy; on arrival at his friend's home town, the boy sprints off, leaving Norman alone, to "begin from nought".*

ffi. *"Mile averages are a curse. So are definite programmes." The Gentle Art of Tramping, Stephen Graham (1929)*

The Book tells the story of a M---------- engineer named C------ H----, alarmed at the deaths of oak trees choked in industrial soot, who set off on a journey to plant acorns. He had had a vision: of a Britain "denuded of trees" (E-Hermeneutics of Fear), a wasteland poisoned by the mills and factories he had helped to build. And so, almost a century before the Crab Man, he had ventured forth in search of a better, more natural, more sustainable Britain, his pockets filled with acorns, determined to put something back. And now the Crab Man was to follow C------ H----'s 200 mile route, to see if any survived of C------ H----'s almost century-old plantings.

On that first morning of his walk, full of potato cake and romanticism, the Crab Man had made his way from the hotel's canteen-like breakfast room, dazzled by the tables of men in hi-viz jackets; it was a short walk to the concourse of the city's main railway station, the local radio station's phone-in ringing in his ears: "the most memorable TV adverts of all time".   All time?

He passed the statue of a prime minister who had once urged everyone to "cut down a tree for Progress" (f9).

The Crab had been preparing for seven years for this moment, practising different kinds of walking, inspired by theatre on mountains (f10), in boats (f11), in derelict hotels (f12) and under the sea (f13). He had researched the thoughts of explorers of the ordinary streets, botanists of the asphalt, rediscoverers of the abandoned (E-List of Exemplary Ambulatory Explorers). He had studied geography, theories of space, critical philosophies, military theory and the history of art. He had trained himself in the craft of making connections. He saw forms in landscapes and architectures, in the leafiest glade he could sense the marks of power. Despite his shell he was sensitised to the slow drift of the earth's crust and the rushing commerce of ideas. He was a mythogeographer. (f14)

But all this might come to nothing because of a bad knee.

Anxious to get going, he'd arrived too early and decided on a 'pre-journey journey', wandering through an arch between two shops at the top of the station ramp. In a wide car park expanse of early Saturday morning a middle-aged Asian man in a charity shop suit was being questioned by two police. The Crab ambled over, a witness; an ethical role he had learned from contemporary theatre. Yesterday, just a few yards from the car park, looking for somewhere to eat, he had come across several uniformed men swarming on a young black man. "My head, my head, my head, my head, my head!" the man was shouting as they held him down in the gutter. "My head!" mocked a passer-by. The uniforms had shone with logos the Crab Man usually associated with groceries.

Until he had bought his OS maps he hadn't realised how close he would pass to Grantham.

The man in the hand-me-down suit was waving a crumpled identity paper.

"This – where they kicked me." The man points between his eyebrows.

There is something disconnected about the way the man moves and speaks. The Crab senses that this kicking took place far away, with consequences that have followed him.

The Crab interrupts to ask one of the policemen for directions. "Down the L…. Road…" says the policeman, swivelling his hand.

The same left turn at the station Hurst took almost one hundred years before.

"Hello! Hello, P---------! Hi, J----! Hi, hi! Good to see you! Really good to see you!! How was the train up from Crewe? Great! Brilliant to see you! We're just waiting for A----. What time is it?

Hold on… this… Excuse me, are you looking for… A---! Hi, good to meet you after all the emails! This is P---------, and this is J---! Guys, this is A---. Well, we're all here. Shall we just get going?"

f:9 William Gladstone.

f:10 Francis Alÿs, When Faith Moves Mountains.

f:11 Wrights & Sites, Pilot Navigation.

f:12 Geraldine Pilgrim, Two Hotels.

f:13 Jun Nguyen-Hatsushiba, Memorial Project Nha Trang, Vietnam: Towards the Complex – For the Courageous, the Curious, and the Cowards.

f:14 See The Mythogeographical Manifesto, page 113.

Consulting The Book, just to be sure, then turning to the left: three psychogeographers (f15) and a crustacean step out. And then they stop. Ten paces from the turn they find an immediately fascinating place. Already the texture of the city is leaping out at them.

A disc sunk into the ground, engraved with exhortations to travellers – "confused by directions, subject to regulations …observe your inclination, toward whatever destination, this is your passage through time" – it's a piece of public art, forgotten now, two light-strips sunk in concrete run to dull walls, and yet… pulling aside a curtain of ivy, dull gun-metal faces peep, twisted either in despair or by the artist's mimetic incompetence. Tearing and cutting at the creepers reveals a lost bas relief of footprints, grinning heads and brassy Coke cans; poorly done, decay and undergrowth have made it dark and pessimistic, the vibrant ordinariness it is meant to celebrate is frozen like Hans Solo after the rebellion's defeat, gloomy and morbid (f16) – art, the everyday, the city and its energy, all grabbed round the throat by Time. Alleluia, they are off! Shit turns to gold. (f17) They like it, and march on.

Along the "direct route" to the hills they cut a slice through an inner city mix of wasteland and workshop, beached-whale ruins and reticent estates, retail units shaped like stunted temples and Hand Car Washes returning high-tech industrial trainees to a labour intensive economic banditry. One of the psychogeographers tells of earth tremors in the city brought on by redevelopment.

The Crab and friends visit a car boot sale, held among the thick stumps of a recently cleared urban copse, but they can find nothing distinctive or eccentric; these are the archaeological remains of a processed culture. Nothing stands out. Until they find a huge erratic to admire in A------ Park, brought here by glaciers. (f18). In the doorway of an old cinema (E - Cinema), P----- sees C----- H----'s flâneur, looking in every direction and adding them up to nothing.

Psychogeographers are students of the art of the dérive. A dérive is an attempt at the analysis of the totality of everyday life, by a sensuous movement through space. A participant may be called a "dériviste" or "drifter". See The Handbook of Drifting, page 118.

f.15

The Empire Strikes Back (dir. Irvin Kershner).

f.16

There has recently been a campaign for the removal of redundant public art. But, of course, this is just when public art becomes interesting. 'Public' is mostly a subjectivity imposed, until redundancy and decay disperses it; in the case of The Withy Man (aka The Willow Man), sited by the M5 in Somerset, only after an arsonist had transformed the work into public bones of steel did it achieve a public quality through withy rejuvenation.

f.17

See For Space, Doreen Massey (London: Sage Publications, 2005), pages 130-162.

f.18

The psychogeographers pass the archetypal English scene – Texaco, Blockbuster, KFC – add living room, car and hot water, then stir. 'Bren's Café (and Lunatic Asylum)'. In the cemetery at H----, they find a freemason's headstone; the compasses and square have crumbled away, but the two pillars are still intact, symbols of conflicting natures, awaiting reconciliation. (f19)

In the market place at H---- close to the general practice of the UK's most prolific serial killer, a monument to violent democrats, only one of their demands unfulfilled: annual elections to Parliament. Almost 200 miles later the Crab Man will realise that this is the last monument-to-change (f20) that he has seen, unless he counts The Saracen's Head. (f21)

Again and again the Crab would see the symbolic frame of the twin pillars. In the remnants of a road sign with the sign part blown off, in salt and pepper pots on the window shelf of a pub, or in his recollection of the silver portal in Phantasm. Not that these constitute portals to other places, but rather that they express the contradiction within the portal, a gateway not to an 'other', but to the tensions always present in the monolith itself. For Freemasonry the two pillars represent the pillars Jachin and Boaz made by Hiram of Tyre for Solomon, setting one on either side of the entrance to the Temple, in commemoration of the pillar of cloud by day and the pillar of fire by night that in turn guided the Israelites in their forty years' wanderings in the wilderness: two manifestations of the one god. So why two pillars for one deity? Suffice to say that in earlier civilisations the gods went in pairs, male and female. It is the splitting of the divine. The twin pillars are usually hollow, constituting an archive or memory. In the correct proportions it is possible to mentally unfold the surface or envelope of such a pillar into the shape of a square, thus a pillar (in its cross-section and then in its surface) contains both the circle of the divine (conceptual) and the square of the world (material).

f.19

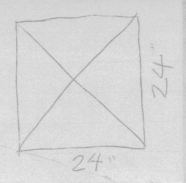

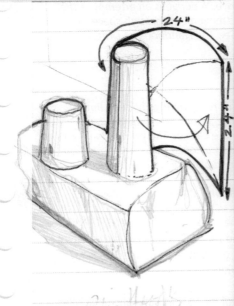

f.20 *It is time to take back our right to monuments; those blind sentinels and anonymous stone butchers that commemorate irrelevance in urban nights. We should embrace those living deaths, celebrate their voracious persistence to no end. We should misplace monumental objects in city streets; steel chests containing items of non-worship such as surgical prostheses, bottles for donated blood, sticks and tops, maps shaped like giant broken haircombs, stone carpets. While transient interventions are both democratic and libertarian, the monumental requires acts of responsibility to the future.*

f.21c *Who is this Saracen? See page 76.*

Then fields give way to suburbs – in a tiny close, residents bid the remaining two walkers cheery hellos. A--- and the Crab Man take a turn past castles of privacy strung along a busy road. Then, it's time for A--- to catch his bus home (E-Disruption) and for the Crab Man to find his night's accommodation on the far side of a blood-on-the-pavement council estate, where two monosyllabic lads are kicking a ball. "Uh? Uh?" They have never heard of Watermeetings Barn; it's a minute's walk away. The Crab Man feels their outrage at his disturbing their private space (in the middle of the road), transgressing their bubble, soiling their invisible living room, flagging down their translucent 'wheels'.

He falls asleep to the soothing clunk of billiard balls in the games room below, and the answers of a contestant called Phil Smith on Who Wants To Be A Millionaire, feeling pleased with himself and his knee. Tomorrow it and he must get over Kinder Scout.

To N------- B------

He leaves the luxuriously converted barn, passing a poster of slaughtered rapper 2-Pac on the breakfast room door, and in five minutes is chatting with a friendly farmer. It might have been at this farm, near C----------, that C------ H---- had stayed as he passed through, a migrant mountain on his way to the Peaks.

The Book was full of clues to where H----'s oaks might be.

"…near C--------" it says in The Book. H---- wrote that he had persuaded his host to plant acorns on the farm. But this farmer doesn't know if they would have put up guests a hundred years before, or anything about the origins of the oaks on his land, so the Crab Man continues along the public footpath through the farm, watching the newborn lambs play, wondering at the trees on the distant sides of fields, and follows the river to a road bending through C--------, past the old mill, where, among the companies now based there is Vico Engineering.

Giambattista Vico was the great Neapolitan philosopher of forests. (f22) The Crab Man remembers a conversation with his statue in the Chiaia neighbourhood of Naples. Vico wrote his own history of civilisation. It starts after the Flood with solitary giants hidden from sun and sky by the great canopy of the all encompassing forest. There were no relationships in this forest; sex was a random and violent event when two met by chance, the dead were left unburied… but, one day, lightning flashed above the branches!! The giants, working together for the first time, made a clearing in the forest, to see where the fire had come from, but the sky was empty and so concepts grew in the place of an explanation, ideas about invisible things; soon there were principles and theories. The giants settled in their clearing. Those who had been having sex when the lightning struck now regarded their act as a sacred one and consecrated it in primitive marriage ceremonies. The dead were gathered together and buried and their graves marked with wooden posts; the first human community literally rooted itself in the soil.

"But if the people are rotting in that ultimate civil disease (cynicism) and cannot agree on *a monarch from within… providence decrees that, through obstinate factions and civil wars, they shall turn their cities into forests and the forests into dens and lairs of men."*
The New Science, Giambattista Vico

The Crab Man puffs as he climbs the narrative of Vico's fanciful history. He feels as though he has already walked and thought a book's worth of experience.

Behind a hedgerow the sight of something familiar catches his eye. He climbs a brambled and rusty metal fence. In the grass lie a pair of bent and damaged ranging rods – the red and white poles that mapmakers and archaeologists use. The Crab Man laughs aloud, for on his tours and for his exhibitions he has often brandished intentionally crooked ranging rods, painted red and white in his children's poster paints, his clumsy way of signalling that sometimes things need to be ruled by wonky measures. His own joke has been waiting for him by the roadside.

Curling up through a gentle valley now, sheep and cattle in the fields – Ruff! Ruff! – farm buildings up ahead – ruff! – dog barking … ruff, ruff! Ruff, ruff! Couple of dogs now – hoooowwwl! Ruff! Howwwl! Ruffruffruffruffruffruff! What the hell is that!! A whole city of dogs howling and screaming!!! The Crab Man prepares to leg it the moment the hell pack appears! Turns out to be a kennels.

He joins a bridleway, admiring intrepid frog spawn in a Landrover track, then Robin Hood's Dicking Rods, two ancient pillars of stone – menhirs – reminders that architecture began not with settlements, despite Vico, but with the marking of those lonely, brutal, random journeys. Beside the Rods are two broken plastic pipes, 'accidental menhirs', part of the Crab Man's taxonomy of space; heaven and earth are twice as far apart here. And what are "dicking rods" anyway? Bent measures?

"Are you going far?" he asks a woman walker, obliging her to ask him the same question. She points him to Burnt Hill.

Where the path meets a busy road, a purple-faced man gets, wheezily, out of a van labelled: 'Symonds Gym, Fighting Fit'.

Whooooosh! Cars pass at speed - 60 or 70 mph – it is a narrow road, no pavement. (See The Spectacle, page 138.) The Crab Man thinks of those lonely giants in Vico's forest wandering beneath their dark screens. Community on the road is a random event. In the litter-filled verge, among the condoms and plastic bottles, something catches his eye. Littering is not thoughtless, it is a planned slow burn of advertising. The something is a notice from a company clawing back some pay mistakenly given under terms negotiated by the GMB union. Among the atomisation of everything, a reluctant anti-fragment of a collective life. Whoosh! Whoosh! The crustacean gets off the road as soon as he can, climbs a stile and begins the straight rising path up Burnt Hill. For the first time he is truly leaving things behind, dropping his burdens, facing something, as the sound of traffic is drowned by the rising wind.

Two miles of straight path.

"Is individualism so bad? Maybe we are returning to an older time: B.V. (Before-Vico). And community's a temporary thing that's run its course, and that's OK."

The Crab Man, like C----- H----, has left his family for a while. "Are we, wandering souls of the 21st century, our own best hope?" he wonders to himself.

"The National Trust is managing this habitat so visitors can enjoy forever the sights and sounds of this special place."

'Forever'?

Yesterday, on a disused building, the Crab had seen the legend "Semper fidelis" – "always faithful". On another: "Always Ready". That radio DJ on "the most memorable TV adverts of all time"…

By the path are marks of another measure of time, a rusting sheet of metal wing, the bleached remnants of an aeroplane engine, the wreckage of forever plunging through time. The peat under the Crab's feet shudders and he walks on quickly. The wind howls, roaring into submission all other sounds. The path, paved with slabs, Bunyanesque, is a stone age strip of celluloid, a long tracking shot. He follows a lone walker far ahead, who disappears.

"Why am I here? What am I really doing?"

Burnt Hill, then Mill Hill, and then he reaches the base for the final clamber to the K------ Scout plateau, crossing the route of the Mass Trespass of 1932. Far below is a shivering plane of reservoir waters and he thinks of the Professor of Geography because he knows she will hate the mythologising and idealising of landscape that he's enacting in his head, reading the reservoir in Euclidean terms.

"But I'm sorry, Professor, I can't help adding these elements of romanticism and abstraction to your materialist and mobile understanding of space. Not because I believe they're there, but because they're the legacy of ideas I've inherited, the ghostly travelling companions of traditional walkers like me, things I have to take responsibility for, even as I try to dispel them, or re-place them."

Sadly the Professor is in Finland today, lecturing; in her email she describes herself walking exactly between H---- and the Crab, 50 years after H----, 50 years before Crab, a girl in plaits climbing M-- Tor and K----- Scout with her family in the '50s.

The Crab drinks from his water bottle. There's little left and what there is tastes of plastic.

The Professor is down to lecture on the 12th in N-----------; maybe he can get there. He, unthinkingly, rubs his left knee as if that is where the future is. In her honour he looks again at the place, and imagines it as one of trajectories, a place still being made. He feels the slow journey of the tectonic plates deep beneath him, the management "forever", the pedestrian motorway traffic of the P------- Way, the historic mass trespass, Jewish walkers singled out for arrest on their return to H------, at the trial the judge commenting on their "foreign sounding names", but the sentences of 2 to 6 months' jail backfiring, uniting conservative ramblers with the radicals. In 1949 K------ Scout was effectively nationalised – a monument to that collective principle walked into this mountain by mechanics and piece workers and engineers.

The Crab, breathless, is on the top now.

H----- had despaired up here. He had wanted to know who he was. But the Crab enjoys the desolation; the broken rock faces and the piles of boulders, the featureless expanses of grey-brown peat and the dry beaches of crystal-sparkling sand. He savours his gothic sensibility, cringing in the face of the massiveness of everything, jumping at the sight of unforgiving heads of stone, plunging up to his knees in Sloughs of Despond, lost in alien landscapes, feeling his own fragmentation, his own particularity, forced to think of the many tiny forces that construct his person, all at the mercy of fields. But these intellectual indulgences are tempting fate, and, thanks partly to some ludicrous encouragement and shoddy directions, and partly to his following ideas rather than reading contours, he is still walking two hours after passing the trig point on the top, missing the obvious descent at G-------------- Clough.

Following the advice of an affable gent with a cut glass accent, who licks his lips at the thought of the beer the Crab "will soon be enjoying", he can't get down from the mountain! Two, three times he tries to descend, paths little better than screes, but his left knee is soon screaming. He climbs back to the main path, walks on and on, feeling trapped. Lured. Misled. Caught by his own art. "Twenty minutes to E----" someone had said back there, an hour and a half ago, 'twenty minutes' in the sense, of that you are twenty minutes from the end of Twilight of the Gods when you hear the opening bars of Das Rheingold! He is shaking now. He can see E----, but the more he tries to get at it the further it shrinks from him.

"Are these real paths?"

And he descends again…

"Ahh. Ahhh! Ahhh!"

And just as… "ow!" … just as he thinks he's finished, done for, the whole mission unaccomplished, the path eases, the slope flattens, the pain lessens. He is going to make it!

But then the path becomes steps. Worse than jolting scree. Painfully, he eases himself down step by step. And then more steps, steeper steps. Gingerly now, he takes them one at a time. Waiting for the jolt that's the cataclysmic last. But then there are only a few left, down to the bridge and up again, and then it's pub, pub, pub!! His knees newborn.

Half an hour, two pints and a plate of Roast Beef and Y--------- pudding later and he's still trembling. It's been nine hours solid walking, two and a half hours in the Twilight Zone, no food, not enough water, high winds roaring like Hyde Road traffic. An April Foolishness. When a woman asks him if she can "pinch that chair" his attempt to make a joke about it not mattering as it "h... h ... has no central n... n... nervous system" is so completely fluffed she grabs the chair away in frustration.

On the summit, around the trig, he had looked for some stunted residue of the "fruitless seed" H----- had planted there. Nothing. He was burnt from the sun, his two for the price of one, something-for-nothing, sunspray lost. Everything was a lesson today. His detached, aesthetic thrill at the desolation had been challenged; too conceptual, unconnected, immaterial... "what am I?" sneering in his head.

With other walkers on the P------ Way there was barely a "hi" or a "hiyah" exchanged, they were hardly less isolated than the drivers on the Hyde Road. All in their regulation kits. Ahead of him at Downfall, he had seen a group all in red and his inner pomposity had reached new heights – "bloody management bonding!" Turned out they were the mountain rescue. He saw the stretcher. "Doing an exercise?" "No, there's a casualty round there."

A few minutes later and further on, unnecessarily no doubt, he waved the helicopter towards the injured walker. At last he'd become a signpost. Trying to reconnect with what this journey might be about. To be something other than himself.

A bull in a field puts an extra half a mile on the journey from pub to Youth Hostel at N------ B-------, where he can't relax in the brutal lounge, packed with forbidding sofas, lit like a prison. Outside, a huge moon swings between tall trees. He stands in the drying room waiting for his trousers to finish their tumbling.

There was a moment up there, on his final route of descent, loose shifting scree tugging at his knees. He had passed beneath a huge wall of rock a hundred feet high. At its base was an utter wasting and despair of boulders, remnants of the violent shattering of hugeness, a world in bits, the terror sublime, and he'd felt its actual terror and was trapped in it for a moment. It hadn't been outside him anymore, no longer intellectual or artistic. Every step down that path to make the journey had felt like a step that was destroying his legs – making his art was destroying his materials – he had not sought it, but he had found a metaphor for what he feared things were becoming.

To E---

Next morning the Crab Man walks on blistered feet with a Journalist from BBC Radio 4, nearly falling down a ravine while walking backwards and talking into the microphone. The Radio Journalist turns out to be one of the founders of the old M---------- Psychogeographical Association, magical mappers and walkers of the 1990s who once tried to levitate the C--- Exchange. The Crab Man tells him how the principles of their kind of exploration are used now by the Israeli Defence Force for their incursions into Palestinian refugee camps. He tells him of a passage in *The Utility of Force* by Rupert Smith, former NATO commander in Bosnia, in which Smith argues that all future wars will be fought 'among the people'.

"Then war is permanent," says the Journalist. Their chat off-mike makes a stark contrast to the scrabbling banalities the Crab gives him for broadcast.

After an hour and a half they pass their first human being; she ignores them, engrossed in her mobile. The Crab flags down a car and confirms the way to the village of H--- (Hope), where they meet up with old friends of the Crab; comediennes and their children. One of the comediennes has just finished a course of chemotherapy, so, of course, they explore the graveyard immediately.

On a stone, crumbled like the H--- freemason's, the Crab points out the surviving shape of a scallop shell; whoever was buried here had been a pilgrim to the church of St James, beheader of Muslims, at Santiago de Compostela; the shell is the pilgrim's badge. But the youngest child begs to differ – she thinks it's the grave of a scallop.

After lunch they amble to B------- and bid each other goodbye. The Crab turns down a track to the local Bowling Green. C----- H---- writes that while staying at an inn in Hope he played bowls, but the man unloading stock for H--- Church Shop says there's never been a green in the village. B------ is the nearest.

A man is 'rolling up' on the green! The Crab Man greets him and begins his story of H---- and the acorns, which the man brings to an abrupt halt, gesturing to the sign above the clubhouse door: "Founded 1985". The old green was elsewhere, next to the pub, but it's a bungalow now. Just as the Crab Man had thought he was about to plug directly into H----'s journey, elusiveness rises like a ghost. He pays the bungalow a symbolic visit, but it cannot compare with the dashed hope of rolling a wood on the same green as H----. (f23) Absent, the bowling green assumes an ideal form, an arena of etiquette, as unreal and as commonsensical as de Certeau's tactics of the everyday. (f24)

The Crab Man may have forgotten where he is. In Derbyshire the game is played rarely on the flat greens where he learned the etiquette of the game, but mostly on crown greens.

f.23

The French critic Michel de Certeau famously proposed that the behavioural structures of the city are like the structures of language, non-negotiable, but that the small tactics of everyday life – the making of informal routes and pedestrian gestures – are like speech acts. And that it is in the making of the details of behaviour that the city is effectively produced by its poorest and weakest, in the space of the ordinary, changing it each and every day.

f.24

He surrenders far too much, but in that he is not alone. There is an assumption among a number of influential thinkers, including Deleuze and Guattari, that the qualities of the everyday are by their very nature resistant to power, automatically subversive.

Not without a body for the new flesh.
(see Footnote on page 77, "If you put Brian…")

Others, including the geographer Doreen Massey, have pointed out the trap in all of this: luring the weak onto the streets where they are weakest, onto terrains that are ephemeral and transient, where victories, if ever possible, are short-lived and non-incremental. The various documents in this publication cannot solve this problem, for they are constructed from it. They see no choice but to start from positions of weakness, and seek out whatever shifts of balance they can deploy to turn these positions to their advantage, aware that the finessing of everyday urban etiquette represents no making of the city by its quotidian peoples, but rather their marshalling within the broad structures of their masters' making.

One deployment of weakness is attractiveness. There is an uptake of 'our' ideas by unexpected consumers. Both Eyal Weizman and Slavoj Žižek have noted the study of the ideas and tactics of Foucault, Debord, Deleuze and Guattari by officers training for the Israeli Defence Force (IDF) (see the Crab Man's conversation with the Radio Four journalist in the text above). By luring the powerful into the realms of weakness, do giants begin to flounder where the weak swim like fish? Or is 'everyone out to fleece you, is everyone vulnerable'?

Spectrality works both ways: the masters may be largely absent, in both senses of 'invisible' and 'non-existent', but before they disappeared they 'outsourced' the business of repression to the repressed. Rearranging the meshings of the compound renders it an open prairie of illusion.

A couple of hours later, having passed the birthplace of the inventor of the Paragon umbrella frame at B-------, (f25) the Crab is rounding the Barrel Inn at B------, with "limousines only" parking, and takes the footpath there, from H-------- Edge, down toward E---. But not before renewing his role as signpost; this time for a lamb he almost treads on, the wrong side of the gate from its mother. He tries to coax the tiny thing back into the field, attempts all kinds of encouraging noises, holding the gate open he leans his body as far away as possible from the entrance, the mother calls, the lamb complains. Now, he worries that the mother will race out of the field. Finally, the silly lamb rushes at the gate, slips on the step, and scares itself so much that it darts off in the wrong direction! It is now, after ten minutes of what the Crab's Nan would have called "performing", that he notices the gap beneath the gate. (f26) This lamb can come and go as it wishes! He shuts the gate and leaves it to its own devices, heading downhill to E---, and passes through the magical works of Fine Grinding Limited.

f.25 *Is there such a thing as a non-reactionary conservatism?*

Since 2001, in Halberstadt, Germany, musicians have been playing Organ 2/ ASLSP (As Slow As Possible) by John Cage, a piece that consists of nine sections, each of 71 years duration. New pipes are constructed as required to play the notes as the players come to them.

Our galaxy, The Milky Way, is shaped like a drum and vibrates as a low C major chord, approximately three million octaves below the middle C on the organ at Halberstadt. If it has one yet.

We found a broken musical box in a garage sale; it plays one note a day.

f.26 *In the 1980s, at Greenham Common USAF base, the fences became art galleries. (ffa) Walls become networks when they are walked: Marina Abramovic and Ulay planned to use the Great Wall of China for a romantic stroll, but by the time they had cleared things with the bureaucracy they had split up. Morsels of the Berlin Wall became tourists' trinkets at such a velocity that they were dispersed like dust, the incremental proliferation of the atomised monolith – like splinters of the true cross, or the lucky bark from the cork tree of Combeinteignhead, or the trading floor set up within Enron – the resulting mass is far greater than can be sustained by its origins, like the contemporary historical process itself. Kinga Araya walked the Wall's atomised spectre to celebrate her own walk to freedom.*

ff:a *In an act of Khlestakovian (see Khlestakovian Inscrutability, page 154) helpfulness, similar to those habitually offered to the forces of the state by The Clandestine Insurgent Rebel Clown Army, women peace protesters from the Greenham Common Peace Camp sought to improve security at the nuclear weapons base by securing the gates with a super-strong chain. In a sequence from the film Carry Greenham Home (dir. Beeban Kidron), police and military are seen to produce a parade of ever larger bolt cutters, each, in desperate displays of impotence, failing to shift the chains. In frustration, the police rush the gate en masse and drag down yards and yards of adjoining perimeter fence. (fffi)*

ff:i *(see pages 92-3, Walking, Writing and Performance (ed. Roberta Mock)*

The materials for the business of Fine Grinding Ltd, banal in a handful, are epic and heroic in their great quantities here. It is the sheer massness, the thingness of it all. Bulk and accumulation, qualities often judged as functional, ugly, but not here, not by the Crab. The wasteheap is, in its shades and shapes, if not quite in its scale, every bit as impressive as K------ Scout. The heaps and piles of shimmering crystals and richly overturned mud are like those works made in the USA in the 60s and 70s by Land Artists, huge pieces of art made with dumpertrucks and bulldozers rather than paintbrushes and chisels. Through the glass door of a portakabin-like office the Crab Man sees the wall around a tallyman's hatch; it is decorated by a thousand hand prints of grime, like a Richard Long mud drawing. One of those art works constructed from one simple pattern – Daniel Buren's stripes, Rachel Whiteread's ghostcasts, Eleanor Antin's 100 Boots, the rock pattern found on his delivery round by the Postman Cheval – the repetitious process is not one of addition, but of multiplication, each unit affecting every other unit, not just the next in the chain. This is its attraction to the mythogeographer.

Object – repetition – variation – structure.

Crab Man had thought of Robert Smithson when he saw the aircraft wreckage on Burnt Hill. Maker of the Spiral Jetty in the Great Salt Lake, a huge twist of rock in the water, Smithson had died surveying marks he had made on the ground for his artwork Amarillo Ramp; the pilot, distracted, stalled and flew into the side of a mountain. In making his work Smithson ended the possibility of it:

"There is no escape from matter", wrote Smithson, "there is no escape from the physical nor is there any escape from the mind. The two are on a constant collision course."

At Fine Grinding Ltd the art is accidental and there is no admission price.

That night, nursing his blisters in The Miners Arms, the Crab Man wondered about the oaks he'd found between H--- and B--------. They might have been C----- H----'s. If C----- H---- had played bowls in B------, and was planting while he stayed in H---... they were the right sort of height, about 35 feet tall. They might have been his.

Was it all going to be "might"? Like the bowling green? Too late to be certain?

He drank another pint of Old Peculiar. In his notebook he wrote about "Hereness". H---- had that. Able to be with what is present. Not with an idea of it, but with the thing itself. What tourists do not have. To be anxious, maybe, frightened even, but not absent. H----'s arrogance and know-it-all-ness are prices worth paying for being Here.

Earlier on at the village of Great H-----, the Crab had passed a pillar on a plinth.

"The Buttercross", it said. He took it, at first, for a mediaeval artefact, but the plaque said it had been "restored". The original was too fragile to re-install. The 'original'? So, what was this? The plaque revealed, further, that the cross's restoration had included a re-siting. The intense non-Hereness of the Great H----- Buttercross shook the Crab.

After that everything he saw seemed fabulously placed and "here" and full of meaning! He stopped worrying about not being able to name birds or trees and simply enjoyed their alien-ness, their cries – little dinosaurs! "Weepa weepa weepa" – "Ugh stewit stewit stew!" The orange sunset in a bird's plumage, the octopus tree, the sentinels, the sacred grove, the lightning canopy. He invented his own classifications of species. (f27)

f.27 *Disrupted walking is a kind of rolling thought experiment, in which unlikely aesthetico-political actions can be mentally enacted in preparation for their material realisation; for example, as he walked through this part of Derbyshire, the Crab imagined assembling all the world's AWACS aircraft on the lawn of Buckingham Palace to perform Rachel Rosenthal's KabbaLAmobile.*

He passed Silence Mine. Shhhh.

Crab's equivalent to H----'s factory soot was sound – mobile phones playing tinny pop in the train buffet, radios in the B&Bs and Spar shops. Never left alone to discover his own mood! He decides to have one final pint, waving to attract the barmaid's attention, but she is texting.

To M------

In the morning he left I-- and J-----'s friendly B&B – the former Rose and Crown. Like many other private houses in the village, once an Inn. E--- is a place still in transition from public to private.

"Follow the E--- Visitor Code!"

He heads out of the village, as it rains for the one and only time in his 16 days on the road.

Past the Riley Graves.

He realises what was most wonderful about the Fine Grinding works – it was open! – no gates, no closed door, no guard dogs or threatening signs, no big fence, just an arrow to an alternative path if he had wanted to avoid the works traffic. Up till then everywhere else had been guarded, shut, cut off, padlocked, defensive. He had more than enjoyed looking in at the works office, that once white wall smudged by a thousand drivers.

He climbs over the stile to the graves – plague victims – Riley is not the family name of the victims, but the name of the place: Roi – King, and Ley – Field. The graves in the King's Field.

For the train up to M---------- the Crab had bought a copy of New Scientist magazine. Two articles had grabbed his attention: one about how the human brain, to avoid seasickness, cuts out most of the signals from the eye, focussing on about 1% of the information from what is around us. The human being is physically programmed to mostly not see! The other article concerned plans for a quantum gravity computer. This computer dispensed with the "if" followed by the "then", the "input" by the "output", instead computing across fields of space, tiny and yet linked to everything, moving not from a to b, but simultaneously influencing and influenced by spooky actions across huge distances, a computer that would have glimpsed its result before it had begun its calculations, using the hereness of what the universe is made of: great sheets of probability. And as he walked, the rain settling in a misty cover across a bed of stone-enclosed pastures, the Crab Man enjoyed the metaphor of disturbing and being disturbed by many fields rather than simply tramping a solitary line. He crossed an empty pasture and, looking back, the sign on the gate said: "Bull In Field". He shrugged. There or not there, there is always, in some sense "Bull in Field".

He passed a young man carrying a plastic lunch box and a pickaxe thrown over his shoulder, looking like a refugee fleeing history.

"Off for a day's work?"

"Definitely."

It was a long walk that day and he'd started an hour early. J----, from the B&B, rang the Crab Man's office to say she was worried for him. His blisters were bad, but he walked through them, the skin bursting and hardening. The pain was hungry, it wanted to eat up his concentration. Today, he must actively look in order to see.

Beside the Derwent, wreaths had been laid. A bucket improvised as a gate latch. Signs told of voles, brook lampreys and great crested newts. He had the names now, but he could not see the animals. He became lost in some fields and then emerged along a road where the backyards were like miniature memorial gardens and theme parks.

"No Respect For Old Lane" says a headline in a discarded newspaper.

He climbs Curbar Gap and onto the moors.

"Good morning!"

The Crab salutes a couple walking their dog, just out of their car.

"Going far?"

But their walk is a private affair and they don't want to talk. Nor any walker or cyclist he meets this day. And so it becomes a day of private journeying. Listening to the monologue in his head. Forcing his consciousness out of his blisters and into the fields and moors he's passing through. The road stretching two miles ahead, vehicles shimmering in the distance like the demon's truck in Jeepers Creepers. He enjoys the space of this place. On top of the Gap he'd looked back and seen the rusting shape of a barn he'd passed, like a Monopoly hotel, a piece of geometry on a rucked carpet of green. Things spread out, thoughts disperse.

He thinks of The Small Vicar (f28) who's coming to walk with him in N-------shire; an Anglican priest who uses walking as part of his ministry, soon to make a pilgrimage parallel with the M62, Hull to Liverpool, devising an urban theology of place as he goes. The Crab wants to join him for a day, and ponders how his walk will differ from The Small Vicar's. And how he, the Crab, had begun, thirty five years before, on his preliminary training for the priesthood, cut short by studies that led him to a materialist philosophy, and how that same materiality, on the road, dispersing the self across numerous planes, had brought him back to something disturbingly like spirituality, to a universe not of cause and effect, not of a to b, but of things spreading, shutting down the inner monologue, pulling apart the complex of identity, throwing him back to early memes, when, what has lasted and remained, is also what can best be changed.*

 Rev. John Davies, author of Walking The M62.

* Publishers' Note: the passage above was removed by the editors. We have restored it on the basis that it is does not contradict the Mythogeographical Manifesto's principles of mixing respectable with non-respectable knowledge nor the interrogation of information in that information's own terms.

And all the time he was looking for a sign, a symbol on the skyline: the shape of three trees planted as a Trinity, spaced equal distances apart, and then four trees planted together to make a mutant atrocity of tangled trunks. Somewhere out there. On a hill with a view of C-----------.

He stops for a plate of duck and two Franciskaner Hefeweißbiers at the newly refurbished Highwayman at E----moor. There had been a time when the taste of this beer had meant he had arrived, fully and completely, in Munich. It was the taste of that place. Now it is part of the flux, of the globalised flow.

The food and drink are good, but this is not a pub. The customers sit at separate tables, the smiling staff repeatedly check "Is everything OK?" but each time they are already walking away before the Crab can answer. It is a place that is not a place, a motorway for the transportation of imagery, a conduit for the flow of commodities.

At I-- and J----'s this morning the Crab realised that the paintings in his rented room were for sale, a catalogue sat on the dressing table. He had been sleeping, partly, in a retail opportunity.

A small party of elderly ladies, perhaps regulars under the previous regime, enter The Highwayman, gingerly. They look, shrink and leave.

The Crab walks on and is inspired!! The road seems mythic now!

He sees something like a human brain in the verge. It puffs up dust when booted – an old wasps' nest! A dead cat suns itself on a wall beside a strapped bottle of water, the crumbling edifice of a Texas Chainsaw Massacre (E – Trash) farm matches the yellowed out light all around: it is as if he is being filmed on 1970s grindhouse movie stock. Fifty or more Special Brew cans are crashed out on a short verge. More than halfway through his 20 mile day and his knees are fine. "Iron Man!" he shouts and waves at the sky. He is bingeing on isolation. A discarded mattress reminds him of a dream. Each infrequent little tin of loneliness – neeeeow! – whizzing by, only heightens his happy exposure to sun and wind.

Four and three? Three and four? H----, who loved to visit churches, expresses nothing like religious faith. Three and four? Four and three? He plants three for the Trinity. And four? For the elements – earth, wind, water and fire? He was an engineer. Would he choose numbers lightly? Is he signalling some esoteric belief that includes, but does not stop at, Christianity? (E – Esoterica)

That human brain of dust by the roadside had reminded Crab of H. G. Wells' plan for a 'World Brain': a worldwide web of libraries offering the same collection of texts, serviced and managed by local selection committees under one global soviet. A great shared field of ideas, contradictory, inescapably bureaucratic, but a global community… the Crab makes plans for a spectral version.

C-----------!! The ground to his left has fallen away and there's the city and its strangled spire, the sight of which twisted H---- into a "fantastic mood".

The Crab had been there once, for Tony Benn's 1987 C---------- Conference of left wingers, hyper-democrats, republicans and environmentalists. What would C------ H---- have made of that gathering? Last night J---- had read aloud from his copy of The Book, a passage where H----- tells cottagers along this very route to quit Britain, avoid cities and go to Canada to escape "the

landowner and… the oppressing farmer". "Seditious," says J----. The Crab, staring down at the city below, remembers trying to stop a hippy from hitting his friend, a Sikh, for advocating an independent Khalistan, and standing up and pontificating at a meeting on Ireland when Gerry Adams walked in.

"O!"

In sight of C----------, standing on a hill are three trees, equally spaced, half a mile away, silhouetted against the yellowy Hills Have Eyes backdrop. The Crab rubs his left knee furiously. Half a mile out of his way – and still a long way yet to go today. But this is the mythic road, two bottles of Weißbier, brain, cat and numerology… have to do this kind of thing here!

Running back and taking the turning off, the trees seem to get further away. Then the road bends and C--------- appears again, it feels more and more right! The trees slowly rising up, empty branches, that's right for oak this time of year, they're behind farm buildings, the trees about the right height, right spread, but … they're on the farm. Dogs, sure to be. Well, can't be frightened now! Not on Mythic Road! He walks through the yard and knocks on the door. Neither dog nor human. He begins to walk to the trees.

"Helloo? Can I help yuh?"

A tiny, resilient Irish voice.

"O, good afternoon!"

The Crab explains to the old lady what he's doing, but the three trees are ash. And that tangle of four trunks there – is sycamore. It's like a trick!! Four and three – and it makes nothing for Crab!

It's harder walking back up the hill. And Mythic Road is more desolate now than when he left it. The endless beer cans speak of isolation, the opposite of H----'s defence of the pub as the seat of conviviality, and of beer as the freeing of the inarticulate to philosophise and debate.

The straight Mythic Road crosses another and loses its metalled surface, a dirt track now, pitted with craters, littered with concrete erratics and scattered rubbish. A car, unfeasibly, weaves slowly around these obstacles, rising and falling like a small boat on a big sea.

Crab finds a porn mag, open at a page entitled "My Story", illustrated with various pictures of "Rebecca". It is unlikely that the text has any connection with the body, but apparently it all "boils down to a basic truth. I like sex." At the bottom of the page it says you can receive Fiesta by text. Beside the track, broken trees are rotted, their trunks snapped, a devastation, a miniature Tunguska. Crab rubs his knee. Loneliness, isolation, nakedness, display – are those really "my story"? "Are we being sold our own individualities and desires back to us – like they do bottled water?" He rubs his knee. "Buying what we've already got, we lose even that?" The crazily veering car passes. The driver, with a cryptic, half-hearted gesture, "something bad's coming" or "why did I do this?", jerks away from the Crab Man's glance. The Mythic Road turns into the woods. On the asphalt a dead pheasant is splayed, as if frozen in flight.

"Ow!!"

He had known. The moment he shouted "Iron Man"! The old lady in the T--shelf cemetery would warn him about taking things for granted.

For the final hour of walking, as the road falls away into M-------, he limps.

Earlier that day he'd forced his consciousness out of his boots and blisters. Now he sees and feels nothing but the inside of his left knee and the empty space that is the rest of his project. Each painful step sucks at his senses. Making the journey, he destroys the journey. (f29) In order to save the village it is necessary to destroy it.

He'd been exultant at escaping a to b, but now, limping heavily, all he wants is to get to the 'B&B'.

There are ways of journeying which are constructed almost entirely from this contradiction. While under house arrest in Turin, Xavier de Maistre created his A Journey Around My Room. In The Right Place, C. E. Montague describes a journey entirely of planning and preparations, and then, at the last moment, not going.

At the Riverside Guesthouse, the Crab lies on his bed, and, but for one brief limp to a Chinese Restaurant, he does not stir till breakfast. Applying extra magic ointment. Stillness. Anti-inflammatory tablets. One of the worst feelings of his life.

He remembers how a virus once took all his taste away.

He remembers how, that morning, from one of the plague cottages in E---, a man had appeared with a computer and hurled it into a skip.

His journey is no more than a frame now; inside, the picture has gone.

Everything tastes of cardboard.

On the news the hostages in Iraq stand in front of maps pointing to national borders drawn in the sea. (f30)

Everything is turning to mush.

Then grey CCTV images: a scheme to reprimand by tannoy those committing anti-social acts. "But our postmodern world is 'anti-social'! That's how it works!"

On the bedroom wall are prints of bookshelves.

f.30c *See footnote to A Scrapbook of Places, page 196.*

To Pl---ley

Next morning, levering himself down the stairs, he finds, by the cereals, a child's handwritten prayer of thanksgiving for "healthy bodies".

OK. Confession time. He takes a taxi. (f31)

f.31 *This might (charitably) be interpreted as a 'catapult'; a Lettriste device, an artificial stimulant a walker can use to disrupt themselves. Leap onto a bus or train without knowing the vehicle's destination, walk against the wind, follow the first animal you see.*

On this part of his journey, through country between M------ and C----------, H---- had sat for hours in churchyards. Checking the map, Crab can see there are no churches along the five miles of main road from M------ to M--ton.

So what if he cheats? His walk was never going to be some great feat of endurance. His distances are a stroll in the park for serious walkers. And, anyway, Crab doesn't know if his knee will work at all, less the five miles or not.

This is about something else.

The taxi driver's a Derby County fan. They talk football. He drops the Crab off at the first houses. He's glad he did, for no sooner is he carefully putting one foot in front of the next than he notices that the oak tree on the other side of the road has a metal plaque. "O, come on! Surely not!!" But it's nothing to do with H----. The plaque says this is the "centre of England tree". He has, accidentally, arrived at the geographic heart of England (or, rather, one of many), marked by an oak, anonymous to the motorists on the busy road.

"Oh, it originates from years gone by" a resident helpfully informs the Crab; the tone of his voice implies that 'years gone by' is an exact historical era.

There is little danger of going lonely in the graveyards of M--ton, T--shelf and T----sal. Barely does the Crab Man get his tired torso onto a bench than he's engaged in fervent conversation.

Grrrrrrrrrrrr!

Grrrrrrrrrrr!

It is a large, silvery-grey smooth-coated beast, and it growls as it circles him.

"Taking a photo?" (f32)

The owner of the huge grey dog…

Grrrrrrrrrr!

… is making his way up through the graveyard. The Crab is a little embarrassed, he has been taking a photograph of the headstone of a man surnamed Skull.

In the South D------ town of N------ Abbot, an agitated man had approached a 'drifting' $f.32$
group who were pausing at, sketching, noting and arguing over a sessile oak set in a small grassed bowl of land within a suburban estate. The man was angry, accusing the group of being property developers, come to take away a fiercely defended space of green. But on learning the functionless and vague nature of the group, his anger melts (see paragraph beginning "This space of recent past/fake present" in E – Myth) and he explains how this dell, when full of water, had been a decoy pond where ducks were lured to their deaths. Later, redundant, it became infested by rats and was drained. He invites the group into his garden where he serves tea and cakes, and the drifters admire an eel swimming upstream in the small rivulet at the bottom of his garden. This is part of an elastic journey, for both eel and drifters. In the case of the eel, one that has crossed an ocean; a journey that was once a short swim downstream, but over aeons has stretched as the continents divided, and beginning grew further and further from the end.

Walk like an eel; let your journey be stretched by what moves around you.

"Get down!! Get down!" he shouts ineffectively. At the dog, not at the Crab, who is frozen like the Hans Solo figure in the M----------- wall.

The owner is an old man who walks on four legs, two of them metal sticks that click at each step. Crab cuts quickly to his story and at the third attempt the big grey dog is consigned to an adjoining garden. Its owner introduces himself as the man responsible for the re-pointing of the church tower in the 1970s, mixing linseed oil in the mortar. It looks brand new.

"Do you want to go in?"

And he disappears. The dog eyes the Crab. The old man returns with keys.

"Just 'ad the organ refurbished – but there's no choir now. Bell ringers, though. I've been coming here for over fifty year – since I moved in next door, the wife's lived here all her life. I'm eighty now. I were churchwarden for twenty years. Between the vicars – y'know, the interregnums – I've run many services. And I'm still an undertaker. I was at a funeral yesterday. But I have someone who helps me run the business now. There's a lot of folk that are fetched back to be buried 'ere, you know – Surrey, Paignton, all over. O, that's the Turbot family, there – three fishes, see. And the rood screen, that were cut in half and made bigger, cut in the middle so you can't see the join. That pulpit weren't there either, that's been moved. And this were me churchwarden's seat, chap who was churchwarden wi' me, he ran off wi' the cleaner. Still wears a cross round 'is neck, mind. My name's Eric. Nice to meet you. Somewhere 'ere there's a history o' the church, m' wife's father wrote it – no... um... 'old on... gi' me y' address and I'll send you one. Us wanted to put a plaque up to 'im, 'e were a devout man, but the church wouldn't 'ave it, they said: 'it's a privilege, not a right' – submitted plans, local stonemason drew them up – "not acceptable". Well, good luck on your journey. You're welcome." (f33)

f.33

Eric of Morton was not alone in showing civility to the Crab Man on his walk. It is a quality that has taken on increasing significance for the Crab. One of the virtues of practising strangerhood. On his walk, such moments of civility were momentary pleasures that served to make his route a plateau of enjoyment. More recently he wonders if such civilities might not be even more useful, more strategic. To think civility a little wider he has read the philosopher Epicurus and of his conception of pleasure in a measured agreeableness. Epicurean suavity is like the O in Roger O. Thornhill; what matters is not what it stands for, but how it stands.

In the shuddering absence in the world of any alternative ideology to that of bankers, generals and liberals (it is always best to have the liberals when there's a choice, the bankers when there is no choice) the Crab Man has been driven by desperation to the thought that Marx's doctoral thesis addressed a positive sort of 'egotism', and to that strain of similarly self-pleasuring ideas lost in the steeling of scientific socialism under the demands of violence, such as Oscar Wilde's manifesto for individuation, The Soul of Man Under Socialism.

A self of patterns and fragments offered a more helpful psychological alphabet, achieving through new media and spectrality what Lettristes had failed to achieve constructing new letters for the overthrow of an old, oppressive language.

The ideology of competition suggests that one person's pleasure is always at the expense of another's. That there is a limited supply, as if it were a fossil fuel. But what if pleasure is limited only by death (but not taxes) and this very misunderstanding? That, while we have an organism to experience it, the more one has of pleasure the more there is for everyone else (it is Girard's theory of mimetic violence in reverse!) Fear that what is good is vulnerable to others drives us towards the negation of the very thing we want to protect. Protecting their freedom, the rich wrap themselves in metal panic rooms, gated 'communities', strong nations, while selling cheaper versions down the chain of fear. Of course, all such ideological terrors have a fragment of truth in them (without such fragments where would lies be?): but it is a self-fulfilling prophecy-machine. For while there are those who are militantly selfish (and some who are 'desperate'), they are un-happy people, and, in a strange silhouette of the egalitarian pleasure that they never seem to get, they (rich miser and desperation-junkie alike, the system practising the twisted-egalitarianism it preaches) are keen to share their unhappiness with those who are otherwise contented. Resist their 'generosity'.

(Perhaps you have noticed the inversion of that nineteenth-twentieth century thang? The end of Mass Society has drawn a new and invisible collective onto the edge of the social stage, a nervous ghost hanging on the curtain for support: the excluded. Where the driving force of old-style, heavy industrial economic progress contained its own contradiction in the huge numbers of technologically included, often skilled, time-disciplined and tightly packed proletarians – demanding immense acts of violence for their distraction or intimidation – the organisers and out-sourcers have finally caught on, intensifying inclusion for some and removing it entirely for others, while keeping porous the line between the two groups. Collectivity is rendered relative, and the progressive – even revolutionary – contradiction has been transferred from the totality and back to the contradiction itself. Thus the contradiction is twisted more tightly: the insecure rich increase their private security at one end of the torus, while at the other the desperate poor have a route through crime into inclusion (at best, for them, by successful violence and extortion – becoming, literally, petit-bourgeois mini-bosses – and, at worst, for them, as clients in the justice system: "the right place for them"). For the excluded, however, there is only the everyday left: streets, bodies, genes, ecology, childhood, animals, food, psychology, architecture, pleasure – these are the new battlegrounds; the cell is the organisation that is neither isolated nor included.)

Of course, this is not to say that selfish, rich, violent or criminal people never experience pleasure; of course they do. There must be some reward for all the effort. But it is a frustrating pleasure – a temporary release from, and oblivion to, competition, which, when faded, is replaced by anxiety and tension before the next release. The result is a narrative drama, with its climaxes and longeurs, staple fare of treadmill melodrama, soaps and celebrity (reality) TV. Epicurus would not have enjoyed Eastenders in the way, one *fears, Aristotle might.*

But there is a geographical solution.

This is a model drawn by the poet Basil Bunting to represent the structure of a Western classical symphony.

It is a model Bunting used in the construction of his long poem 'Briggflatts', which somehow transcends the limitations of this frame. In simple terms the model evokes the tension, the delays, the deferrals, the releases and the depressions, the climax and return of the dramatic-symphonic form.

This is the Peace Pilgrim's own diagram of her spiritual progress.

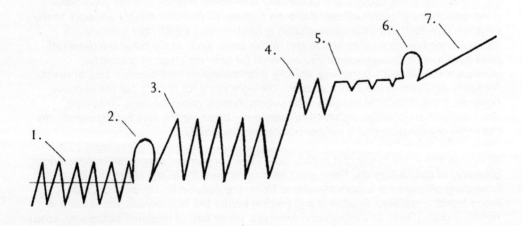

And this is an urban skyline.

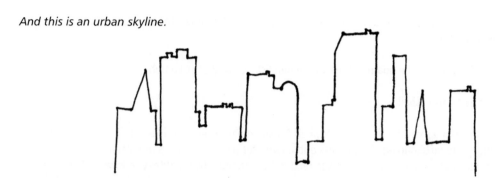

But there is another model.

(First, let's be clear, the tidal force and wavelengths of great symphonies like Beethoven's 7th or Mahler's 5th, the concertina and release of classy thrillers like Mamet's or Lynch's, are no treadmill melodramas. This is not an argument about art. This is an argument about politics through the geography in art.)

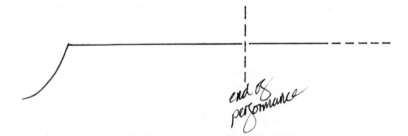

end of performance

Kathakali dance-theatre is the other model, not because of its dramatic structure, but because of the absence of one and its replacement by the scaffold of experience. The musicians warm up and then play an introduction, the tension rises, the first performers prepare for their entrance, the inadequate coverage of the half-curtain only jacking things up further, generating an effect like that of watching athletes limbering up before running on to the field of play. Then, the entrance of the performers raises the tension and excitement a little higher – and that's where it stays – the performance abandoning structure for a plane of consistency, a sustenance of differences without tension, a massively extended climax stretching through the performance, a cosmic plain, with the narrative weaving over and under it, and the level of pleasure remaining all the time as a kind of universal default.

In other words, fewer spikes (for all their temporary piquancy) and more tables, planes, plains and plateaux. Crossed by the graceful slither and slide of the cells of the ecstatic and the excluded as they weave over and under.

Eric's directions and distances are wonderfully precise. He knows the measure of things, being an undertaker.

The Crab passes the boarded husk of the derelict Live And Let Live pub.

Gently on to T--shelf.

On its boundary is the churchless T--shelf Parish Cemetery, laid out like a B&Q necropolis, like edge of town shopping: easy access and a large car park. The graves are recent. In traditional churchyards even the modern graves tend to be restrained by what they fit in with. But not here, the place is a census, a stone poll of resonant images for the recently deeply moved: teddy bears and giant rabbits, landscapes, horses, new-age angels, a cricketer, a Derby County badge and numerous engraved footballers. The Crab sits on one of the benches. Taking plenty of breaks today. Beyond the gravestones is a large fenced field. A place waiting. For the dying that has not happened yet.

The Crab thinks about football and what it has become. The taxi driver has given up his season ticket, because the players "weren't tryin'". Football on the radio is all profits and boardrooms. The Crab's in-laws are Arsenal supporters, he takes his son to see their local team, but it's Rooney he knows about. And here, in T—shelf, the brand survives even death.

A mile or so on, in the traditional churchyard of St Peter's, are the four remaining Whitebeams of five planted "in a block" to celebrate the release "of Mr Terry Waite", part sponsored by the Bass Charitable Trust. One of the five is missing and around another someone has placed fresh orange flowers, perhaps for the hostages in Iran. The Crab is puzzled by what he sees on the News in his B&B bedrooms. The TV people seem to be pleased that the hostages are playing along with their captors – "it's our fault, but we're being treated marvellously". He fears he knows what goes on away from the cameras; they'll be blindfolded, they'll hear guns cocked, sounds of their graves being dug, and yet is it not the point that you do not give in to that? This hostage-taking is more like a Health and Safety exercise than a war of ideas. And yet maybe that IS the point: being willing to suffer humiliation, to NOT die for your cause, but biting your tongue and swallowing your pride is what avoids the war of ideas - The Holy War - is what keeps things kicking along…

The Crab photographs the surviving hornbeams and steps back from the path to allow an old lady to pass.

He bids her "Good morning" and she begins to cry.

"O dear, o dear… I shouldn't…"

He tells her: "it's ok, you can cry."

That seems to take away the helplessness of her tears and she looks up at him with extraordinary eyes. Rheumy balls with frayed black pupils that when he looks deep into them are nothingness itself. She wears a blue quilt coat and a kitchen frock.

"You'll think I'm bizarre, me husband's not dead yet, 'e's slipping away. I've been to look where there's room for him, that's where they put the cremations. There's room. Can't abide the idea of that Parish Cemetery out there, in that field? That's 'ow I think of it - that field, I'm not going in there! He worked at the pit, you know, loading the wagons, a very devout man. We came here…"

She nods toward the church.

"… for two years, but… something happened and we'd not been welcomed after that. You know, strange it is, but I feel calm, strangely calm, that's the Lord, he 'as 'is 'and upon me. I feel 'e's calling me to witness, y'know. Me 'usband's only 75, just got 'is free TV licence! I'm flippant about these things, but… it's good to talk, folk 'ave avoided me recently, seem frightened, frightened o' tears… we've 'ad a very 'appy life together."

She cries now, at the mention of joy.

"'E would give talks, you know, on spiritual matters, to the Chapel's house meetings, never prepared a word. I'd say, night before, 'as the Lord come through yet?' And he'd say: 'no, but He will…' O well, I might just catch the butchers … God bless."

The Crab tells her that he'll think about her on his journey.

"You have to accept Him you know, you understand that?"

Walking through the villages, no more than strings of houses, without public squares or communal spaces, the Crab is depressed by the constant threatening — "beware of the dog" — and its variations: "never mind the dog beware of the kids", "beware of the owner" (a picture of a hick with a gun). He is passing through a nation terrified of itself. Even of its tears.

Yet under this public face of fear, people are warm and generous…

Later that day, the Crab stands, his fingers curled through a grid of wire fence, his face against the metal, speaking to a security guard on the other side.

After the sudden draught of huge trucks as he crossed the bridge over the M1, and the giddiness as he passed the sign of the pilgrim, the scallop from Hope, appropriated by the Royal Dutch/Shell Oil company: "site of the first inland oil well in England", he was pleased when the route at T----sal turned onto a disused railway track. His knee was holding up. As if all the sitting in graveyards had revived it. The cutting was pleasingly geometrical, it felt like sliding down an inverted pyramid. He had had brief chats to cyclists, a gang of kids up ahead armed with sticks had chucked them into bushes as he'd approached and raced by on their bikes with "hiya", half cheeky, half sheepish. And, at the tip of the pyramid, had been the large obelisk, shimmering, and all the time growing.

The tall menhir turns out to be the chimney of Pl---ley pit, shut 1982; now, a massive tourist trinket, framed in a bizarrely clean-cut gravelled approach, like a mansion's driveway.

"O, in twenty years time it'll be a tourist place – café under the pithead wheel there, I've seen the plans, it'll be lovely. They've spent ten million putting the roof on that engine shed already, off a boat it is, the steam engine. Runs on electricity now, but they want to get the steam back. They have parties, schoolchildren – Thursdays and Sundays. Volunteers – ex-miners, mostly – run it. And that 'ut, 'istorian 'as that. There's a twenty four hour watch on it all, – good job or they'd trash it…"

"Trash" – the same word as J-----, at the Guest House this morning, had used to describe a room of hers, damaged by guests, and why sometimes she turns people away. "You get a feeling", she said.

"Gippos came in wi' a truck and a chain and they took the old gate off. They got through that wall with sledgehammers – three foot thick that is …didn't take anything…"

The guard looks about him, wondering if he should say the next thing:

"There's pieces of brass in there… that big!"

He holds his hands in the shape of a football.

The Crab passes The Book through the wire for the guard to see. The Guard takes it and turns it over in his hands. He's a stocky man, and his frame is cut into squares by the wire between them. The Crab tells the guard he is staying at Appleby Guest House at Pl----ley…

"That's not in Pl----ley!"

And he opens the gate and becomes a man rather than a grid of information and attitudes.

"I know Appleby 'Ouse! It's in New ------ton, come here! You don't want t' go into Pl----ley, that's down there! Appleby 'Ouse were the pit manager's 'ouse. I knew 'IM! There, see that big roof over them trees – that's Appleby 'Ouse, that's where you're going! 'Ere, this gentleman, will show you!!"

And he waves over a dog walker, who directs the Crab across the busy C----------- Road – "HASLAM OUT!" shout posters on the lampposts – another football boardroom row. Animatedly describing the directions as if it were a trip up the Amazon, the dog walker bawls at the Crab: "there's a layby you can walk up – they've blocked it off to stop travellers – go up there, you won't 'ave a path, you'll 'ave A ROAD!!"

And he's right.

To E-----stowe

Next morning, after playing the 1950s pinball machine, the Crab leaves the friendly grandeur of Appleby Guest House and walks again through the layby. These are a bejewelled few minutes, for the layby has been retaken by greenness. Entered through the twin pillars of a sawn-off road sign, though only two yards from the roaring traffic of the dual carriageway, thick growth of small budding trees and shrubs holds back the noise, birds sing, the strip of sky above throbs with blueness, below glittering emerald mosses creep to meet each other across the macadam, shimmering green dewy shoots push apart the road surface, bees, moths, butterflies, a future world in which roads have returned to the earth… very suddenly. (f34)

The flags of St George flutter over the New -----ton council estate as if it were under siege. The Crab had ventured onto the estate to buy his tea from the shop. He'd asked a woman why the name "Occupation Road"?

"I don't know – and I've lived 'ere since I was six months old!"

She must be 70.

See Life After People (dir. David de Vries).

He had heard his first duck of the journey – "alright, me duck!"

Now, he leaves the future of the glistening, shimmering blues and greens of the overgrown layby for the brown-sign nostalgia (f35) of Archaeological Way, a route constructed by the

Groundwork Trust, and yet it is their signs that are the ruins now. (E-Things)

f.35 *The maternal side of the Crab's family had once been well-to-do farmers. They lived for two centuries in a large farmhouse not far from the industrial city where the Crab was born. Then, 150 years ago, a reprobate ancestor squandered the family's wealth, lost the farmhouse, and ejected his descendents into the army of labour. In the 1940s the grand farmhouse was demolished and the contractors found a secret room without windows or doors, like the room in Gustav Meyrink's novel The Golem. The house, freed of its foundations, walks now (see Footnote on walking cities, page 107), and, together with the Crab, explores those things secret even to itself. It makes for a walking consciousness that is self-aware of its partial emptiness and enclosure. Like the room, in the house and in the Crab, nostalgia's significance is relativistic. As a utopianism of the past it can be radical or reactionary; a rosy and exclusive spectacle, or a springboard to the best of all possible worlds (an inverted memory that repeats the changes of the past without their failures). Repetition is the first step towards New.*

(MGF) He follows their path by streams jammed with tyres, picks his way across the scattered smithereens of motor cars, he is thrust again into the crisis that is coming. Then the path rejoins the road at a gate to some works. Dogs bark ahead and he wonders if it is guarded. He looks about for clues.

There is a man leaning against a van. The Crab walks over. Thick lumberjack shirt, knitted hat. Working boots. A big man with huge hands. Thirty minutes later he will have taken the Crab on an extraordinary journey through England, and yet neither of them will have moved from their spot.

"That's where they 'ad the gun emplacement, see – by that chimney, when they made bullets in Number 2 Mill... now if you want to walk... do you know the Cat and Fiddle? Not that bloody road there, don't take that one, next one, leg it over the field there, that's a wonderful walk, don't take bloody Derby Lane, though... are you goin' t'Welbeck! I don't bloody go round there, I leggit through – go and 'ave a look at them tunnels – big as that 'ouse there – some Duke wi' syphilis built 'em, visiting the girls in the village, get someone local to take you in – there's an underground ballroom there, y'know – been through E---, you say? Did you see that road that goes nowhere, 'Surprise View', built to gi' the men some work to do? You know the road by the pub, not there, take the next bloody right and leg it up there, at the top there's a kissing gate there – don't go down bloody there, go through the field..."

The Crab has no idea where any of these places are, but it doesn't matter. The woolly-hatted psychogeographer is taking him on a fantastical trip; up roads to nowhere and down tunnels to underground ballrooms. The generosity of his knowledge is intoxicating.

"I sub-contract for 'council, — there is always work digging 'oles."

He gestures to his JCB.

"'ere, you're not scared o' heights, are you?"

Yes, the Crab is, he is terrified of them, but the thick-handed dériviste is not waiting for an answer and drags the Crab up the fire escape on the side of Number 1 Mill. Four storeys up, the Crab clutches the wall.

"'ave a look in 'ere!"

And they plunge into the renovated mill, snaking through corridors and down flights of stairs, a labyrinth, each corridor identical to the one above, same doors, same carpets, same decorations, a hall of mirrors that might go down and down into the earth forever, an endless repetition of small business.

What a man! A true psychogeographer in a worker's hat! An accidental guide to the underground imagination and the economic labyrinth! (See Taxonomy of Spaces, page 203.) This is a materialist magician and the Crab shakes, with great pleasure and sadness at having to get on, the man's huge hand.

Passes huge mills, like mountainsides. Cup of tea at a stall — "Friendly Service" it says on a sign, but no one cracks a smile. Locked churches. The sun is beating down, the Crab, having lost his posh sunspray, has bought some cheap stuff from a Spar, vanilla scented: it's like rubbing dessert into his face.

"Hiyah!"

He passes many walkers, they really walk in D-----shire and North N-----!

A van man, taking a break for a stroll, tells him: "I used to walk down there by t'stream — farmer'd threaten t' shoot us!"

The Crab burrows through a narrow tunnel and feels for a moment as if he might be entering the JCB man's secret England.

He passes a distant shimmering metal conspiracy, a movie anonymity in a desert of yellow earth: S----brook Regeneration Project.

Follows a glistening brook, pondering on C------ H----'s own thoughts as he had passed through here on his way to S---- wood Forest. H---- was bothering himself about "the end and purpose of humankind". Does there need to be one? Nothing points to it except some people's need to have one. Not every culture accepts a purpose, and the Crab thinks of the Gnostics and their alien god and his botched universe, the work of an evil divinity, a thing best left to destroy itself, and all remaining of goodness is one divine spark deep and dim in our souls, like a tiny translucent crustacean, shell-less in an allconsuming niche (f36), the merest rumour of something bright, alien and almost completely inaccessible.

The Crab catches a glimpse of something in the stream - it seems to look at him! A strange stone? It doesn't appear to be alive, yet it seems aware. It's the same colour as the sand in the brook. He presses across the stingers and the thorns, using his walking stick… the bottom erupts in great clouds of silt, but after ten minutes of pricking and stinging struggle he manages to prise it from the stream bed and bring it to the bank.

f.36 *Lobsters seek out niches on the sea bed. Occasionally, when the niches are tight, the animals become wedged in their homes. This is not always fatal, as many lobsters are able to survive on the food that falls to the bottom, attracting it to them by making turbulent the waters around their mouths. These lobsters grow into the shape of their niches. The planet becomes their shell. This is an image to be carried in the mind by dérivistes.*

It's a plastic pencil top in the shape of a frog. With its big alien eyes it will do as an incomprehensible maker of a mysterious universe of absurd animals and dread places. The Crab puts it in his pocket.

In the last few miles, stone walls have changed to hedgerows, there are crops in the fields, rather than sheep and cattle. And he's passing through layers of butterflies: Brimstone, Peacock, and now Tortoiseshell.

At last a church is open! J--- and J----- are cleaning up the dust and sand from crumbling mortar inside S---holme Church – they need Eric's linseed oil! – getting ready before they put in the Easter flowers. But first, they must clear the altar of decoration. Good Friday tomorrow, the Crab thinks of H---- planting his Calvary on the hilltop.

Vooom voooom, vooooeeeeeerrrrrrrrrrrrrrmm… – J---- turns off her Hoover.

The Crab tells them his story, and that today he's heading for the Major Oak in Sh---wood Forest. He knows he won't be able to stand inside its hollow trunk, as H---- did. And as, it turns out, J--- did too, she and her school friends packed in to test how many the trunk could hold. Such visits compacted the earth, rainfall wasn't reaching the roots. Above the three of them, the carved face of Christ looks down, his head exploding in the spikes of an unusual halo. At first, the Crab had thought they were thorns. They look a little like the lines he'd seen in Pl----ley churchyard, carved around a skull and engraved against the shape of a pyramid with its top lopped off, like those retail units in Manchester, like the decapitated pyramids of Anton LaVey who worshipped earth, excess and individualism.

J--- and J----- tell the Crab about a man who died two years before who spent half of his life in this church, mending, cleaning.

"A building needs someone like that," the Crab says.

"Yes, YES!" they say.

He tells them of Eric at M----.

"Yes, YES!" (f37)

Nikolaus Pevsner asserted the symbolic nature of materials in gothic cathedrals: lime = love, sand = earthly labour inspired by love, water = the uniting of heavenly love and earthly labour. In the church at S-----holme the mortar was drying out. At M—ton, Eric had used linseed oil.

And of staying in Brancepeth Castle, near Durham, where at night, to get to the lavatory the Crab would make his way along dark corridors…

"Yes, YES!"

"Ahhh!" He's scared by his own reflection in a long mirror!

"Yes, YES!"

Down the armoury…

"Yes, YES!"

Oak panelled rooms with false doors that once concealed safes full of Pyrex patents.

"Yes, YES!"

Through rooms painted green by the army…

"Yes, YES!"

And to the ruins…

"Yes, YES!"

If the big-fisted sturdy man in the lumberjack shirt and knitted hat had been his magical guide, then J---- and J--- are the Crab's fabulous companions on a remembered journey, encouraging him down those old corridors again. For a moment they are all travelling together!

Then they implore the Crab Man to tell his story to the people at the Visitor Centre in the Forest.

"Show them The Book! They'll let you stand inside the oak!!"

"I'll say: 'J---- and J--- sent me'!"

The Crab Man takes his lunch at The Gate Inn, Market W-----.

Just outside of the town he had passed a small encampment on the banks of a stream. A family were tearing branches from hawthorn trees to feed their bonfire. Flag of St George towels flapped demonstratively over picnic chairs. Yapping dog. Sausages. Against his better instincts, he'd liked the scene and wished he'd seen more like it.

A terrace in the town, kids in the street, a 1920s photo alive again. An oak in a hedgerow. Hmmm, maybe on his path now.

The Crab Man enters Sherwood Forest.

For two miles he walks through the Forest.

He sees no one.

He is alone with a million trees.

Giant oaks lean over and reprimand him for his ignorance, for his mistakes, for underestimating the seriousness of their predicament. They point at him with snaking, sclerotic arms. Of course, he knows such humanising of alien trees is wrong, but this is a human-made place. It is all about humans. From the wide paths, to the swathes of different species. And yet the sheer immersion in wood has its effect. He turns off the path to plunge through the roaring underfoot of crackerjack twigs and silverfoil leaves. He finds another Tunguska – a massive levelled area where, among the thin stumps of other species, huge old oaks lie like burnt out fuselages. (f38)

Passing the Centre Oak, he is baffled by the signs, to 'Major Oak' and 'Fairground', and one with two arrows pointing in opposite directions, both to 'Visitor Centre'. Finally, he finds the Major Oak. Fenced as he'd expected. Unmagical. An unengaged party of French school-children file morosely by. A family play spot the weird shape in the bark. He starts to walk around the fence, because H---- had processed around the tree and he can at least partly imitate H----'s circumambulation. The fence leads away from the path, through briars that he forces himself through, then ankle-deep in dried oak leaves, then, again, along a velvety path of lush green moss, he follows it, bending, through the low branches, and right... whoops! – to the Major Oak itself! – unintentionally, climbing no fence, lifting no latch, he has arrived right at it... a couple of steps and he can be inside its mighty waist.

See David Blair's film Wax: or The Discovery of Television Among the Bees. It is clear that the death of hives is related to problems in the human media. Just as the aeroplanes used by the Crab Man are maintained in flight partly by his fear of heights and his utilisation of this anxiety to power the engines of the plane, so all hive-like behaviour, including mass media, is field-like, sustained by the mass-anxieties of collective pleasure-seekers. The fragmentation of the media into ever smaller franchises has damaged this field and hence the hive, as an institutional model for bees, like everything else, is collapsing. The bees are the first victims of this minor flaw in the generally impressive self-regulation of the Spectacle. f.38

But he cannot.

Two feet. Hardly going to compress the earth so much, is it? Two feet.

But the symbolism stops him. There is an agreement here. To keep this thing alive. "I'll ask at the Visitor Centre," he lies to himself. "There'll be someone who knows the history, who'll listen to the passage from the book, who as a special treat will bring me back here, I'll tell them J---- and J--- sent me."

As the day's journey began in the green magic of the layby, it ends in the plastic horror of the Visitor Centre, with its Information Room (a looped video playing to empty benches), The Robin Hood Experience (an insulting 'exhibition' and shop), and the Heritage Shoppe (a heritage of horoscopes and plaster cottages paid for with poverty wages), and, in the spaces in between, a man with an enormous lens photographs a pair of peeling figures. The Crab Man reels at the trashing of the myth.

Here are all the myths: of rough justice, of the generosity of multiple natures, of robbing the rich to feed the poor, of bravery and hospitality, of breaking bread and popping corks together, of Arcadia, of the egalitarian Garden. And here they are trashed.

The Rangers' office is locked. The only people here are cashiers. Should he tell one of them? Or just buy his S---wood Forest Key Ring for a keepsake – "What car did Robin drive? A Reliant."

"Please, mister, can we have our myths back?"

(E-Fake Places)

Leaving the forest the Crab Man finally meets a Ranger – not a tree man, sadly, but the Ranger explains the Tunguska: "the Forestry Commission cut down everything round there except the old oaks. The first big storm blew them over… lack of communication", he says.

After dinner at the Youth Hostel the Crab sits in a cosy communal room and chats with Youth Hostel enthusiasts – convivial and collective – about Guernsey, white water rafting, bicycle repairs, youth hostel chores, youth hostels in the 1960s, assembling flat pack furniture, dot.com companies – nothing riveting or speculative, nothing remotely Crabbish – a safe exchange between strangers with an appetite for company. They are talking on the dotted lines.

"Do you think there are the same characters about as there used to be?"

The Crab thinks: "isn't it our job to be the characters, now?"

When the others have retired to their beds, the Crab Man stays up a while, and finds on the communal bookshelf a collection of improving tales written by his first sweetheart's great grandfather: C.H. S---geon, the Baptist evangelist. In the book, S---geon comments acerbically on church gravestones that extol the virtues of their incumbents — "where do they bury all the sinners?" S---geon wonders. (f39)

Everywhere the Crab Man goes, everywhere everyone goes, he/they find/s some record of themselves (if they look for it). This is the nature of everywhere/everyone, exemplified by the Pudong New Area of Shanghai, see Michael Winterbottom's Code 46: although, at first, it may appear slippery and unmarked, it is thin and field-like.

At a dour workers' hostel in the North of England, commuting by bus each day through a chemical plant, the Crab Man found the only reading material in its social room was an Aeroflot inflight magazine; he recognised the byline of a revolutionary full-timer to whom he had once delivered supplies of instant coffee in St Petersburg. Utopia's connectivity is always in the cracks of the now.

The night before, on the landing of Appleby Guest House, the Crab Man had found a row of old volumes addressing a variety of subjects and yet identically bound. He had taken up the one entitled "How Much Do You Know?" and begun to read the first chapter: "The Wonderful World We Live in":

"Why is the sky blue?"

Apparently, because particles in the air scatter red and blue light differently, and we see more of the blue.

"What are the seven seas?"

"Where are the bad lands?"

"Where does platinum come from?"

"Why is the white race dominant?"

Apparently it's something to do with the weather.

This had not arisen out of the blue (particles of red scattered differently). One of the many earlier questions had been: "Are There Stone Age People Still In Existence?" and rather than the obvious answer — "yes, the editors of this book" — it turned out to be "Yes, the Australian blackfellow. They have no houses worthy of the name and no pottery", and then there was a list of many of the other things that they did not have, though strangely omitting weapons of mass destruction and Enron. Also, there was nothing about what they did have; nothing about a navigational system based on storytelling called the Songlines, nothing about a mystical-geographical mapping called Dreamtime not unlike quantum gravity computing.

In bed, in the Maid Marian room, the Crab Man began to realise that, beginning anywhere, he could remember every part of his walk in sequence. As if he were a crustacean Charles Fort measuring a circle. He felt unnerved and it was all he could do to prevent himself reliving the whole walk. He imagined sliding back into a deep, watery niche and fell asleep.

To Holly Lodge

At breakfast the Crab began to realise that everyone else had come to the Youth Hostel – IN THEIR CARS!!

This is the Fueltime mystical-geography, its badge the Royal Dutch/Shell Oil pecten, pockets of beauty and nature linked by Songlines of in-car stereo.

He overhears one of last night's companions say of somewhere: "they're returning it to real wild". It's a good description of what now passes for authenticity – a re-creation of innocence. Half-pregnant.

Setting off through E----stowe, passing Maid Marian's Secrets lingerie store, the Crab thinks of the Ranger, telling him how the authorities will soon close the Visitor Centre in S---wood Forest in order to build a new one in a distant field. The present one attracts too much damage to the forest. The Crab, dreamily, imagines the present one, left to the forest's tender mercies, like that layby at New -----ton, adapting, managed by the forest for the benefit of "forever".

The Crab's mood – acidic – does not improve in S---wood Pines Forest; a grid of roads and cycle-paths with large incidental quadrilaterals of trees in between. Assuming the turnings are exactly perpendicular, the Crab gets lost, spectacularly. He enjoys an imaginary soak in a dumped bath. And contemplates the sinister sublime of a rusty railway, its tracks almost concealed by the low branches of the trees seeping to the forest floor. A kindly cyclist sorts him out and after three hours he is finally able to leave the forest for a dark, black and grey expanse.

"This must be 'The Desert'," says one passing walker to another.

The old pit yard stretches for nearly a mile, a quarter or so across. The Crab wanders among its lunar landscapes and miniature dry river beds. For almost half a day now he's been looking for a

pond – to have one to sit beside like C------ H---- – and now he finds it in the middle of the black slag dust. Nothing alive, but there are bird and deer tracks to the water's edge, and not far away, basking in the sun, an umbrella frame spider. Could it be a Paragon umbrella? And a broken piggy bank.

Under the pit railway are parallel tunnels: one functional, the other obtuse and hermetic, with back to front steps and cryptic graffiti that wed the A of anarchy to the broad arrow or 'Awen' of the benchmark and trig point. A burnt out car rots symbolically.

Crab bumps into the two walkers again – he's a lorry driver, she's helping his father write a life story – "a true Romany," she says. Identity trips everyone. In the sky, contrails make a halo of spikes. It's Good Friday.

A burst of bowling green at Rainworth relieves the bleakness of concrete walls and shuttered shops. A brilliant purple light in the gutter, turning as electric blue as the skin of the Hindu goddess on the calendar in the T--shelf shop. Reflected light from a sliver of cd. At a junction, a decorated tree … but there's a broken, fragmented feel… and coming closer, the Crab sees that this is not a celebration but a memorial, a car smash. "A true lass," says a card.

The Crab is fastened upon by an 82 year old Ukranian man…

He's in B---worth ("Blid'uth") now, past the smelly pond in Tippings Wood Park, circled by Quad bikes, through the magical edgeland where, on an extended slab of concreted abandonment – a real playground, dangerous and educational, of decomposing directories and used targets – a lad with a shaved head has given him precise directions to a road that the lad's already admitted he's never heard of. Broken glass sparkles at their feet. The two walkers pass him as he phones ahead for directions.

"Where do you think I'm from?"

The man tells the Crab that he didn't want to go back to the Ukraine after the war.

"The Communists would have killed me."

And then, as if there might still be a threat:

"Not that I was against the Communists, I was against the Germans! The Germans want me to fight in their army, I say: I'm not German, I'm Ukranian."

He talks to the Crab as if he's answering accusations.

He wears an RAF beret.

They pass a girl walking a ferret on a lead.

He says he was in the army.

They part at Tescos and the Crab passes a woman tending wallflowers shaped like two vampire fangs. In the churchyard of St Mary of the Purification a frail lady tells him of tunnels beneath their feet that lead to big houses. Beside them a concrete model of the church disrupts all sense of scale. Will Scarlett is buried here.

The Crab surfs a wave of change – from the shaven head, the cloudy pond, flooded warehouse and a forest of cherry pickers, a family who seem to be living in a caravan in their garden, the Ukranian, the ferret and Tescos, the hill and houses now become cottages, property prices rise, pub, church and into Ricket Lane, farms, scout camp and Holly Lodge. Little is revealed from snapshots when change is unfolding like a wave.

Ann S---side serves tea and scones and the Crab sits and chats with her and her husband in their conservatory.

"eat it and eat it and eat it!" sings a bird in the garden. Later the Crab takes a walk in the S---sides' wood and phones home.

Bang! Thud, thud, thud…

The cork from a bottle of German beer bounces off the walls of the immaculate bedroom. It somehow avoids the ornaments, zig-zagging in the gaps.

(MGF) And these are the best bookshelves of the journey! If it wasn't for the oaks he wants to find, the Crab would have skulked for days among the illustrations of Bunyan's The Holy War.

/|\ On TV – the hostages have been released. And a friend of Prince William's has been killed by an Iranian-backed bomb, they say.

One of the books here was taken out at H--on Green library one hundred years ago – that will be quite a fine. And this on an erratum slip in Old Nottinghamshire by J. P. Briscoe (1884): "page 11, last paragraph, leave out the words "the late" before Mister Boyce's name"!

This time the Crab places a towel over the second bottle before removing its cork.

He sits up late and reads I Lived In A Village by one Tom S---side. In the early hours he leans out of the bathroom window to catch a view of the Druid's Stone.

To L---ley and S---hwell

At breakfast A-- reveals that Tom S---side, blacksmith at Oxton, chronicler of country life, got a concession to sell bikes and ended up with five dealerships for the Morris Motor Company, moving into Fountain Dale, the local country house with 'Friar Tuck's Well' within its grounds. To which A--'s husband was an annual guide.

After clearing his abundant plate, the Crab takes a detour to visit the site of Bessie Shepherd's murder. The killer's name is spelt differently on the front and back of her stone. Bessie is unusual, for being better remembered than her assailant. Why did he kill her? The killer couldn't answer that. He said he awoke and felt compelled. The scene today is coloured by this meaninglessness. Bessie's mother passed the murderer on her way to meet her daughter. He was carrying Bessie's umbrella. Was it a Paragon frame?

Always check the backs of monuments.

T---- is the gatekeeper at N--stead Abbey.

"We had the BBC Springwatch here a while ago…"

They chat about her work and about walking.

"We hoped Bill Oddie would come, but he didn't – and there were thousands – people sat in cars waiting for two hours when they could have walked it in ten minutes. At times I was playing 'chicken' – jumping in front of the cars! O, I walk! When I lived in M---field, every Sunday we'd walk to Hardwicke Hall and on the way we always passed through this village and at the same time each week we'd see these same three old men with their walking sticks toddling along – just like Last of the Summer Wine."

"Oh!" cries a peacock, like a woman surprised.

A customised plate goes by. T---- says the woman who runs Bubbles Balloons has one that reads: "LATEX".

The Crab Man takes the recommended path through a dry tangle of rhododendron stalks. The shape of blue sky framed by the ruined wall of N--stead Abbey reminds him of the Daily Mirror's dissing of one of those American Land Artists, James Turrell, who came to Cornwall to make one of his sky pieces – he designs places that intensify the perception of light (f40). As the Crab walks through the outskirts of H--knall, enjoying cracked concrete driveways, he improvises a speech:

"In daily life we only use a tiny part of our capacity to see – "is that too steep?" "Will I slip?" – we are physiologically inclined to sensual short cuts and generalities. But if we learn how to trip up our evolutionary efficiency we can over-see: textures, details, hidden shapes and frames, the marks of history, clues to the crimes, mistakes and coincidences, (f41) to see myths at work in ordinary places – then our lives can be lived, every day, as if at Alton Towers, as if on our Hen Night, as if playing for England, as if falling in love, as if on the beach, as if watching the last 90 minutes of Peter Jackson's King Kong on a big screen – ludic intensity, not just when you pay for it, but any time you want."

f.40   *John R. Stilgoe in Outside Lies Magic suggests cupping your hands around your eyes, to intensify your perception of pigmentation.*

f.41   *A 'drifting' group found a pair of tiny plastic breasts on Mamhead Hill, so named for its mammary shape. The soiled pink breasts had been eroded by heat and frost, a history of ice and fire rising to the climax of now, as if it saw something coming, had some design upon her, so that she might characterise herself so, and suddenly see herself as others saw her, as 'other', other than herself, and seeing through others' eyes made those eyes excited, set them a-shifting in their sockets, rolling back in their heads, so that she liked herself and began to shift queasily in her bed of humus, and what had been a passive wateriness became a skittering moistness, a shuddering in the forest beyond the sandy lips of the shore that now started up and flaunted its limbs. In the centre of a single glade, a priapic trunk, a prehistoric protector of seamen, tipped, spilling combs and crumbs of soil, pecking against soft mounds of moss, pushing back a furzy bush, its bole swaying above the shivering rock as far as the twin peaks that now grumbled and rose, their summits hardening before the puckering explosion…*

Action: practice eroto-topography. (E-City.)

If you stop the thing in your head that says "ugly" about things, you start to enjoy them.

"Brian, what the hell are you doing?"

The Crab is in St Mary Magdalene Church, H--knall and the vicar is being ticked off by a woman lay helper for making a mess of dressing the altar. The Crab has just taken a stone from a bowl.

Laid out on the chancel floor is what a sign calls "A Journey of Life" – and the first step is that one must take a stone…

Next day he sets out on quite a different journey. He is going to walk from L---ley to S----well. C------ H---- had made a day trip to visit S----well Minster, walking there and back. The Crab would follow his route, for H---- writes that he plants five acorns on the way, and identifies the road he planted them alongside.

Neeooow! Neeooow! NNNNNNEEEEOW!!

An overtaking car almost touches the Crab. He feels the draught run through his meat. He'd entered the road at G---lston…

Later, at the Earl of Chesterfield Arms in S---ford, David would tell him something of G---lston…

Neow!Neow!Neow! Neow!Neow!Neow!

Six motor bikes – doing over 80 … the road is literally a racetrack!

Paaaaaarp!!! – the only car to toot aggressively at him the whole journey…

Part walking on the road, part on tiny verges, he starts to get scared. There are plenty of tyre marks where dozy drivers have missed their line and run up where he's now walking. He's

relying on there not being one today. He finds a shrine to a car crash victim.

Taking the stone you must think of someone who has helped you. The Crab thinks of C------ H----
who would never have imagined he would help the Crab. But he certainly thought about others
and about a future. Holding that thought, with the stone in his hand the Crab sets off along the
Journey of Life, which is a riverbed of plastic pebbles on the chancel floor.

O, my goodness! O – my – goodness!!

It could be a H----- tree… It is!! It is!!

Carefully crossing the road, the Crab is lost for what to do. Kiss it? Hug it? Photograph it, he
supposes. He reaches out and touches it.

Neeow! Neeow! Neeow!!! And now he's here, all he wants to do…. Neeow! Neeeow! Neeow!
Is get away as soon as he can! Neeeow!

He backs away. One last glance and leaves it. Head down. Walking again.

Up on the moor – between M--lock and C----------- – the wind blowing in his ears had blocked
out the sound of each car approaching from behind, until they were right on him. Nothing for
ten minutes and then – woosh again! If he stepped out into the road to see what else might be
com… neeow!!! – he needed to throw himself back to avoid being run over, more than once
… and then a tailgating car nearly knocked him down – no car for two miles either side and it
tailgates!

Like that moor, there's something pilgrim's way-like about the S----well Road. Horrible, but it
releases something. To be walking with a destination that has nothing to do with doing, nothing
to do with obligation, everything to do with meaning. He feels the loneliness suddenly and
doesn't mind it.

Neeeeeow!!! Neeeeow!!!! The smashed up sports car on the H--- Road. He doesn't mind it.
Neeeow!! The burned-out wreck near the old pit yard. He doesn't mind it. Neeeeow!! The one
hundred plus empty cans of Special Brew on the road into M---lock…

Neeeeow!! Neeeeow!! And with a stone in one hand and the plastic pebbles under his feet he
takes a few steps down the Journey of Life towards a cardboard tree…

It will get harder to walk later today – taking the wrong turning yesterday he had somehow
ended up at the N------shire Police HQ, a dead end. "Security Alert Status: Standard", said a

board. The extra distance had taken its toll on his feet. "You can't take pictures", the guard had said and mimed looking about him, as if playfully unsure whether to say the next thing. "There's a lot of undercover people here." People fill silence with things they shouldn't say.

The blisters were getting to him, but he so wanted to detour through C--verton. Twenty five years ago he had sat in the Miners' Welfare Hall there and watched the first performance of the theatre company he'd helped to found, given to an audience of a dozen souls. A quarter of a century on, the company performs more English language theatre in non-anglophone countries than anyone else in the world, is watched by a quarter of a million people every year. The day the Crab had left home he'd got an email from Shanghai – a standing ovation for their new show at the People's Liberation Army Theatre. Now he wants to stand on that first stage, sit in that hall, acknowledge a marker on the Journey of His Life.

Beneath the cardboard Tree Of Life are paper leaves, and an invitation to write the name of someone for whom he would like to give thanks.

"Remain in me and I will remain in you. No branch can bear fruit by itself…"

They are no longer serving lunch at the huge plastic pub beyond the Police HQ, he'd missed it by one minute and makes do with a packet of crisps.

Hobbling on his blisters into C-- verton, he asks for directions, and after visiting the Miners' Welfare Sports Ground and the Calverton Working Men's Club, he finally arrives at the site of that first performance twenty five years before. It is now a housing development called Old Hall Close. (f42)

Neeeow! Neeeow!!

Yes! Yes!!!

It's another! Finding the second H----tree on the S----well Road is just the same as the first! The Crab dodges the traffic to reach it. A quick photo, he brushes the ends of its branches with the tips of his claws and then turns away.

There's no time. There's no ease. There's no way of staying. He must move on. To be on the go. To get away.

f.42

Performance is a process of dematerialisation. There is no satisfactory form of documentation for performance. But there is a half-life of fading, in-between spaces, where performance continues to be; not re-enacted, but decaying. The theatre itself acknowledges this, with its physical borders, footlights, aprons, curtains. These make spaces for performers to perform (not on, but) into. Beside the point is where performance lurks: not 'in', but 'in the vicinity of', 'beside', 'next to'. (Millions must have felt this before Mike Pearson articulated it.) This is its usefulness for us; not as a means to communication, but as a means to let go, to release, a means to lurk and stalk in the between spaces.

The beat of his feet on the hard road begins to take its toll. But he is passing landmarks too. A college and, checking the map, he's nearer than he'd thought, nearly there. He trips on the remnant of a bollard – trademark: Bigfoot.

"The Woodlark Inn!!! It is! It's his!!! It's his!"

This isn't on the road to S----well. This is the Crab yesterday evening, coming into L---ley and seeing the Inn at the bottom of the road. After a gulp of Timothy Taylor's Landlord, he's with Gill, the landlady, she's showing him round the pub. This has to be where C------ H---- stayed! The skittle alley H---- describes is roofed and now a steak room, but it's there! In the back is the brick building where he described the landlord making surgical hosiery: now a toilet. And the stream where H---- washed Pontiflunk passes just behind the pub. The church is just the right distance for H----'s five minute stroll while his breakfast cooled. It ALL falls into place.

The Crab stands in the doorway of the Woodlark and watches Pontiflunk, a mongrel dog, sheepishly creeping across the road outside. Making its way towards H----. The Crab is on the very mark of their first meeting!!

It's Gill's birthday, but she makes time for the Crab. Tells him how she came here. What they've done to the pub – a bar moved here, a wall there. It's like being with Eric in M--ton Church – places are fluid things. "But we'll never sell it!" she says. Takes him down to the cellars. "Eyes are always following" one of the staff reckons. A clairvoyant came and said there were two monks – annoyed at the refurbishments – Gill doesn't believe in clairvoyance and then tells him the extraordinary story of what a Romany told Gill about herself. "I love the trade," she says.

There is a fabulous feeling here, something different to anywhere else the Crab has been on his walk. Local, but welcoming to this stranger. He gets talking to Wendy and Mike – another lorry driver – they've walked over the fields from A-nold. Theirs is the perfect, civil chat. The Crab is beginning to think that Gill is a kind of wizard. She introduces him to J--- who farms much of the land around the village, and when the Crab speaks to him it is in the middle of a scene like that of a Spanish village square, different generations sitting together enjoying the last hour of sun.

"Sylvia!!! Put those candles out!!"

The Crab has stayed at a colleague's house overnight, avoiding the bare live wires in the bathroom that she's refurbishing. Places are fluid things.

She has accompanied him to The Holy and Undivided Trinity Church at L---ley. The Crab cannot stay for the service. He has arranged to meet J--- at his farm at ten. But they've time to pop their heads into the church before the service starts. The Sylvia in question, an elderly lay helper, has begun to light the candles, forgetting that it's Easter Sunday and today they are lit from the Pascal Candle.

"We've a fine example of mediaeval cleric over there," says one priest of another, as The Crab examines the fabric of the building.

"He looks very well preserved," says the Crab, "Is he Grade One Listed?"

"Grade One Certified," he quips back.

On the paper leaf from the cardboard Tree of Life the Crab writes the word "Pan" – he is struggling to find a word for 'everything'. But more than 'things'. He ties it to the cardboard tree and continues along the laminated path towards the pile of stones at the altar.

"You are being watched," the sign says at the entrance to Jericho Farm.

In J---'s Four-by-Four they find four good H---- candidates – oaks of the right size – and the Crab knows from The Book that H---- was planting on these hills. There's two above Hanging Field, another two over the main road beside the fields of Oil Seed Rape. But it's impossible to be absolutely certain.

"What is this?" he asks J--- as they shoot along a green carpet between two shining fields of yellow.

He's told J--- about the excitement of last night's discovery that the Woodlark is the Inn in the book.

"Well," J--- says, "there are three inns in the village with skittle alleys, they'd all have had workshops out the back, and one of the others is also near the stream, and nearer the church…"

The green carpet, like an artificial Journey of Life, like the velvety grass that led him unwittingly to the foot of the Major Oak, is an airstrip for J---'s airplane. "It's an aid to field management," he says. "You can see all your cock-ups!" For a moment the Crab fears that J--- will suggest he takes him up to look for oaks. The Crab presses himself back in the seat of the Land Rover as he did against the wall of Number 1 Mill. He thinks of Robert Smithson and the wreckage on Burnt Hill. He sees (f43) the land stretched out like a model railway set with little green florettes of oak below!

f:43 *Looking: all the time we are presented with the circumstances of particular ways of looking, the circumstances that make the gaze and the gaze that makes the circumstances. On a family holiday the Crab discovers that they have unknowingly rented the former home of a notoriously Soviet-friendly churchman: the Red Dean. An oar from Summer eights hangs on a wall – "four bumps". An expansive bay window contains the arc of Ceredigion Bay. And what did the Red Dean see through this glass? A generalisation, an aristocratic 'in parentheses' of monotony, the waves as a constant traffic, a machine egalitarianism without cause and effect, a steady state universe, fatherless but avuncular?*

By not going up in J---'s plane, the Crab Man sees from above, through empathic vertigo, which is not a fear of heights or falling, but a desire for leap-space. (f44)

"Everything is as it is because of human management," says J---. "Man intervenes and then man has to manage it to right the balance again. A lot of people don't like what we do." (f45)

And they discuss killing. Neeeeow!

Well, at least he is sure of the trees by the murderous road.

Five acorns. Neeeeow!! Two trees. Neeeeow! And it's definitely C------ H----'s road. Definitely the journey of his life. The sides of the road rise for the cutting he describes in The Book, and here's the view to L------shire!

The Crab Man eats the small chocolate Easter egg his colleague has hidden in his rucksack.

f:44 *A low level vertigo might be added to the low level paranoia (see page 178) as another useful mental tool for the scuttling walker.*

f:45 *"if humanity were to abruptly stop its immense industrial activity and let nature on Earth take its balanced course, the result would be a total breakdown, an unimaginable catastrophe. "Nature" on Earth is already so "adapted" to human interventions, human "pollution" is already so completely included in the shaky and fragile balance of "natural" reproduction on Earth, that its cessation would cause a catastrophic imbalance. This is what it means to say that humanity has nowhere to retreat to..." In Defense of Lost Causes Slavoj Žižek*

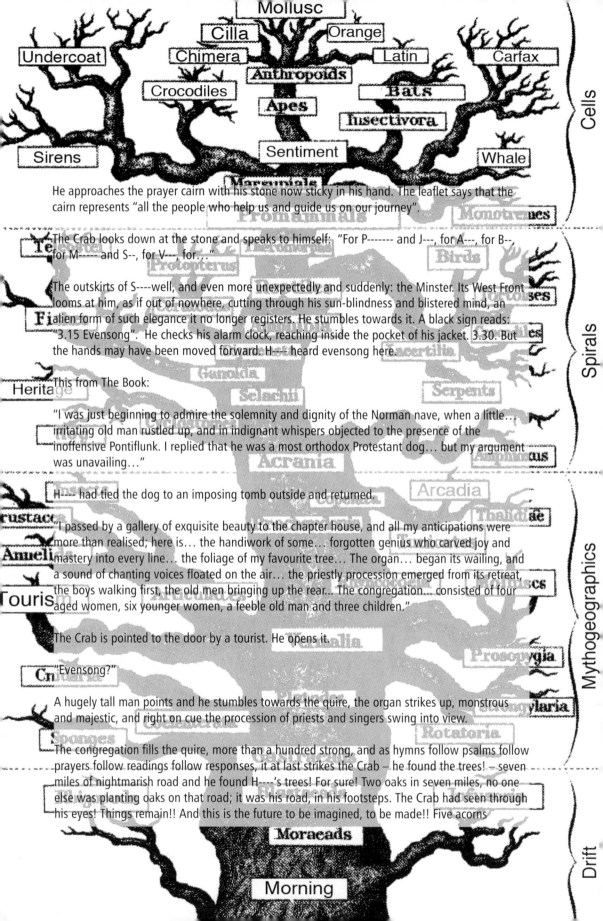

Mollusc

Cilla Orange

Undercoat Chimera Latin Carfax

Anthropoids

Crocodiles **Bats**

Apes

Insectivora

Sirens Sentiment Whale

Cells

He approaches the prayer cairn with his stone now sticky in his hand. The leaflet says that the cairn represents "all the people who help us and guide us on our journey".

The Crab looks down at the stone and speaks to himself: "For P------- and J---, for A---, for B--, for M----- and S--, for V---, for…"

The outskirts of S----well, and even more unexpectedly and suddenly: the Minster. Its West Front looms at him, as if out of nowhere, cutting through his sun-blindness and blistered mind, an alien form of such elegance it no longer registers. He stumbles towards it. A black sign reads: "3.15 Evensong". He checks his alarm clock, reaching inside the pocket of his jacket. 3.30. But the hands may have been moved forward. H--- heard evensong here.

This from The Book:

"I was just beginning to admire the solemnity and dignity of the Norman nave, when a little… irritating old man rustled up, and in indignant whispers objected to the presence of the inoffensive Pontiflunk. I replied that he was a most orthodox Protestant dog… but my argument was unavailing…"

Spirals

H--- had tied the dog to an imposing tomb outside and returned.

"I passed by a gallery of exquisite beauty to the chapter house, and all my anticipations were more than realised; here is… the handiwork of some… forgotten genius who carved joy and mastery into every line… the foliage of my favourite tree… The organ… began its wailing, and a sound of chanting voices floated on the air… the priestly procession emerged from its retreat, the boys walking first, the old men bringing up the rear… The congregation… consisted of four aged women, six younger women, a feeble old man and three children."

The Crab is pointed to the door by a tourist. He opens it.

"Evensong?"

A hugely tall man points and he stumbles towards the quire, the organ strikes up, monstrous and majestic, and right on cue the procession of priests and singers swing into view.

Mythogeographics

The congregation fills the quire, more than a hundred strong, and as hymns follow psalms follow prayers follow readings follow responses, it at last strikes the Crab – he found the trees! – seven miles of nightmarish road and he found H----'s trees! For sure! Two oaks in seven miles, no one else was planting oaks on that road; it was his road, in his footsteps. The Crab had seen through his eyes! Things remain!! And this is the future to be imagined, to be made!! Five acorns

Moracads

Morning

Drift

planted! Two oaks grew and persist!

The choir sings: "It is better to trust in the Lord
Than to put confidence in princes.
All nations compassed me about;
But in the name of the Lord will I destroy them."

The layby at New -----ton reclaimed by the green, the oaks by the busy road.

"They compassed me about; yea, they compassed me about:
But in the name of the Lord I will destroy them.
They compassed me about like bees…"

Neeeeoow! Neeeeow! Neow!

△ The remnants of cars along the Archaeological Way.

"They are quenched as the fire of thorns;
For in the name of the Lord I will destroy them."

The burnt car at the old pit yard. The four wheels in the stream.

Neeeeow! Neeeow!

"Thou has thrust sore at me that I might fall:
But the Lord has helped me."

The Crab stands without cringing before the oncoming traffic. He thinks of the artist Chris Burden, crucified to a Volkswagen. The organ is apocalyptic.

"I love you more than the Assyrian's" reads the priest. "For your sake I will send an army to Babylon."

The Crab places the stone on the cairn, a monument beside those to Byron and his daughter, Ada Lovelace, author of the first computer software.

And the Crab begins to cry.

"Alleluya! Alleluya! Alleluya!
Ye sons and daughters of the King,

Whom heavenly hosts in glory sing,
Today the grave hath lost its sting. Alleluya!"

The BBC had rung up – 'will you be discovering one of Mister H----'s oaks on the 10th of April?'
Now, in the nave of the Minster, with the psalms and hymns and the responses ringing around
him, on the 10th of April, the Crab at last knows what he's looking for – for the future. H----
made his mark. He made a difference – but the answer to one question only begs another –
what kind of difference should we make? The Crab who spends his life looking for and making
connections between things wants to know – what happens next?

He stands with the congregation, now gathered around the font and the priest renews the
baptismal vows of the people, wafting leaves from some 'Holy Land' plant and splashing the
crowd with holy water.

Swoooosh! Swooosh! Swooosh!

"Is there anyone I haven't splashed who would like to be?"

Afterwards, the Crab wanders about the Minster, buying a licence to photograph in the Chapter
House. The carvings of oak leaves are accompanied not by human figures, but by strange
animal-human hybrids… Bigfoot! Crab Man! … back in the nave he's drawn to a small
opening to 'The Pilgrims' Chapel'. Inside, a tapestry of pilgrims, donated by the N---------shire
Constabulary. Had they imagined themselves Knights Templar, escorting scab miners through
Moorish picket lines to dark Jerusalems of coal? He almost misses the life-sized sculpture, clearly
modern, in cream-coloured stone, above the door. Happening to glance back and up, he sees a
representation of a young man, clutching a small towel to cover his modesty, a mixture of Nazi
monumentalism and boyband coiffure.

"Excuse me…"

The Crab approaches a lay member of the Minster staff who is emptying collection boxes.

"Do you know the significance of the modern sculpture over the door to The Pilgrims' Chapel?"

"Oh, you mean the prancing queer?"

His younger colleague twitters and cringes – nothing that's actually a word.

"Perhaps I shouldn't have said that."

The Crab maintains his Klestakovian Inscrutability. (f46)

"It's supposed to be a pilgrim," continues the lay official, dismissively. "They promised us a plaque. That was four years ago, but this is the Church of England."

Yes. Yes, it is. And, no, no it isn't.

As he turns to leave, without telling them of his mission, a woman enters the Minster leading a handsome, black dog! Outside, he meets the woman and the dog again, now with a man in tow – and, telling them his tale and of Pontiflunk's exclusion, he asks if he might take their photograph. The man commandeers the dog and as the Crab touches the shutter the man says:

"There you are: 'Verger and Dog'!"

f.46 *A tactic for obtaining things from a position of weakness – as with the security guard at Nottinghamshire Police H.Q. – called "Khlestakovian" after Khlestakov, the hero of Gogol's play The Government Inspector, a waster and wanderer, mistaken for an important official, who, thanks to his inscrutability and passivity triggers ever more elaborate attempts to impress and pleasure him.*

That evening the Crab splashes out on dinner at the Saracen's Head in the oak-panelled room where H---- had eaten his dinner. Bottle of Merlot, black pudding starter, lamb for main, consumed under the lurking presence of a hulking royal coat of arms, and an over-solicitous head waiter. H----, fervent in his dislike of Charles the First, might have enjoyed the place's title, for the page of history in Crab's bedroom explains that 'Saracen's Head' is a reference to the common belief that Charles was beheaded with a Saracen sword taken during the 'Holy War'. The 'Saracen's Head', then, is Charles's; a forgotten insult to a royal and magical body once hidden from democrats in this very oak-panelled room.

What was he going to do now?

He'd found two H----s. Was it now just a matter of how many?

In his room, with its half-timbered bathroom, Gideon Bible and phonebook was a copy of 'HRH The Princess Anne' published by Country Life. Commander-In-Chief of the Sherwood Foresters, apparently she has the power to dissolve Parliament (on the sovereign's instructions): "if she wasn't who she is she says she would probably be a long distance lorry driver."

The couple in the restaurant pay their bill and go, leaving the Crab alone within the oak – compensation enough for his exclusion from the heart of the Major Oak – but not before they have exchanged a few words with Crab and tell him of their son's walking from M---field to P--mouth to mark the family's move from one to the other.

Was the Crab's walk over? Despite the good food and wine he felt unaccountably depressed.

Alone inside the oak he imagines the other tables filled with great walkers, living and dead – Arthur Machen, Stalker of Rome, He Yun Chang, the Peace Pilgrim, Simon Whitehead, Sophie Calle, Guy Debord, Maureen Stone – and he sees them arguing furiously with each other… the 'project' was still alive.

"Come on," he tells himself, "you didn't really ever think this was just to do with oak trees, did you?"

The arguments at the other tables suddenly recede like the sea before a tsunami. The Crab feels their eyes upon him.

Nothing was ever going to be certain.

The other walkers were getting up, suggesting to each other a drift in the night air…

He rises as if to join them. What if this was nothing to do with oak trees? If H----'s acorn planting was some sort of a trick – or sign – to hide – or reveal – something else… something quite different… what was H---- trying to say? What message had he left?

He moves to leave with the drifting group (f47) of walkers. But they have gone, left him. He is forming the thought that any solo walk is no more than a preamble to learning how to walk in drifting cells, when he sees the figure at the table in the shadows, furthest from the royal coat of arms.

It was C------ H----.

If you put Brian O'Blivion (Videodrome, dir. David Cronenberg) in a blender with V. I. Lenin *what you would get is the biopolitics of the New Flesh; the struggle of what Antonio Negri calls "the general intellect" (those ideas and attitudes resistant to co-option, work and wages) to manifest a body, a physical expression. Atomised – or perhaps, better, particularised – by the velocity of capital and the reach of commodification, the best that postmodernism can offer so far is something at the molecular level. Hearteningly organless (free from the totalising control of an organism-like political totality or a natural history), the New Flesh is open, not only to temptations of constructive, cosmetic surgery, but also to its manufacture from within, cell by cell. "What is required is a demiurge, or rather an external vanguard that can transform this flesh into a body, the body of the general intellect. Or perhaps… could the determining body of the general intellect be* determined by the world that the general intellect itself articulates, in such a way that the general intellect becomes the demiurge of its own body?" ("What to Do Today with _What Is to Be Done?_" Antonio Negri in Lenin Reloaded).

"My dear comrade, has the scope of your philosophical reflections ever included the consideration of the marvellous mystery of your own individuality? Speaking for myself, I am a being with certain faculties, organs, desires, aversions and weaknesses, whose usual mode of progression is upright upon two legs... but, my friend, who am I?

"Two months ago I left my wife and family on affectionate terms and have walked to this place. Of my future route and destination I am, as I was two months ago, as ignorant as of my fate after death.

"And why?

"Can you imagine this island denuded of trees? I am not one who prates on the degeneration of the English race. I have great confidence in the future of this country... BUT, there is a tendency among us to forget natural beauty in the fierce stress of social and political questions. And I have no talent for those. Yet, I can do some service – wherefore I have quietly stolen aside from the clamor to perform a task which requires nothing more than a little enthusiasm and a sound pair of legs. To leave a track – in the form of a noble line – a lineage – of oaks."

And he took from beneath his jacket a small wooden box, of which he proceeded to lift the lid and produced an acorn.

"Stay there, Ponty! Good fellow!"

And then addressed himself to the Crab again: "The setting of an acorn is an important matter. Let me describe my method. First, select a suitable spot, then remove the turf very carefully... Received a letter this morning. From that fine fellow who sends me these seeds... I next prod the ground thus cleared and remove all large stones, roots, worms, slugs or deleterious matter."

Putting down the acorn on the field of white linen, he took an opened envelope from his pocket and extracted the letter.

" 'per favour of your poor deserted wife... if you would return immediately I think some of your friends would not altogether throw you over, but I would advise you not to strain their forbearance by a continuance of this folly...'

"What do you think of that? Hmmm. Pat the loose earth and leave a hollow in the centre about three inches in diameter, one and a half to two inches deep. Place the acorn in the hollow…Since leaving Hope I have averaged about twelve a day. Cover with some soil reserved for the purpose, pressing it down so that the soil touches the acorn on all sides."

He rucked the tablecloth to achieve his effects.

"Yesterday on the road here I planted five. And more on the way back. And when we returned I felt light hearted…– indeed, by way of a little diversion I promoted a concert at our Inn in Lambley, offering a small prize for the best comic song!

"…and then sprinkle a little grass to hide my labours."

He took toothpicks between two fingers and dropped them over the acorn.

"And the last thing… the whole operation takes about fifteen minutes – I place a few thorns around the spot, as a fence.

"After all the songs I had mentally adjudged the award to a retired puddler with a bottle nose who favoured us with "A Tear Fell Gently From Her Eye", but in consultation with mine host, and in deference to general opinion, it was given to a merry cobbler who rendered "On It Like A Bird" in great style!!

"Finally, I address the acorn, mentally: 'Now good hap seize thee, little seed; grow in any manner worthy of thy noble parents, and be delight for many weary men whose light is not yet blown in.'"

He shook his head.

"Twelve a day. It is not such a great deal. And barely two or three miles covered between each breakfast and sundown since Hope. But the results of my actions may be visible for a thousand years! – they are, I think, well worth a little care."

He stood and began to make for the door to the hotel lobby.

"Come, Ponty! We must, at least, make some show of progress for those who chart us! Come!"

And he clapped his hands. And something like an idea seemed to cross the floor of the restaurant.

"Good boy! Let us climb over yonder hill!"

And he was gone.

H---- had adopted the dog at L---ley, soon winning its trust, washing and trimming its coat. Together, they explored the land around the Trent, while H---- concocted unlikely schemes for the dissemination of his ecological mission, floating messages in bottles down the river, idling about the villages and meadows, assisting in the capture of a wily horse, searching fruitlessly for a large, vicious, black rabbit, and drinking. Moving on when his supply of acorns was threatened.

If C------ H---- was walking a symbolic message into his account, the Crab never cracked it. Instead, it seemed to the crustacean critic, that H---- was being walked by the walk itself. (E – Strolling)

Under pressure from home to realise some function in his mission, he resisted this, conniving to misrepresent the miles he walked, avoiding every opportunity to end his amble, wondering if his journey might be years in the making. (E – Permanent Drift)

Reluctantly H---- had visited N----------- to collect money and some supplies, the first city since leaving M------------. There he ate at the Flying Horse Hotel and made his way to the historic Castle, leaving a prohibited Pontiflunk in the care of a policeman, while, inside, he set, unobserved, two acorns on the East side of the castle.

Almost a century later the Crab and his friend, the Academic, were struggling in the same place.

"Can you reach it? Yes, that's it! Pull that one down! There! Got it! Go on! Well – what do you think? Is that anything like an oak bud?"

His voice rings out around the grounds of N--------- Castle. A minute previously, the Academic had spotted a strange portal, an eighteenth century front door set in a solid wall of rock, "it's Alice In Wonderland!" she says.

And there is an atmosphere of unreality in the grounds. No one will let them pay for anything. Arriving before the ticket office opens, they wander up to the castle. Peter, at the desk, brushes aside their proffered fivers, whispering solicitously, "say you're on a project". He directs them to another Peter, the gatekeeper, who they are to ask about oak trees.

The Crab Man knows from The Book (f48) that the man he has been following these last ten days planted the two acorns here, on the East side of the castle, and there are two trees, the right size, in the right place – and, just as the magical door seems to be opening… they find it's built into a wall of stone.

"But is it a bloody oak?"

The Crab Man rummages in the fallen leaves.

"About half-past two o'clock we left the Flying Horse and started for the historic Nottingham Castle... a conspicuous notice stated: "dogs not allowed in the grounds". I approached a policeman at the gates and asked if he would take charge of the harmless Pontiflunk... I begged him to examine a really exquisite silver coin and told him that if he collected such things he might have this one. This banter secured him. I passed through the grounds and approached the grim fabric of the house. After making the round of the galleries, I managed, by a little stealth to plant, unobserved, two acorns on the east side of the castle; and then returned to the gatehouse where I was pleased to find Pontiflunk on good terms with St Peter..." The Book of the English Oak, Charles Hurst

"I just don't know – they can grow straight like this, if the top bud survives! And there are oak leaves down here! But others too! I don't know – ahh! Ahh!"

If only these were them! Perfect twin pillars!!

Peter the Gatekeeper knows nothing of trees. "Well, you're in now," he says, with a dismissive wave of the hand, "don't worry about a ticket."

The Academic whispers to the Crustacean: "Do you have to be called Peter to work here?"

The thing about a walk like this is, want it or not, it becomes a kind of pilgrim's progress; every place visited, every gate opened, every fence climbed, every person encountered, all begin to play some part in a bigger journey than the one you'd meant to go on, in a bigger story than the one you'd set out to write.

Peter goes off to find the gardeners.

If H---- were here today, he'd happily have entrusted his dear Pontiflunk to this Peter.

When he returns it is to say that the gardeners are having breakfast. But Peter's had a word and, apart from a couple of young oaks nearer the outer walls, there are none they know of.

"Ooo, that's hard on the eyes!"

The Academic and the Crab emerge from the labyrinth of caves under the castle. Like H----, they've joined a guided tour, but find no minotaur, no secret that explains it all. Instead, they emerge from a passage carved with stone bird cages and sandstone texts scratched by a King's fingernails. (f49) The guide explains that the Alice In Wonderland doorway really does go nowhere – the Crab looks through the letterbox – she's right. They're not going to discover any secrets here.

_f.49_   "The past was really, _really_ weird." (Mike Pearson)

If only he had learned a few simple things – like the shape and colour of oak buds… (f50)

Similarly pricked, H---- and Pontiflunk had walked into L-----shire. Their pace fell "grievously". While H---- worked gathering hay in the fields, Pontiflunk would lie under the shade of trees or haycocks, the flow of tears from his eyes now stopped up. In S--mford they found accommodation at The George, an old inn, "wiring home for shekels and a further supply of acorns". And recruited four unemployed men to plant a grid of trees in a coppice five minutes walk from All Saints Church. (f51)

A few days after this sudden outburst of practicality, H---- and Pontiflunk left S--mford and walked in a south-westerly direction through the edge of N----------shire and then into R--land. The sky was cloudless, and the atmosphere heavy, the good weather seemed about to break. In the middle of the day, man and dog "obtained a frugal meal at a lonely cottage standing in a patch of shrubby ground". As they sat in the cottage garden consuming their respective repasts H---- engaged the dog in a discussion not on the subject of oak trees, but of the nomadic

(E-Nomadic) life, adjudging Pontiflunk's reaction one of approval. It were as if H---- performed a psychological act at this point, affirming his betrayal of missions, targets, completions, making his final break from the engineer's agenda and adopting a way of being: in place of his practical project he adopted The Project.

The Crab Man returned later to Nottingham Castle, at a time of year when the leaves were on the trees. Those 'twin pillars' were elms. However, beside them (in the usual location of the truth of things) WAS an oak tree, thin and tall and uncharacteristically shaped against the vertiginous slope. Right place. Right age. When the Crab Man proudly announced this to a passing gardener, telling how Charles Hurst had once secretly planted acorns there, the man said: "Well, in that case, I'd like to kick his ass – the roots are undermining the castle!!" *f.50*

We then wandered about the pleasant little town, admiring a very fine steeple, All Saints I think it was, when I was accosted by one of the strangest specimens of human architecture I have ever seen. *f.51*

"Can you give me a copper, mester?"

The man had intensely red hair, wild wandering whiskers, a complexion like a male stickleback, large protuberant eyes, spindle legs and a fat paunch:

"Give you a copper? I can very easily do that, but whether I will or no is another matter. Why should I give you money?"

"I must live."

"I fail to see the necessity of your existence. If we were both struck dead this instant things would go on pretty much the same."

"You're a hard un, guv'nor."

"I should be a soft one if I gave you my hard-earned coins for nothing. Why don't you work?"

"Can't get a job in my trade."

"Why, what trade is it?"

"I am a snow-shoveller in summer and a haymaker in winter."

"Right, friend. I owe you one!"

But as I spoke I saw him give a wink to a group of three equally eccentric individuals – a fat man, a blue-faced man and a melancholic.

"Friends of yours?"

"Yes."

"Of the same profession?"

"Rather."

"Now, look here, I can find you all a job! With better pay than you ever got before, lest you've been cabinet ministers and bishops!"

And I led them to a small coppice I had noticed from above the town, showing them the acorns, explaining that each would receive two-pence apiece for every one set. I walked about the coppice and indicated the positions for the seeds by twigs thrust in the ground. Pontiflunk and I then took up our positions on a large stone and I spread about fifty acorns on my handkerchief. Each man received an acorn with instructions and the encouragement that their earnings depended on their exertions. I held a small book in my hand wherein to mark the amount due to each man – striking it on the stone as the signal to commence.

Shades of Sherwood, what a sight!! Four curious creatures displaying frantic energy beneath the blazing sky, casting off one garment after another, an hour of tremendous activity, until not one acorn remained on the handkerchief!

Red man, 12. Melancholy man, 16. Fat man, 11. Blue-faced man, 15.

"My good fellows, you are my brothers, and I love you, but in this extreme heat I love you best a few paces' distant – there – thank you. Now, I have a few coppers remaining... I'd like to reward some of you further. Which of you are teetotallers?"

"Me!" said the red and blue men together.

"Then I am sorry we part company so soon, for I am about to ask my two friends here to join me at The Red Lion to quaff a flowing bowl of cool beer, capped with an inch of delicious creamy froth. But! I won't dissuade you from your beliefs. Good-day!"

These words were greeted with a yell of fierce laughter, so infectious that the blue and red faced men soon joined in.

"We were only having you on, guv'nor..."

"Your sin is forgiven. Come on!"

And like Comus to this bedraggled band of curiosities, I led the way to the inn, paid for four pints of ale, and amid their good wishes, left them cooling.

The Book of the English Oak, Charles Hurst (abridged)

At five o clock that afternoon, H---- and Pontiflunk arrived in the small village of M--cot. They found accommodation in a blacksmith's tiny cottage, close by the church. Attracted by the "picturesque" qualities of the building, H---- took his dog to explore the church, and it was in the road running alongside this porch that Pontiflunk was killed, (f52) crushed under the wheels of a passing motor car. Just as suddenly as H---- had broken from practicality to Project, he now terminated the whole business, impossible alone, and returned to his family in M----------. The long interruption was over.

I entered the cool silence, and, seated in a pew, mused awhile on schemes for the efficient display of gummed slips promoting the setting of acorns in which cows, pigs, horses and dogs would form innocent propagandists.

f.52

I then rose.

Pontiflunk was waiting patiently in the porch. Pleased at my return, he ran ahead of me, down the path, through the gate and stood in the middle of the road.

Paaaarp! Paaaarrp!

I could hear the panting of a motor car! Paaaarp!

The thing swung round the corner and into view!

Pontiflunk, his gaze fixed upon me, did not seem to hear.

Paaaaarp! Paaaaarp! PAAAAAAAARP!!!!!

The sudden blast startled him, looking round he saw the thing upon him, closing, and stood petrified with fear.

The driver, believing no doubt the dog would run, did not slacken speed, but...

PAAAPAAAPAAAR!!!

And before I could make a movement the wheels passed over my poor creature, and he lay writhing in the dust. I ran to him and raised his head. But...

"Alas!!"

I could see he was done for. His agony was pitiful, but he seemed soothed by my caresses, and endeavoured to lick my hand.

I looked around for help and saw a man approaching me with that peculiar gait that comes of much horse-riding.

"Is he hurt?"

I answered him not, but gently raised my companion from the dusty road and carried him to the churchyard and laid him on the grass.

"I'm sorry this has happened, but my man thought he would clear out when the hooter blew. But I'll make it right with you. What's he worth? I'll give you a fair price. What breed do you call him?"

I looked at the man.

A smile!!! A smile hovered around his lips!! Almost imperceptible – but A SMILE!!!

"Fair price? Breed? What are you smiling at, you heartless rascal?"

"Don't be impertinent!"

"You damned villain!!"

My fury was uncontrollable, and gave me a temporary advantage over my powerful opponent. The conflict did not last long, however, for his man rushed to us, and the women ran shrieking to the scene; men darted from their cottages and we were soon parted.

"This fight must go on! This knave has smiled at my dog's agony!!"

By now the men from the neighbouring cottages stood between me and the smirking villain. I would listen to none who spoke on his behalf!

Eventually all dispersed – and only my friend the blacksmith remained with me and the dog.

"He's done, there's no doubt about it."

"I think he is too," said the blacksmith. He fetched a cushion and we carried Ponty to his house. His wife attended to the poor creature as if he were a child.

Pontiflunk died about nine o' clock and the good blacksmith buried him at the bottom of his garden.

Adieu, my affectionate little comrade. I will not know how to tell them at home of this. My return, so pleasantly anticipated, will be, after all, a sorry affair.

I walked next day, the rain in my face, and planted twenty acorns. That night as I lay in bed I knew that all joy in my journey had ceased. I rose early in the morning, walked to Northampton, and took an express to Manchester. Arriving in the grim city, in a little more than an hour I was seated in my usual chair at home, with my slippers on.

The Book of the English Oak, Charles Hurst (abridged)

Now Crab did not know what to make of H----. The more of The Book he had read, the less sure he was that H---- was serious. Twelve acorns a day?

And who was he, Crab, kidding?

Had H----, like Crab, discovered that at the heart of his mission was something that didn't make sense any more? Was it the acorn itself?

Because it grows, because it isn't a simple dimension of space. It must have been like carrying time in your pocket. Every time he knelt and set one of these, he saw that space a year ahead, a hundred, five hundred years ahead. Twelve times a day, over two or three miles, he'd feel himself stretch across time. Against all the odds, a bluff, practical man, with his sensible clothes, working boots and antiquated ways and words had begun to time travel – he'd slowed down, his closest friend was not of his species anymore, on the one hand he'd become a farm labourer, on the other he commanded the unemployed in work gangs, he slipped between classes, he acted out an economy like a theatre performance, dreaming of the ruin of mills, wandering among redundant hills, becoming space itself, a stroller on the way to Nowhere.

A few days after the Crab's own "what is this all about?" crisis, between S---ford and B---ham, he passed the yard of G. J. Pick Pallets; ravines of wood, three times the height of forklifts, stood in a grand canyon of timber. The smell!!! The enormous smell of the wood! Released in tiny particles, like the scattering of acorns, like the identity of a person on the road.

It seemed clear to Crab that after S----well Minster, H---- was walking to work out "how to be".

Crab left S----well first thing in the morning, passing the well that gave the town its name; the plaque was obscure, the well more of a spring, hidden and dry, its future seemed uncared for.

At the level crossing at F---kerton, M---, the signalman, welcomed Crab into his signal box, all still manual. Crab imagined the thousand feet of steel that M--- must pull to change the most distant arm. Slow, gentle work – a couple of trains an hour, plus freight – but M--- is a former painter and the slow solitude of a signalman is like the slow solitude of an artist. He has swapped careers for a regular income and a pension and he shows no signs of bitterness or any sense that he has exchanged a greater cause for a lesser one.

As Crab walks on he enjoys thinking of M---, and T---- at Newstead Abbey and the Peters at the Castle. They are the gatekeepers, regulating the flow, marking the hello and the goodbye, keeping people safe.

But he's sad to leave M---'s signal box, it's a 'border' place; part machine, part lounge, a generator of 'character'. In a few years it will be computerised.

The sign for Caythorpe had been changed to Gaythorpe.

Crab sees many ads for Pilates classes; given that it's Easter he can't help mis-reading them as promoting sessions of washing hands and avoiding responsibility.

His arrival at the Trent is almost processional; through a mini-avenue of trees at F--kerton. But the path along the bank is a pedestrian motorway, as characterless as a High Street full of national chainstores. Crab walks in step with passing gin palaces and then cuts inland, towards L---ley once more. The well-heeled villages are beginning to get him down, with their security fences and their angry dogs. It is a relief to get to L---ley, then up over the hill south of the village, just as in The Book, the view to B--voir Castle. All around the Crab on the hilltop are oaks of the right age. Perhaps his first dead H----; a fallen trunk, come down maybe in the last ten years, lying by one of the perverse ponds that sit on the hilltops here.

He crosses the metals at Burton J---- and looks up the track towards M--- in his machine-lounge.

At The Ferry Boat, Stoke Bard--ph, "Isn't she lovely!" wails over the speakers, a notice promises a half hour wait for Harvester-type meals. Crab declines and takes his beer outside, un-permitted, but away from the smell of cooking oil and the ching of overpriced drinks. He sits watching a ferry that isn't there anymore.

The man catches his eye – dusty grey coat, work boots, unshaven chin, swarthy and gap-toothed, makes for Crab like a shark, like a question mark. But Crab is quicker and fends off the moment of appeal with his own questions. The man is from C--lton, "one of the millions of unemployed", his father was a miner at G--ling, everything in N---------- in the last twenty years has been for the worse. Crab reminds him of the Victorian-style policeman who called 'last orders' at Yates Wine Lodge thirty years ago. The man tells Crab that the copper's name was "Tug Wilson" and that 'they' should put up a statue to him in the Market Square. Crab asks him what the future holds for N-------- and the man says, simply, "I don't know." They sit in silence, time travelling stupidly.

That night the Crab Man is staying with S-- and D----. S-- picks him up from Burton J---- and drives him to As----ton, past piles of horseshoes, like banks of good luck, and a Romany caravan on a village green, a knife-sharpener on his annual visit. S-- says that she is trying to persuade the As----ton congregation to keep their church open at all times, but people say "the kids will vandalise it". S-- says: "which kids? Your kids?" D----'s a trustee of the cemetery; offered a seat for mourners to use, the other trustees wouldn't accept it. Scared of each other, people are handing their public space over into a void, (f53) generating the dread spaces that are meat and drink to a drifter like the Crab Man. In protecting and defending what remains of public space, the authorities turn it into holey space, the terrain of choice of the resistant wanderer.

Maps and their expansive boundaries create the illusion that we live our lives across planes of possibility when in fact we move within narrow corridors, with sudden airline leaps in summer. We need a new set of maps, made in strips, unfeasible, like our lives.
(E-Maps)

$f.53$

Action: create a series of pulpits – in city centres, deep in woods, in the middle of fields – open for anyone to use (ramped), without locks, constructed from material that will last longer than human speech, platforms for public speech and silent indictment.

In the morning, when S-- drops him back at Burton J----, the Reverend J--- D----- – The Small Vicar – is already waiting for him. It's wonderful to see him again. They have walked once before, in central London, when J--- D----- was thrown out of a gift shop for photographing shelves of identical resting policemen the Crab Man had just described to their gang of wanderers as looking like riot police, two streets back from the fighting, having a breather. They practice H----ian strolling along the bank of the Trent. (E-strolling) And at this gentle pace, out of the path of dog walkers and on the sandy edge, they find numerous accidental pieces of Land Art – a chance Richard Long here, a freakish Nancy Holt there, and then a fortuitous David Nash. They walk in a matrix of accidental beauty. A kingfisher scintillates by. The Crab has never heard of David Nash, so as they walk the Small Vicar describes Nash's piece Wooden Boulder, carved from a single trunk, a boulder of wood, released into a waterfall and moving seven times downstream in more than twenty years, turning black like stone, edging towards the sea. The Crab likes the idea of a decaying art released to perform its disappearance.

On the shore is something wrapped in a knotted red cloth – the shape and size of a human heart. The Crab opens the fabric tentatively. A coconut.

The Crab's phone rings. His old school-friend M---, the Curator, he's in a cab somewhere between N---------- Station and the two walkers. They meet him on the bridge at G--thorpe.

89

It is in the nature of these walks that the Curator is not only the Crab's oldest friend but also a director of the National Museum Wales and curator of David Nash's most recent exhibition.

From now to N---------- they count possible H---- oaks, on the S---ford meadows always a few fields away, framed and inaccessible, like old landscape paintings. (f54)

After a perilous hike on the edge of a narrow road the three find the one pub at S---ford, only candidate for H----'s Inn. The place looks shut, its sign fallen and leaning drunkenly against a wall in the car park. There's evidence of building work. For the sake of form they approach a side door and it's open. S--, the barmaid, is playing computer poker.

"Are you open?"

"S--!" encourages a man behind the bar.

The Crab attempts to take a crafty snap of S--, but the fellow behind the bar catches him… "S--, he's taking a photo of you!"

When others "ooo!" at some hillside vista or expanse of green valley, do you also see fences and property? In Simon Pope's London Walking it is the sites with generous vistas that seem to provoke suicides. It seems there is a certain affordance in these places, that we perhaps mistake for the place remembering past events.

They wait for her to finish her game. There's no food on sale, in the second bar two men are constructing their own sandwiches, laying slices of bread on the counter. It's all a little uncomfortable until the Crab chances his tale and everything changes. He reads to S-- the passages about the pub in The Book. She calls over a customer – D---- who begins with a Pinteresque conversation with S--: "You've missed him." "He rang – do you know what he wanted?" "Did he say?" "I missed him." "O. He's gone now." "Ah." "You've missed him." "He didn't say what it was?" "What was it?" "I wish I could remember." "Why don't you ring him?" "What shall I say?" "Ask him." "Ah. Where's he gone?" "Round to see you." "Ah." – and moves on to a free-ranging chatter, on place names, the Saracen's Head, mill work and pub games. D---- says he moved south reluctantly to please his wife; from G--ling (a mile to the north).

After they leave, D---- races after them in his car to tell them of the fifteen old fire insurance signs that once decorated S---ford's cottages. Until they were mentioned on Down Your Way. Then thieves came with ladders and stole most of them away.

The three reach the south bank of the Trent. It's a scene from Apocalypse Now: fires burn all along the edge of the river. The Small Vicar tells them of Rae Gates' website Entrances2hell which gathers photos of ordinary portals that portend dreadful things. They're going through one now. Fastening on the queasiness, quad-bikers drive them uphill, away from the river and they take a late lunch at The Trent public house at R--cliffe. The Afro-Caribbean landlady is disproportionately amazed at the Crab's story, staggered that the three might now walk to N--------- and when the Crab gives her a pack of the little maps he carries as presents she gives him a warm kiss – an unexpected tenderness; planting an acorn in his heart.

Touched, the three walk down a dead end that isn't, though the residents would like everyone to think it is, pass the vast, dreadful and un-shimmering endlessness of a rowing lake that planes off into an infinity of pain, and approach Forest's ground and the Brian Clough stand, chatting about stadium rock, U2 and the Crab's Mum's terrible faux-pas with Bono in his hotel ending calamitously with her request for "anything from Phantom of the Opera?"

D----, in the S---ford pub, had told them of some un-marked graves in G---lston churchyard, a dark place shadowed by yews. When the Crab had asked the Easter Sunday congregation at L--dham some questions about G---lston church, their answers were all wrong, as if the place was putting out a cover story, like in a black op. The bodies of children. Under the yews. Victims of mill work. Expendable London orphans. Mass graves. No headstones. Such was the slaughter,

D---- says, that the bodies began to be distributed about the various local churchyards, to hide the numbers. Such grievances are not quickly forgotten because they are generalised.

That night the Crab dreamed he lived in a world where writing was dangerous. Where police sought out anyone in possession of it. He wandered through this world in various states of humiliation, not particularly frightened by investigators, but more by social clubs, mores and manners, pecking orders and sports, knuckleheads, elitism and upper class sexiness. His only way to stop sinking into the contempt of others was to sing poems, their unexpected phrasing expressing the detail of feelings, different from appearances. As he sang, a young woman sought him out; she is Integrity, they embrace, but as they make their way to her room a bell rings and she, along with hundreds of others, begins to march. The Crab loses her in the crowds, some of whom begin an orgy, and for the rest of the dream he searches unsuccessfully for this girl with short blond hair, as he drives ludicrous wooden carts with sails, and then a car – driving from the back seat, unable to reach the steering wheel – careering through a wedding party of the well-to-do. He is with E--- S----, one of the actors from the company that had begun at C---erton. Maybe E--- S---- has some news of where she is? But police approach and arrest E--- S---- for possession of some scraps of paper. The Crab manages to persuade them that these are insignificant notes. The Crab is not frightened for himself, only of losing her. But he is uneasy in the fraternity houses, unable to be quite placed. Unafraid of authority, but lonely in the face of casual status.

M---, the signalman, has an itch inside his working boots. He can't get at it – "do you ever get that?"

To S---ford Again

Next day, after dinner and an overnight stay at D-----'s and C----'s, the Crab sets off for the centre of N---------- with The Academic, a lecturer with a special interest in site-specific theatre and performance, and, most recently performance linked to transport.

At the centre they ask after the Flying House Hotel where H---- and Pontiflunk took their dinner before visiting the Castle. It is now part of the Flying Horse Shopping Centre, the fireplace of the "cheerful room" where engineer and dog enjoyed their repasts still evident, though piled with Benetton cardigans. After their ambivalent visit to the Castle, Crab and Academic head out of the city.

On its borders they experience a key space-moment, familiar to these walkings. They'd got down by the edge of the Trent, by a roaring weir, approaching that part of the river bank that the Small Vicar, Curator and Crab had been driven off by quad-bikers the day before. But this is a lower part, closer to the water and here there is a climbable wall. But what if the bank runs out further down? What if the water rises suddenly? They're hard up against the same red cliffs that H---- had passed under. It could be a long walk back if the path peters out. The Crab might not have taken such a path without The Academic. She's using the walking stick he'd been lent and she occasionally stops to perform alarming exercises to get her ballet-damaged knee back in order. They scramble over the wall, into a rich web of twisted elegance, drapes of sandpapered driftwood and bleached plastic, shoes, bottles, thin shifting sands beneath their boots, python-like trunks enfolding a wonderland of miniature, bleached beach-ness, playful and apocalyptic. A little nudge to say – this world is going to be pleasurable, right to the end.

At S---ford, they start thinking about how The Academic can get back to her car and so a bus turns the corner. They flag it down and in a moment she's gone.

The Crab sits with a pint in the car park of The Chesterfield Arms, waiting for S--, noting the van parked exactly adjacent to the back wall, invisible to the road. Two men emerge and something in a plastic bag is transferred from its boot to a flatback. One of those days in England.

To B--tesford

Next morning the Crab leaves S---ford, passing a dead greenfinch by the road, killed by the draught of a speeding car, and the dispersing particles of wood from G.J. Pick Pallets. He arrives in B--gham – "The Vales Housing development – the place to start living!" - and turns off the main road and along a disused railway line, now the Linear Nature Park. A dumped and cracked blue plastic scallop-shell sandpit lies abandonned. "Harness my talents" begs a graffito. The Crab stops to chat with a man whose dog is taking him for a walk. The not-quite-in-control beast has seized a giant stick and racing by his – ha, ha –'master' the stick cracks the man across the shins. He's greeted the Crab with "lovely day again."

"I've had this for twelve days," Crab says.

"As long as it doesn't turn into a drought – I don't know if it is global warming."

They agree that it's difficult to know what to believe.

"They want you to turn your remote off – fat lot of good that'll do! That Al Gore, he's a big one for this, but they say his house has got more light bulbs than the …"

He can't think of anything that has got less light bulbs than Al Gore's house.

"I fly four times a year to see my daughter in Majorca, I'm not going to stop that. There's too many people. They complain about China and India, while we export our shit! It was alright in the 60's, people had a Morris Minor or a Volkswagen, but now they want a BMW…"

It's a remarkable conversation. For it contains all the possibilities and resources necessary to change the world, and all the short-sightedness and individualism that make it impossible.

"Nice to have a moan," he says as they part, still rubbing his shin.

"Miserable old sod, that farmer – but you've got the right of way – it's the show jumper, Whittaker, it's his farm."

O, great.

The Linear Nature Park begins as a cut in a hill, but changes slowly into a raised embankment with a sweeping view of a valley floor. The Crab can tell from his map that the old line soon runs out and he must cross a farm. That might be H----'s preference, but not Crab's. They share some qualities: arrogance, love of beer and their own company, but the Crab is not at ease on a farm as H---- is. Uneasier now, thanks to the brief exchange with the disgruntled walker, the Crab negotiates the footpath, slipping down the side of the embankment. To a small wooden bridge across a river. He's barely placed a foot on its boards when he sees a horse rider in the field on the other side, at the same moment as the rider sees the Crab and steers the horse towards him. Crab slows. But the horse hasn't seen the Crab and when it does it shies and rears and the rider barely hangs on.

O, really great now.

Crab steps back onto the bridge as the rider (presumably Whittaker) steadies his mount. Crab begins to apologise.

"That's all right, you spooked him because he didn't see you. You can use the footpath."

"Is that all right?"

"Just keep outside the electric fence and it'll take you to the stile into the next field."

"I'm sorry I scared the horse."

"Don't worry, it's in his character."

Later, when Crab jumps high as a steeplechaser as a startled hare races from a hedge, he wonders if it's in his character too. Is it the ability to be spooked that harnesses our talents?

At the 'Marquis of Granby', at Granby, Crab stops for a pint of Marquis. S---- the landlord is washing his dog. Crab tells him of Pontiflunk's ablutions and takes a photo.

He makes good time to B---esford, checks in at The Thatch and then, slightly bizarrely, takes the B---esford train back to N-------- and room A42 of the Sir Clive Grainger building, in the University of N--------'s School of Geography, to hear the Professor (f55) address forty or so academics and their students. The hulky ones in rugby jerseys hide on the back row. She is here to speak about London as a 'world city' – what's that got to do with H---, with E---, and L---ley?

She speaks of a contradictory London, of a place where people come to be free, but are often escaping impoverishment inflicted by a globalisation originated in London. So what's that got to do with G--alston, with N----- B----, and South W--ham?

The Professor had warned the Crab in her email that her paper might not be relevant to his walk, but at the end he tells her of his conversations in village homes and B&Bs; of an engineer just back from a Chinese province, of a granddaughter buying for Marks & Spencer in Sri Lanka, of surveying in Malaysia – "the villages are just as connected".

It is clear from the content of the address, that the Professor in question is Doreen Massey, Professor of Geography at the Open University. The Crab Man's interest and enthusiasm for Massey's work sits in distinct contrast to Massey's pronounced lack of enthusiasm for the situationist tradition in which the Crab seems to place himself.

f.55

This passage allows the Crab Man's walk to be dated, for documentation exists placing Massey at the University of Nottingham in April 2007.

In her paper the Professor brings together her involvement in the politics of London – she's an advisor to the Mayor – with her lifelong obsession with the way people talk about 'space', and she has three propositions for what space really is:

One: it's the product of practices – we make space. Two: it's a multiplicity, it's the thing that allows more than one thing to happen at a time, it's where other people are. And three: it's never finished, it's always being made.

But the world as it is doesn't seem to fit her space. In its flows, where everything we do affects other parts of the world, politics is organised territorially! From parliaments to parish councils. The government deals with wars, the parish council with verges. But what if you could cut across this, if every local place had some kind of international politics… (every Parish Council should have its Office of International Relations).

Things flood the Crab's head – which tends to happen when he listens to the Professor – beware of the dog, faded signs declaring M--------- a Nuclear-Free Zone, N--------shire villagers living in houses still largely built around mud walls, "the day a nig-nog comes through that door, I die!", the Franciskaner Weißbiers at The Highwayman…

Stop seeing the local as the product, the victim of the global. Because it's at the local that the global is organised. Each thing and everyone is made up of many things, so – show hospitality to the 'other within'. Then there's another geography, that looks outwards… and the key to that is taking responsibility, not just for what we do, but for what has made us. And again the images come rushing in!! Of all those dispersing particles, suddenly thrown into reverse – clustering into a pallet, and then into pieces of timber, and then a tree, and then an acorn.

He feels the seed, planted in his heart, start.

Identity is not a claim on something or somewhere, but it is the acceptance of a responsibility.

For the first and only time the Crab wishes he had brought some acorns.

To South W--ham

Next morning in B--tesford, the Crab buys a film for his camera. The DJ on Radio Spar Live announces that the company is giving away trees to schools. "Spar – rooted in the community".

Last night the train had stopped at As----ton. In the shelter four lads and a girl mucked around, mock-fighting, in the intermittent purple light of a malfunctioning neon strip. They were having fun, but it looked like a nightmare.

Climbing towards B--voir, the mist comes down. Wooosh! A sports car shoots by, reminding the Crab of an early sequence in O Lucky Man!, another narrative of incoherent wandering through a representative England of unexpected corruptions and mass productions. Rather than a shell Malcolm McDowell wears a gold suit. The bleak industrial architecture of B--voir Fruit Farms. B--voir Castle closed and hidden in the mist. A friendly chap directs the Crab past the castle grounds and onto the wide Jubilee Way, which almost immediately brings him to an unsigned three way junction. He chooses the way with the stile, but disturbs a field-full of monster geese, who organise themselves into squadrons of aggressors, swooping out of the mist at him, then disappearing into the mist again – each time diving lower and lower, closer and closer. Until the Crab panics, turns and jogs back the way he's come.

And so begins a day of something like nightmare. For, to get off the roads, the Crab elects to walk The Viking Way. Soon he realises why it's called The Viking Way – because until he came

along no one since the Vikings has been stupid enough to walk it. It's not a bridleway at all; gateless, it's been churned to mush by cross-country vehicles and dried to rock-hardness by a fortnight of sun. To avoid a broken ankle he must walk with his eyes fixed to the ground. He meets no one. On the hills he can see his own breath.

Fixed to the ground he begins to disappear inside himself.

This is the opposite of the walk across Derbyshire moorland with all his particles dispersing. On The Viking Way he is forced into a single point of unhappy effort. After three hours all the parts of his self have collected about this point and formed into a material object – a pint of beer. A huge water tower taunts him, lures him. Into Buck--nster where the pub is shut for a private function! This is the cruellest privatisation of public space yet!! And on screaming blisters he limps to S--stern, harassed by a pair of weedy but malevolent hoodies on mountain bikes, where at the Blue Dog he consumes two pints of Bog-Eyed in quick order. In the bar three guests for the Buck--nster 'do' are warming up. One man regales a couple, occasionally dropping his voice, nudge-nudge, with tales of screwing bridesmaids in Belgrade – "they're not like us" – the predicament of a mutual friend with two women on the go, shootin', owning a Labrador, interesting roadkill; it's Billy Bunter meets Ben Dover. An old man totters past and warns the Crab that the little white dog at the bar is fine when you come in, but "'e won't like you leavin'"!

Great.

The Crab decides on a third Bog-Eyed. On the walls – coronation parade 1953, first aiders 1969, a tribute band, various pub dogs, fancy dress parades, a spectacular fall at a steeplechase… this didn't come as a job lot from the brewery. The wedding guests, with their opportunistic morals and their shootin' and roadkill, consume the ambience without giving it attention.

The three pints and his unwanted and involuntary eavesdropping leave the Crab in a changed mood as the landlady puts the white dog in another room and he heads off. He is no longer the dispersed and open pilgrim, but steely, closed and angry, sick of harshness, sick of the lack of communality, sick of the assumption that you have no right to the road without a machine, sick of the swathes of property, sick of 'beware of the dog'. He stops waving to motorists, cuts through the country as sharply as he can, until he's mellowed by the friendly village of South W--ham.

There he feels as though he passes beyond something.

There is something special about South W--ham. Something changing. Something in shapes. Just before the village, he's attracted to a hill on his left. He likes the feeling of it… the shapes and shadows seem to draw out his anger. And on the right side an edgeland of collapsed sheds, crime scene tape and decoration opens up – a theatre of young dreams. Houses cluster round a dried out and turfed village pond. Later, in a book borrowed from his landlady, P--, he will learn that he's passed the site of the former Satellite Club, that the hill is Temple Hill and its shadows the grid of a Knights Templar complex, and that those gigantic roars from the mist are from military aircraft (f56) at Cottesmore: "Harriers, Tornados and AWACS" says P--. And we are still at war over Jerusalem. He drinks a pint of L------shire Bomber at the Angel Inn.

f.56c See footnote beginning "Tourism as an organised agency…!" page 223.

To St--ford

Before the Crab Man begins his walk to St--ford, he accompanies P-- to the church of St John the Baptist. She brings the key, but the church is already open when they arrive. There's a mixture here of the sublime and the ridiculous; an ancient coffin lid propped behind some brooms, a Roman grave marked with a traffic cone, the south door flanked by phallus and slit. The bell atop the church, open to the elements, reminds the Crab of the Spanish Mission in Vertigo and suggests the influence of a nineteenth century vicar's Iberian wife.

Then a detour to the Quarry. The young woman on the gate is no M---, no T----, no Peter, not yet, and so he must make do with his imagination; of part of a buried boiler that South W--ham kids dubbed "the sunken train". It's enough.

"Jew Crew" says the gang graffito.

The Crab Man walks for five hours and sees no one. The heat is intense and he's struggling. The footpaths are empty. Apart from a flock of – "weep weep" – birds, possibly lapwings, in a field of marshy grass – "weep weep" – who subject him to more military swooping.

He passes the Jackson Stops Inn at Str--ton, for sale for so long they named it after the estate agents.

At Pickworth a man refills the Crab's water bottle from his kitchen.

And, at the request of its rider, Crab leads a timid horse across a quiet road – it has become frozen with anxiety unable to move. The Crab is unsure who is more scared, as he takes its bridle. Its great eye swivels, and the Crab feels the strength and power of the horse as they take a few steps together.

Walking these almost empty roads (f57) is a pleasure, but the Crab is giddy from the heat.

f.57

*In the UK there are many rural footpaths, some – the green lanes, postal, drovers' and pack routes – of considerable vintage, but don't ignore the joys of the metalled roads. Avoiding busy and dangerous roads (and taking a precautionary route at tight corners), the reward is in the series of unfolding communities. So few people walk the roads now, that the pedestrian gaze is often unaccounted for, affording the walker unguarded revelations of natural, private and civil idiosyncrasy. ***

*Publishers' note: this footnote was originally designated for the Toolbag.

He wobbles down the hill into St--ford: his last chance of H---- trees. He scours the skyline for a sign of that grid of oaks that must have risen from the little coppice. He longs to find a legacy of the red man, the fat man, the blue-faced man and the melancholic. To sit on the same stone as H---- and Pontiflunk. To enjoy the geometry. But the Crab Man sees nothing remotely like it. (f58) And instead makes his way to the Museum, where a helpful A--- digs out a late nineteenth century map in the hope of finding some trace of the coppice. No luck there either. Nor among the locals questioned – no one can think of any substantial group of oaks in St--ford. No one can think of any oaks in St--ford!!

f.58

Glossary of Remote Viewing terms (abridged):

Aesthetic Impression (AI): a feeling and intuitive response to landscapes remotely viewed, inimical to Scientific Remote Viewing (SRV).

Analytic Overlay (AOL): a rational analysis of the RV experience while in duration. When this occurs the Remote Viewer is to declare it and expunge it.

Bilocation: the Remote Viewer's experience of his/her consciousness dividing between the target site and the Viewer's own material location.

Cue: a word or phrase introduced to a Viewer in order to direct them to part of the target site.

Emotional Impact (EI): emotions present at the target site. As distinct from emotions (AI's) experienced by Remote Viewers.

Event – a Cue that locates the Viewer's consciousness at the target site at a time of significant activity.

Scientific Remote Viewing (SRV): the activity.

Signal Line (SL): event stream from the unconscious mind including AI and WI.
Stages: 1: crude contact, possibly a building, 2: colours, texture, temperatures, 3: making a sketch, 4: intimate problem-solving, 5: furniture in the room, 6: guided explorations

(limited intellectual activity), advanced sketching, 7: names, addresses, phone numbers, 8: beer.

Structure: "remaining in structure" refers to Viewers doing as they are told.

Targets: Typical = places, events, people. More difficult = a particular person's fantasies, the cause of an event, even God.

Target Time (TT): date and time of the target, such as 1947 for the Roswell Incident.

Demoralised, the Crab buys some beer for the evening and heads off for a compensatory cream tea at a quaint tea shop he's spotted on his way in. As he opens the door a figure is exiting and the Crab says:

"You're R-- D--------- and I haven't seen you for thirty years."

R-- was a friend at school. He even went youth hostelling with the Curator exactly where the Crab had been two weeks before. The Crab rattles on to him and his family about theatre, about his journey, about H---- and the oaks. But only as they're about to leave does the Crab ask R-- what he's doing now. R-- lowers his voice, like the oaf in the Blue Dog relating shenanigans with

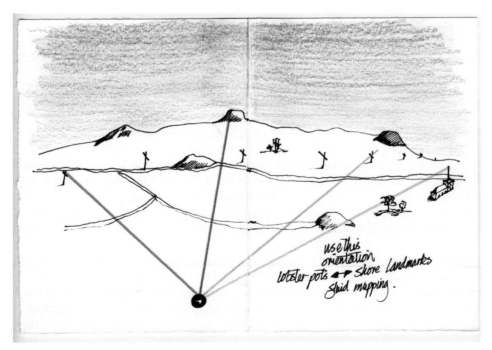

bridesmaids in Belgrade, (whispers) – he's the new Permanent Secretary at the Ministry of Transport, the former Director General of Roads. And after two weeks of meditating on walking, on cars, on what our mobility makes us … the Crab can think of nothing to say to him.

He finishes his tea and heads, like H----, for The George. That night, he watches Blood Diamond at the St--ford Arts Centre. And thinks of the Professor as the light from the projector glints on the jewels of St--ford ladies.

If London is the Professor's 'world city' then St--ford is his world town. Its churches define it, like the towers of San Gimignano – state it rather than confine it. In the three minute walk from The George to the Arts Centre the Crab has listed 30 references to places overseas; from stone fleur-de-lys to designer labels.

The Rutland Mercury reports that 10 out of 16 County Council seats will be uncontested due to lack of candidates.

A huge explosion has rocked the Parliament Building in Iraq.

The papers, yesterday full of hostages' personal stories, are now turning on those who sanctioned them.

In his bedroom at The George the Crab watches, for the umpteenth time, Election – a comedy about imposing democracy at a US High School.

To M--cott

Before breakfast the Crab asks reception if the crypt mentioned on the Hotel's history sheet is accessible. Expecting a polite rebuttal, he's delighted when S---- the Porter is instantly summoned. S---- leads him to the cocktail lounge where he assumes that S---- will unlock some concealed door. But, in the architectural equivalent of one of those "I shouldn't tell you this, but" moments, he begins to move the furniture about, sliding away an armchair and some stools. The Crab is still expecting the door, when S---- pushes back a sofa to reveal a trapdoor, which he deftly opens and the Crab follows him down a metal ladder.

They enter the secret England that the giant-handed, council subcontractor in the knitted hat had led the Crab through before, in thought. Now S---- the Porter, another gatekeeper, a M---, a T----, another Peter, welcomes him into a cool holey space below the cocktail bar. It's clear, even to the Crab's uneducated eye, that there are a number of buildings here, a hybrid: twentieth century concrete, eighteenth century handmade bricks. Most striking though are a pair of vaulted arches, remnants of a hospital of the Knights of St John, companions to the Knights Templar, originators of the St John's Ambulance Brigade.

The Saracen's Head, the roar of the AWACS aircraft through the mist, the shadows in the field outside South W--ham, Easter Sunday at L--dham, Bunyan's The Holy War in Holly Lodge – Jerusalem is always here. Even beneath the cocktail bars. (f59)

The Crab has just begun breakfast when R---mary arrives. She's heard the Radio 4 report of his walk. He explains that this is his last day, his chance to find the resting place of that miserable cur and cherished companion, Pontiflunk. And then J--- arrives; architect of the Rutland Round, parts of which the Crab walked yesterday, scene of avian military operations against him. The guide for the day.

It is hot, and the three are soon tempted into a car boot sale to worship at tables of junk. The Crab buys a display of coins collected free from petrol stations – 'Space Exploration', including one for Sputnik, and J--- tells them of a verse drama he once participated in, the writer insisting on inserting new lines on contemporary events, including Sputnik's launch. Quite a challenge for the rhyming scheme.

R---mary tells the Crab that 'her claim to fame' is to have once climbed around a classroom without touching the floor. He likes this subversion of geography. She sings in a tunnel. He's sad when they say goodbye to her at T--well. He and J--- repair to The Crown for roast beef and Abbot Ale.

"Palestine has been one of the countries most visited by pilgrims and travellers over the ages. The accounts I have read do not describe a land familiar to me but rather a land of these travellers' imaginations… what mattered was not the land and its inhabitants as they actually were but the confirmation of the viewer's or reader's religious or political beliefs… Perhaps the curse of Palestine is its centrality to the West's historical and biblical imagination…" Raja Shehadeh, Palestinian Walks: Notes on a Vanishing Landscape

f.59

As they walk, J---, an organiser and maker of footpaths, a member of Harringworth & Rutland Chowder and Marching Society, lists places, directions, paths blocked, paths opened and re-opened, stiles repaired and refashioned, committees amalgamated and duties delegated. The Crab is dizzy from the spreading map of links, routes, disputes and rules. But it is a kind of Epicureanism. Then J--- tells the Crab of another geography; under Beachy Head, operating radar for the RAF, J--- would enter a subterranean installation through an anonymous bungalow, walking down a sloping underground road. The Crab adds this to the ballroom and the crypt on his mental map of secret England. (f60)

The Crab realises he has not seen a single person in military uniform for these 16 days – another disappearance of the public. (f61)

They follow the edge of Castle Cement's vast quarry at K--ton, the giant roof of the works like the shell of a monster beetle from The Planet of The Bugs, then after quiet roads they arrive at the buzz and hum of Rutland Water and the swish of burkhas. This is where Leicester comes to play on a Sunday. The Crab returns a lost ball to a child and a mother's voice thanks him through the fabric. The road to H-----ton disappears into the water. He savours these subversions of geography.

"At first everything seems to be proceeding smoothly. Slowly but surely, Navidson draws more and more slack rope down onto the floor, steadily lifting Reston up through the bore of th(e) stairs. Then about halfway up, something strange happens: the excess rope at Navidson's feet starts to vanish, while the rope he holds begins to slip across his fingers and palms with enough speed to leave a burning gash. Navidson finally has to let go. Reston, however, does not fall. In fact, Reston's ascent only accelerates… But if Navidson is no longer holding onto the rope, what could possibly be pulling Reston to the top? Then as the stairway starts getting darker and darker as that faintly illuminated circle above – the proverbial light at the end of the tunnel – starts getting smaller and smaller, the answer becomes clear… the stairway is stretching (ffa), expanding…" Mark Z. Danielewski, House of Leaves

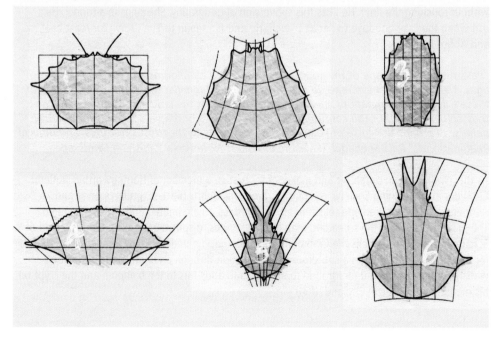

In the city of Z----- at the Walk 21 Conference a commercial company exhibited a small enclosed space which could model various walking experiments, so that street furniture, levels, surfaces etc. could be tested on a human subject. These machines should be purchased in large numbers and set up as publicly owned, free-access theatres without any purpose other than enjoyment. Or perhaps as sacred spaces of walking. Lo-tech versions could be made widely available, but only in public places. Like the chalked Masonic space, but not covert. In the city of E ----- a set of roads are named after astronauts, making the area lunar.

See footnote beginning "Tourism as an organised agency…!" page 223.

ff.a

f.61c

Suddenly weary, the Crab Man begins to struggle, almost wading along the roads. This is the day he must find Pontiflunk, but J---'s snaking route has its teeth in the clock. His feet are suffering. The heat and 16 days. He walks as though these were the streets of N---anton, under Rutland Water.

And then, suddenly, the tape seems to wind forward and M--cott is in sight. The sun is falling. The green fields rust. The village gleams. And the Crab Man and J--- climb the last stiles of the journey. A dog barks.

"He's here!"

And as they descend the final field, the crustacean thinks of M---------- and potato cakes.

Then up the other side and into the village. He cannot quite believe he's arrived – he can't believe his knees have survived. But all that fades, all that's meaningless if nothing remains. He's desperate now to find the site of the accident and then Ponty's grave. And J--- is equally keen for him to see the church. Why the church? Not now.

As they turn the corner of the churchyard the Crab Man realises that he's pictured this scene vividly in his head: a blacksmith's cottage, a proletarian scene, he's seen it like his Gran and Grandpa's council bungalow in C-------, the grave is a version of their tiny garden, but this is completely different, with thatched cottages, golden in the evening sun. This is the place, the corner, the houses, the church and he begins to pace out the scene, his cracked voice rising to a shout: "it would be here, it would here, yes! No! Where's the corner!?! Yes, that's it… the car from there, the horn sounds… the dog runs down the path… which path… where's the porch?"

Of course J--- is right; start at the church. And for a few minutes the Crab Man sits in the church, so full up he cannot think.

He gets up from the pew. Like C------ H----, he makes for the door. The dog rises in excitement from the porch and lollops down the path and into the middle of the street.

Paaaarp! Paaarp!

It's clear where it has to be – perpendicular to the church is a short path to the road, the corner is not the one on the main road, it's in the side street they've just come up!! He can see it all now! The dog just standing there. Transfixed!!

Paaaarp! Paaaarp!!

Run! This time, run!!!

But the dog doesn't. He can't. He's fixed in terror forever.

Neeeeeow!! Neeeeow!!! Neeeeow!!

The Crab Man kneels in the road and mimes picking up the stricken Ponty, carrying the dog to the grass of the churchyard.

That villain is coming up now.

"Is he hurt? I'm sorry this has happened… But I'll make it right with you. What's he worth? I'll give you a fair price. *What breed do you call him?*"

"What breed! I'll give you what breed!!"

And the Crab Man begins to swing punches into thin air.

Meanwhile P--, J---'s wife, has gone to consult the bed-ridden local historian on the whereabouts of the blacksmith's cottage. They've come up with a cottage, but it's too far from the scene. Nearby there was a forge. But was there a cottage for its blacksmith?

Frustrated, the Crab Man begins to ring on door bells, but is driven back by mortar bees.

P-- returns. No, there was just a forge. And a garden that was turned into a cottage.

"A garden? Can we go and look?"

And J--- leads the Crab Man gently, as H---- might have led his dog, to the gate and then into the garden of Forge Cottage.

"Forge Cottage!"

Ah, no. It's a modern cottage… but hanging on the garden wall are blacksmith's tools,   /|\
horseshoes and cogs.

J--- leans into an open window and the Crab Man, discretely, joins him. Through the aperture they can see an elderly lady in a dark dressing gown immersed in the shadows.

"I've been in hospital," she explains.

She can't really help them and yet it seems clear the forge was here or hereabouts, the gate to the farm the forge serviced is directly opposite the cottage gate. It would make sense if this was originally a garden to one of the adjacent cottages and that one of them was lived in by the blacksmith and his wife.

And the Crab Man might now be standing beside Pontiflunk's grave. At last. Right now. He asks if he can take a photograph, thanks the old lady and then gives one look back. Stunned that he could be standing a few yards from M--cott Church, in the garden of Forge Cottage, and still – STILL – be unsure. (f62)

After a day of J---'s detailed descriptions of routes, of stiles, of gaps and steps, of this way and that way, of Crow Acts and bye-laws, of access forums and parish councils, suddenly there is nothing certain, and the Crab had been so sure THIS would be the moment of certainty, closure and completion. And what had he really found? A handful of possible oaks and the understanding that he could leave the way open for others, for them to find H----'s oaks, to find H---- and who he was, to check the 1909 M--cott directory of trades for a blacksmith and the whereabouts of his cottage, to decide whether global warming is caused by our behaviour, to travel wormholes, to define their identity by what they take responsibility for…

At moments like these one might begin to suspect that material geography is even more fluid than Doreen Massey's migrant mountain. That these places might move around like the 'rues sauvages' of China Miéville's story "Reports Of Certain Events In London" in Looking for Jake, or like the predatory cities of Philip Reeve's Mortal Engines, or the mobile locations of Hayao Miyazaki's Howl's Moving Castle and Laputa: Castle In The Sky, or the latter's model in Swift's Gulliver's Travels.

f.62

Going Home

The next day J--- drops off the Crab Man in St--ford to catch the train home. He has an hour to wait and goes to All Saints Church, then walks with his back to the church for 5 minutes, the time H---- said it took to get to the coppice. Keeping All Saints at the same 5 minutes walking distance, he begins to cut a circle through St--ford looking for oaks. He finds not one. But he walks through numerous twentieth century housing developments, any one of which might have been cause for the clearance of a small coppice. About to close the circle and catch his train he passes the St John's Ambulance Brigade hall and then, across the road, sees… an office… an insurance office… Oakwood Insurance!!

"O my goodness!"

Was this it? Had he found the last surviving fruit of H----'s acorns. He gingerly enters the small office. Three women sit at desks at the front of the office, a younger man at a desk behind.

"Excuse me, is this office part of a national chain or are you specific to here?"

"We're not part of a national chain – there's just this office."

"And are you called Oakwood after an oak wood that was here?"

A young man, at the back of the office, stands up from his desk, suddenly authoritative. The Crab Man realises that he is about to learn what is really left, what endures, what drives history and meaning, what remains to point us to our future, safely, responsibly.

"My father founded this company," the young man says, "He called it Oakwood…"

"Yes, but because there was a wood here? Did he want to remember a wood?"

"He called it Oakwood because he thought it would sound attractive to people. Nothing to do with trees, I'm afraid. Sorry."

As the Crab Man leaves, closing the door of Oakwood Insurance behind him, the sound of the hinges is like the rustling of leaves. Behind the window he hopes that three women and a young man are beginning to imagine their own forests.*

* With thanks for their generosity and administrative efficiency to New Perspectives Theatre Company, Nottingham, in whose archives an early version of this document was discovered among the records of a theatrical project.

WHAT IS
MYTHOGEOGRAPHY?

Preface

What follows is the nearest to theory (see Theory, page 168) that mythogeography has got so far. Which may not be that close (partly for reasons of operational flexibility, but also as an act of faith that one day others might fill the void with something helpful). And because mythogeography must always be a mixture of thoughts and actions, and not so much a theory, but a series of approaches, a set of modest survival strategies, a bran tub of prefigurative behaviours plus the honesty to say that no one really knows what is going to happen. So this is more a toolbag of ideas for those wanting to create their own mythogeographical practice and less a guide to the philosophy that may one day strangle it.

So, here goes.

Introduction

In the past imagining Utopia has involved the erection of borders, fencing off a community with a radical identity or putting a distance between now and the future or setting sail for an ideal island.

Mythogeography, however, began in a quite different way; with site-specificity rather than exemplariness, with theatre rather than with politics, struggling to expose people to what was most immediate rather than what was distant and desired on behalf of others. This was more difficult than expected! Participants in early mythogeographical experiments often felt like expelling themselves for their lack of resistance to the lure of the general. No sooner had they managed to fight off the temptation for metaphorical grandstanding, than what they had stripped away came back at them: porous and full of wormholes (f63) to elsewhere. (This is an important but pretty obvious lesson: sometimes getting things wrong helps the most.)

Any illusions entertained by these first mythogeographers about skiing comfortably across the ascetic, cool, smooth, planed territory of specificity, or pleasurably frotting a warm and crumbly local texture, were soon erupted by all sorts of incursions and irritations from the landscape.

During the very first theatrical experiments on quiet canal banks, drunken Land Rovers would erupt from the reeds.

On an early solo drift, tucked behind the veneer of a cemetery noticeboard on Guernsey, there was a card to a dead son: "one day we will find out what really happened on that dreadful night."

On a group dérive, a small notice marking the site of "the only Islamic-influenced architecture in the Westcountry, demolished 1968" was just plain wrong. They soon found another: a seaside hotel with prayer steps and a missing minaret.

Behind a tea shop wall, a discarded plaque of promises for the millennium. (f64)

On the roadside below the former home of the Red Dean, the singed remnants of a wish lantern: "I want to jump like a Power Ranger".

"I particularly want to draw attention to the ways in which walking conjures up other times and places that disrupt any linear flow ... For example, as my body was forced to confront the ... buckled, wooden flooring, I was hurled back to a childhood visit to the Funhouse at Blackpool Pleasure Beach, in which an array of devious contraptions – moving stairs, wobbly stepping stones, huge revolving tunnels – challenged my ability to walk upright." Tim Edensor, Industrial Ruins (See footnote beginning "At first everything seems...", page 104)

f.63

Place a blue plaque somewhere - an imaginary or a material one. It could commemorate a dream. Put one on the house where the heart of sleeping performance-maker Tim Etchells, artistic director of Forced Entertainment, (connected to a monitor), slowed almost to stopping (three beats a minutes) and was then quickened by a dream:

f.64

Old Tiverton Road.

I wrote and asked D. I wrote:

> amusing request below.
> can u rmember the house number?
> was it 105?

She replied:

>No, but 104 sounds more right than 105. Your mum would
>know, so would mine. I'll check. Funny, it should be
>indelibly marked on our memories that house. The
>interior is, but the house number! who knows.
>dx

Tim Etchells
Forced Entertainment

In place of Utopia arose the idea of 'anywheres', though even that modest concept felt like an act of contempt for the eccentric places they had encountered. The very unevenness of what had

been explored, the bittiness, the unsatisfyingly half-interwoven, the tangle, the dissipation; these all began to seem hopeful, even utopian in an un-utopian way, when subjected to wandering.

So, this was nothing to do with replacing specificity with 'everywhere'. It was about a set of uneven and inconsistent 'anywheres', partly experienced, partly imagined. Places where you could seriously map hauntings, places the movies you had always wanted to see were already playing, places where the routes of globalised exploitation hit home with the full force of their ironies.

The first mythogeographers soon found that they were not alone, but had become part of a shaky matrix of explorers and walkers; too incoherent to be a community, too liquefacted to tolerate definitions for very long, too porous to be directors of their own floating islands, but wardens of an idea and of a landscape unabashed by its own illogic. They were fuelled by a self-belief – in the quotidian re-making of space.

This is where 'mis-guidance' came in… for with mis-guidance the everyday is provoked to 'do the business', to carry through what it is always starting – the making of space into trajectories – slipping neatly between the clash of civilisations and the stream of products. Mis-guidance (with its mis-guided tours and various provocations) sites itself somewhere between Britain's Most

Haunted and The Dematerialisation of the Art Object. Rather than mythogeographers performing in the city, the move to mythogeography via mis-guidance is the move to provoking the city to do the performing itself.

The biggest difficulty so far for mythogeographical culture, and for the art and literature of the 'drift', has been the shortlivedness of its residues, its lack of increment.

The opening phase of the 'work' has been, as was predicted at the very beginning, the turning of actors into signposts. The members of the cells have pointed to what is unseen, ignored and already there; superfluous places, maintenance hole archaeologies, edgelands, banal spaces, new menhirs, accidental museums, urban sheep tracks, Z worlds, doubly inauthentic spaces.

But the next step is different. The next, treacherous stage of the 'great work' is to make 'anywheres', to imagine an architecture that is, in the words of Francesco Careri, "taking a step in the direction of the path": a realisation of what is only now an ache: spiral mythogeography. To turn signposts into actors.

Let it begin.

The Mythogeographical Manifesto

1/ mythogeography is an experimental approach to the site of performance (in the very broadest, everyday sense) as a space of multiple layers.

2/ it is also a geography of the body. It means to carry a second head or an appendix organism, in other words to see the world from multiple viewpoints at any one time, to always walk with one's own hybrid as a companion. (f65)

3/ it is a philosophy of perception, always a mobile one; it is a thinking that allows the thinker to ride the senses, and to use those senses as tentacles actively seeking out information, never as passive receptors of it; perceiving not objects, but differences.

4/ the space of mythogeography is neither bounded nor sliced by time, but is made up of trajectories, routes, lines of journey and cargo. The places of mythogeography are defined by the reach and roundabouts of their commerce, traffic, interactions and solidarities. It aspires to a new, mobile architecture of exchange where strangers are changed into friends.

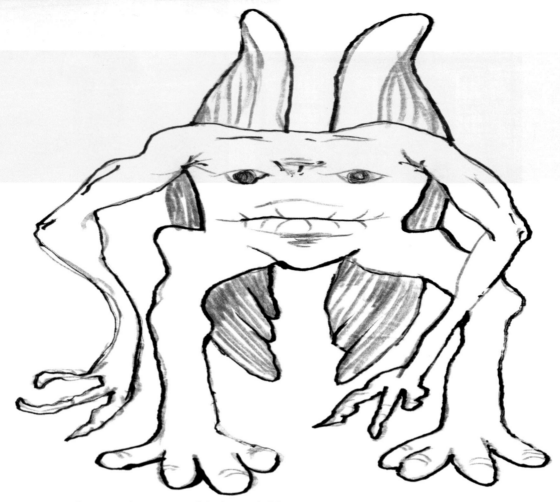

5/ mythogeography as a way of thinking is led from its margins. As an exploratory (f66) practice it is guided by its periphery.

6/ mythogeography is not one discipline, but a setting of many disciplines in orbit about each other; it is not an accumulation of data, but a description of relations and trajectories.

7/ mythogeography mythologises the mythogeographer. Everyone can play their own part, choose their own role. The mythologised mythogeographer's self is one such selected story. The 'self' is a very successful evolutionary category, a super-meme, but mythogeographers can still play 'Nature' and select their own. Then the mythogeographer's self becomes like a discipline, to be practised just like any other, and is set – like all the other disciplines of mythogeography – in orbit. (E-Myth)

8/ mythogeography arose from an aggressive, critical engagement with the monolithic labelling of certain 'historic' places by the heritage industry and by agencies of national and municipal identity-making.

f.65 *See the prostheses of Kinga Araya.*

f:66

(Mythogeographical exploration is not a sociological categorisation of place, but a disrespectful variation on the discipline of geography. Mythogeographical exploration alters the experience of everyday place. Even in the least remarkable of terrains the unfolding narrative of exploration peels back one vista after another (ffa), it disturbs the silt, it turns signage ironical or poetic, it sparks revelatory detail in banal encounters. Each of these adds incrementally to the mobile sculpting of the exploratory walk, as it transforms quotidian spaces into sites of wonder.

> "Outside an isolated village, drifters come upon anonymous,
> wooden buildings. It is a commercial enterprise to which dog
> owners bring their sick pets for aqua-therapy. The place is
> visually unexceptional, only impressive in its utilitarianism,
> but in the context of the mythogeographical 'drift' it becomes
> part of a gathering narrative-weave of water supplies, filters
> and springs. A momentary glimpse of a dog massaged
> beneath the healing waters trips the physiological into the shrine."
> (Notebook lent by non-aligned walker)

The arbitrary narrative of such an unfolding journey gives to the explorer a completely different set of sensations from those enjoyed by the visitor on an organised jaunt.

For a physically inscribed sense of the unfolding of the vistas, check James J. Gibson's description in The Ecological Approach To Visual Perception. Or walk without maps or the need to arrive, experiencing sequence. Maybe walk (but not at high tide) from the tiny railway platform at Llanbedr in Wales to Shell Island, as fields become dereliction, become defunct Cold War, become dread, stream-bitten openness, become multilayered holiday camp canteen where a sophisticated past peeps from behind bleeping fruit machines.

ffa.

9/ mythogeography's weapons against the monocular are the politics and theatre of the everyday, the atmospheres and fictional town-planning of psychogeography, the Fortean processional of 'damned data', and (both analogically and directly) geological, archaeological and historiographical methods. It is self-reflexive in the sense that it regards the mythogeographer, the performer and the activist as being just as much multiplicitous and questionable sites as the landscapes they move in.

10/ mythogeography has not developed in a vacuum, but as part of a growing practice of disruptions and explorations, including those of occult psychogeographers like comic creator Alan Moore, performers and walkers like Lone Twin, ambulatory architect-activists such as those of the Stalker group in Rome, urban explorers like the late Ninjalicious and artists of the everyday like Clare Qualmann, Gail Burton and Serena Korda of walkwalkwalk.

11/ mythogeography uses techniques of collection, trespass and observation, and a mapping that upsets functional journeys. It deploys various means to heighten or change perception. It exercises performativity, embodiment and subversions of official tour guide discourse. It subjects the layers of meaning in any place to a rigorous historiographical (or alternative and appropriate) interrogation, while connecting the diverse layers and exploiting the gaps between them as places of revelation and change. It avoids 'scientific' aloofness, or any kind of collapse into a monocular satire or a capitulation to safe and policed forms of eccentricity.

12/ it practices a 'hermeneutics of fear', it is nervous about the annihilation of human consciousness. It adopts a low level paranoia, beginning with, and then testing out, the over-explanation of things.

13/ it does not discriminate between respectable and non-respectable types of knowledge, but insists on the presence of popular, trash, pulp layers, and the foregrounding of the mythogeographer's autobiographical and non-rational associations, exposing the ways these different layers are received and, through its penchant for try-too-hard/over-ideological trash culture, reaches for a poetics of the Spectacle.

"what is going on in the lower reaches of society is probably very much more potent and effective than what happens in intellectual circles." (Ekkehard Hieronimus)

14/ it studies dynamic forms (the patterns of patterns).

15/ the mythogeographical 'tool kit' cannot be definitively assembled, is mostly invisible (fanciful, conceptual or microscopic), and is banal in its material components. (f67)

f.67 *Note from The Central Committees: for a different view see Mark A. James's exhibition The Itinerant Toolkit.*

16/ mytho-geography can be spelt with or without the hyphen, but it is a hyphenated practice.

17/ mythogeography is not a finished model, neither in its theoretical nor its practical forms. It is a general approach which emphasises hybridity, and does not attempt to determine what combination of elements might constitute that hybridity.

18/ mythogeography is an invitation to practise, to share and to connect, but also to take the risk of comparison and to practise implicit and explicit criticism of each other's practices and theories.

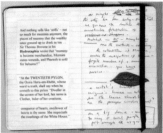

The Handbook of Drifting (extracts)

To drift well, it may be quite enough to know the situationist definition of psychogeography (f68) and simply take it from there. On the other hand, you may end up in a pub, collapsing back into the everyday and missing the whole point. The following hints will save you from wasting time (there's not much left).

1/ If romantic walking – that philosophical walking practised first in late eighteeth century Europe – can be compared (as it has been by some) to the rites of passage defined by anthropologist Victor Turner (first, separation from the community, then a plunge into flux in some kind of liminal space, and then, finally, re-integration back into the community), then the dérive (like Matthew Barney's model of 'situation' followed by 'condition', then ignoring 'production' and feeding straight back into 'situation') lops off the last of the three (re-integration) and short-circuits flux straight back into separation. And keeps doing that until the practice can stand no more repetition and throws off some new, mutant activity.

So… until you get to mutation, avoid ending your 'drifts' in the pub or sinking slowly back into the everyday; it's far better to break off abruptly and go straight home, or just leap back into your ordinary life, into whatever you were doing. That will keep the walk raw, amputated, ready to feed back into the next drift. Drifting is not a leisure activity.

2/ Begin with a theme (for example, looking for sharp angles, angels for sale, wormholes, dead businesses) or use a 'catapult' (start at a weird time, or jump in a taxi and let the driver take you somewhere anonymous).

3/ Sensitisation: get your nerves out. Walk for a while in a fictional state (you are detectives and there has been a terrible crime, you are the last survivors of the mind-changing virus, you can smell colours – 'follow your noses'). Walk slowly and look for meaning in everything.

4/ Get rid of rational way-finding! At worst use chance (dice or sticks) to determine which way to go, but best is to go by instinct. If it feels equally good or bad whichever way you turn, then you have come to a 'plaque tournante' and your life will be radically different depending on which direction you choose (nothing but strength of will can help you make this decision, you are Buridan's Ass, everything else is equal).

5/ Allow the narrative of your walk to develop. After a while certain things may begin to connect and once that starts happening, without obsessively pursuing a story, you can begin, collectively, to 'compose' your drift, allowing what has happened so far to determine your next choices, maybe to seek out certain things, trying for entry to certain places, to accept certain affordances that help to develop what you have already found. (It doesn't always happen that a narrative emerges, and it isn't necessary, but when the offer comes encourage it to unfold.) (E-Composition)

6/ The exploratory element of the drift is not a re-run of colonial appropriation, it's not about slumming and nor is it some kind of zoology of street life – it's a way to rewind, to review, to re-infuriate, to see as if for the first time all the things you already know, as good myth should help you to do (see Journey to the Lower World, Marcus Coates).

7/ Play with the senses and use sense self-consciously. For example, make a drift where you look for horizons. Or use your peripheral vision as much as possible. Or touch everything. Switch back and forward between seeing the landscape as chaotic, unrepeatable textures, and then as ideal, gridded shapes.

8/ All of these 25 ideas for Drifting are offers – only use them if they help. If they don't then do something else – and there's no rule about sticking to one thing – you may choose a theme, take three steps and something else pops up, so now go for that.

9/ Look out for mistakes and decayings in commercial and bureaucratic signage – they can be wormholes to philosophical systems, secret states, changes of consciousness, discussions.

10/ Accidental architectures: you may find unintended theatres or pulpits or bedrooms – act, preach, dream.

11/ Ruins – watch out for yourselves (Ninjalicious's Access All Areas will tell you most of what you need to know to keep you safe) – and then press your body to the decaying textures and /|\ morphing shapes (Tim Edensor describes it better than anyone).

12/ Boredom is a prelude.

13/ Don't be satisfied with irony – insist on double-inauthenticity.

14/ Avoid art, mostly. Enjoy rotting, splintered, stained, overgrown or torched public art (fuel for mental détournements).

15/ Teach yourselves (or amass as you drift) your own complex taxonomy of places: new menhirs (bollards, radio masts), almost places (shops under new ownership but not opened yet, new plantations). (See Taxonomy of Spaces, page 203.)

16/ Generally avoid shops, cinemas and galleries (unless you intend to use them for something for which they are not intended). Instead, seek those public places that are 'hidden in plain sight' and visited by very few people; public galleries in court rooms and councils, for example, are often harsh cross-sections that cut against the grain of social structures. Be 'witnesses', keep changing your characters. There are a range of less accessible sites that you can try to get access to; use Khlestakovian Inscrutability, there are plenty of "good, corrupt janitors" (Lenny Bruce) out there who will let you into private and secret places (morgues, flower factories).

17/ Drifts do not have leaders or guides. If they do then they have become something else. If someone is initiating the whole thing then they need to think about how they hand over to everyone else. A good drift is led by its periphery. The people at the back and at the edges of the group should be the ones who call everyone else to stop and see the gem they've missed. Leadership from the periphery means the drift can keep going off at tangents (the spine of a drift is made up of tangents).

18/ Between 2 and 7 is a good number of people for drifting. Any more than that and you'll probably split up into smaller groups.

19/ After the drift, write to each other, email, send each other fanciful maps, dinner mats or plates decorated with images from the drift, or cryptic games based on your findings; each documentation or memento of one drift should contain a provocation for another, or for something else. (Warning: straight descriptive accounts of drifts are very rarely of any interest to non-participants.) You might seed a future exchange by leaving messages on ansaphones as you drift.

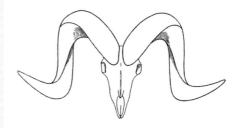

20/ Displace your erotic feelings for each other to the landscape.

21/ The dialogue among the drifting group is its most precious thing. This is the real meaning of "university". William Hazlitt wrote in his famous essay On Going a Journey, "I cannot see the wit of walking and talking at the same time." His problem is the singular "wit"; walking and talking requires multiple "wits". The best model for this is the alien played by David Bowie in The Man Who Fell To Earth who watches multiple TV screens in order to fill up his sensual capacity. The dériviste should develop their sensual capacity in the same way; while walking, listen to your companions, compile taxonomies, chew blackberries, frame reflections in windows and watch the landscape.

22/ When you encounter strangers, LISTEN to them. (E-Stranger) Ask open questions, give them as much space as possible, leave them gaps and silences, so they speak of what they want to tell you. Don't try to recruit them to your agenda, let them speak so you can find out how you might connect to (or understand or criticise) theirs.

23/ When you meet mutable things on your drift, build with them. Construct images of futures from the ruins of the banal past. Fallen trees and boughs, driftwood and flotsam and jetsam, garden waste, collapsed walls, dumped building materials – from these make heroic and hopeful monuments. From trash and ephemera make landmarks. /|\

24/ Most importantly and preciously, for the opportunity rarely arises (though this is what the drift is 'for') when you come upon mutable situations then also build with them. Construct models of future behaviours from the gestures and circumstances of the banal present. Fallen souls, drifters, the wasted, the waiting and the collapsed, the cheated potential, the hidden materials – from these make heroic and hopeful events. From trash and ephemera make history.

25/ Take things with you on your walk. Tiny models to place. Gifts to give. Chalk to make gnomic marks and symbols. (See E-Trash.)

"the study of the precise laws and specific effects of the geographical environment, consciously organized or not, on the emotions and behaviour of individuals"

End Notes

note. E-letter of explanation (email received 13.5.-----)

Dear S-----,
As you may know, during the last few months I have been working on a text for publication. To support my research I briefly rented a small room in a building earmarked for redevelopment in the vicinity of the Cathedral Close, E-----, on or near the site of the former Mortar and Pestle public house in what was an area of brothels in the early nineteenth century. During the short period I worked there I came to meet and befriend one of the other tenants – one A. J. 'Tony' Salmon – a rather shadowy and unambitious young man whose room possessed no window nor outlet of any kind, hardly even a door. For some reason we made common cause, discussed our various works and interests. Without wishing to be vain, I believe that 'Tony' became very interested in my work. I flatter myself that he had begun to follow – or at least become influenced by – some of my research ideas, though his personal investigations were, I think, very different from my own; less academically reliable, more emotional and politically driven than my carefully sourced investigations. I wish this story had a happy ending, but it has no ending. One morning I arrived to begin my day's work and my fellow tenant had absented himself, never to return. And this, just as I thought I might learn something from him. Perhaps you will think me 'out of line', but when Salmon failed to return to his room for some days I took the liberty of entering his abode. I found an essay in an opened file on his personal computer, still on. I assume that he wrote it shortly before leaving the room (I should have checked, I realize now.) To his room and to this document he did not return as far as I know. Not long after this I completed my researches and terminated my tenancy. More recently when I returned to see if 'Tony' had reappeared, I found nothing but the shell of the building surrounded in scaffold and thick plastic sheeting.
I am afraid to say that I found no evidence in 'Tony's' room to support any of the assertions in his essay: no minutes or emails, no 'notes' concerning any walking group or movement. All that I can confirm are those parts of the story where he has clearly borrowed from our conversations. It may be of some significance that a single dog-eared anthology of horror tales (though I think the damage was done by many similar), the Machen story included, constituted the sum total of his book collection. The postcard of Anonymous was also there.
I liked A. J. Salmon, I liked him a great deal, but he was not everyone's "cup of tea". I would like to believe that what he wrote, indeed that he himself (!), had more substance than a collection of borrowings and posturings.
As a mark of respect I am placing his essay in the public domain, confident, given its derivative nature, that any plagiarism is Salmon's rather than mine.

Or possibly that the principle of plagiarism itself is the point of this whole exercise, including our friendship and his abandonment of it (me, room and document). I hope you will take a moment to browse the work.
I also pass on some of the newspaper cuttings from 'Tony's' wall. Though I fear they, perhaps intentionally, throw more darkness than light on these matters.
In honest enquiry,
(no name)

The first part of the Salmon Document is to be found above at page 14, the second part of the Salmon Document is to be found below at page 220.

E – H----

note.

"The Engineer" is Charles Hurst.

(Photograph courtesy of Hurst and Lamb families from the U.S.)

Born in England in the second half of the 19th century, Charles Hurst was a skilled and innovative engineer. He created floating concrete piers that were used in both World Wars and published several textbooks, including Care and Management of Stationary Steam Engines and Valves and Valve-gearing.

As a young father, he moved about the UK, following the available work. He lived in Burton Joyce, near Nottingham, in Manchester and on the Isle of Sheppey.

He was a talented water-colourist.

After the First World War, with work hard to find, and young men returning from the trenches, Hurst moved with his family (wife Hanna, daughters Mary and Joan, and sons Jimmy and Jack) to the southern USA, arriving in Dallas in 1921. He first found employment in a men's clothing store, later returning to engineering. There are reports of him designing a large cement plant near Dallas/Fort Worth, and also designing or organising the construction of an electrical power plant in west Texas.

Hurst began investing in local newspapers. He seems to have had some interest in a newspaper in Abernathy, where his daughter Joan met her future husband; later Joan and her husband moved to Ruidoso, New Mexico, where the husband became editor and publisher of the local weekly newspaper.

Sadly and ironically, given Pontiflunk's death, Charles Hurst was killed as a result of a car accident in west Texas.

Today many of Hurst's descendents continue to live in the states of Texas and New Mexico, and a number retain connections to the newspaper business.

The route of Hurst's Walk, as re-walked by the Crab Man:

(While certain parts of Hurst's route are easily and exactly deduced from The Book of the English Oak, other parts are vague. Those wishing to re-walk the route are advised to consult Hurst's book and make their own guesses.)

London Road Railway Station, Manchester (now Manchester Piccadilly), Hyde Road, Denton, Hyde, Compstall, The Pennine Way, Kinder Scout, Edale, Nether Booth, Hope, Bradwell, Great Hucklow, Eyam, Curbar Gap, Matlock, Morton, Tibshelf, Teversal, New Houghton, the Archaeological Way, Warsop, Sherwood Forest, Edwinstowe, Sherwood Pines

Forest, Rainworth, Blidworth, Newstead Abbey, Hucknall, Calverton, Woodborough, Lambley, Lowdham, Gonalston, Southwell, Fiskerton, The Trent, Burton Joyce, Stoke Bardolph, Gunthorpe Bridge, Shelford, Radcliffe-on-Trent, Nottingham, Nottingham Castle, The Trent, Shelford, Bingham, Linear Park, Granby, Bottesford, Belvoir Castle, The Viking Way, Buckminster, Sewstern, South Witham, Clipsham, Holywell, Pickworth, Stamford, Tinwell, Ketton, Rutland Water, Morcott.

Possible 'Hursts' sighted by the Crab Man:

Numerous - on the road between Hope and Bradwell.

2 - on the road (A612) from Nottingham to Southwell.

1 - on the east side of Nottingham Castle.

Most of the potential oaks that Hurst planted and noted in his book were not found by the Crab Man. They await the explorations of other walkers.

E-Book

note.

The Book is The Book of the English Oak written by Charles Hurst and published by Lynwood, London in 1911. It describes Hurst's journey from Manchester to Northamptonshire, planting acorns, in response to the damage done by pollution to oak trees in the industrial areas of England. Hurst apparently intended to walk for just a few weeks, but his mission lasts several months. Eventually he makes plans to walk as far as Devon, but he ends the pilgrimage shortly after the death of an adopted dog, Pontiflunk, at Morcott in Rutland. Very few copies of Hurst's book remain, though there are some in the reserve collections of the UK's public libraries, and these can be borrowed through any branch library using the Inter-Library Loan system. Ask at any UK library for details.

E-The Crab Man

note.

The Crab Man was born in 1956, in a central working class area of a car city in the Midlands of the UK. He grew up on the suburban edge of this city, with easy access to 'Shakespeare's countryside'. He became a playwright; in periods of theatrical unemployment he worked as a grass cutter, warehouseman and library porter. He was active in left social-democratic and then revolutionary politics in the 1980s and 1990s. He worked for a while co-ordinating the

publications of an organisation for working class writers in Bristol. In his fifth and sixth decades he turned increasingly to walking as a political-aesthetic activity, earning his keep by lecturing and researching at various universities and as the company dramaturg of a Munich-based touring theatre. He lives with his partner and their two children.

"There are no nomadic or sedentary smiths. Smiths are ambulant… Smiths may have a tent, may have a house; they inhabit them in the manner of "an ore bed"… like metal itself, in the manner of a cave or a hole, a hut half or all underground. They are cave dwellers not by nature but by artistry and need." A Thousand Plateaus, Gilles Deleuze & Felix Guattari

note.   E-Cinema

"I noticed a man stood in the identical place and attitude that I saw him five years before when I had occasion to pass this spot. He looked anxiously down each dull street, as though he were expecting some remarkable event. He was doubtless an unproductive thinker; an inarticulate philosopher who desired no market for his speculations; a self-contained dreamer whose thoughts enriched not the blood of the world." The Book of the English Oak, Charles Hurst

It is appropriate that Patricia saw Hurst's flâneur, one hundred years later, standing outside a derelict cinema, looking anxiously about him, as if some Dealer from Hell was about to materialise at any moment.

Cinema, apparently modernist, is an ancient space. Feasting, immersion, darkness, hush, spectacle, dreaming, furtive sex, all these take place in the ritual space of the studio. The cinema is a place of hope, where we experience virtually and are analysed simultaneously, collectively. (Along with electricity substations, cinemas will be radically misidentified by alien archaeologists, though more precisely understood by them than by most of us.)

note.   E-Maps

The universe was made by a god who botched the job.

Therefore, we must proceed mostly by abstract and fanciful maps, rather than by empirical observation. We need tabernacle-shaped maps, enclaves of words, maps that grow like 16th century Italian cities.

The role of coincidence is not a manifestation of the supernatural; it is that state when map and landscape overlap.

Whenever the Crab Man spoke of moles, helicopters would appear.

In some handwritten notes to his Document, the Crab Man recalls sitting next to his crawfish father, in the bucket seat of a Triumph Herald, navigating on Treasure Hunts.

We must make treasure maps for strangers.

E-Things

note.

Thesis: The truth of a thing is always somewhere other than in the thing itself. Antithesis: Representation of a thing is a concealment of the thing it represents. Negation of the negation: that in concealing the thing itself, there is a deflection, which, if the angle (f69) is correctly computed, reveals the displaced-truth of the thing (not as something we might recognise as "truth", but as something rather more useful).

So, truth is not in things (f70), though it need not be wholly relativistic, for it occurs materially in the "and and and" of connections, in other words (to make any social or dynamic sense) it is in the 'patterns of patterns' (see Patterns of Patterns, page 174). But that is still not enough, for truth lies in these connections not as some generality, but in the specificity of each "and". "and" is a space of nothingness (the ultimate 'weakness') because it is a space of trajectory, simultaneously both a context and a shift within it (like the duality of wave and particle) and this means that its direction and position are never identifiable at the same time. (Hence the resistance of revolutions to timetables.)

See Patterns of Patterns (first paragraph), page 174.

It's not about authenticity. But how would you tell, anyway?

f.69c

f.70

E-Fake places

note.

Fake places are key to establishing a materialist mythogeography; they are exemplars of multiple-ambience made physically manifest. Examples include the concrete Stonehenge at Maryhill overlooking the Columbia River, the complete Parthenon Marbles in Tennessee, the stone circle and pyramid at the Glastonbury Festival site, Las Vegas in toto, Philip Johnson's Chippendale twiddle on the top of the Sony Building, Clough Williams-Ellis's Portmeirion, the model of the Hungarian Parliament made from four and a half million fossilised snail shells in Keszthely, the £40 million copy of the Taj Mahal being built close to Dhaka in Bangladesh by Ahsanullah Moni, the bedroom in Fellini's City of Women, its monstrous window beaten down upon by huge-leaved, storm-tossed plants, the stage world of the Sharmanka Theatre.

Failed place: Habbakuk, 610 metres long, 91 metres wide, an aircraft carrier made of an adapted

ice (ice mixed with wood pulp, called 'pykrete' after its inventor Geoffrey Pyke). (f71) Weighing 2 million tons and capable of accommodating 200 Spitfires, Habbakuk was never built.

There is a virtual equivalent to fake and failed places: the non-existent trap streets inserted by map makers to protect their copyright, such as Lye Close in the A-Z of Bristol. Textual equivalents are known as Mountweazels, Nihilatikels or Esquivaliences.*

* Publishers' Note: this is not true. "Esquivalience" is not a term for such trap words, but is a trap word, inserted in the Modern Oxford American Dictionary.

f.71 *"Surprise can be obtained from permanence as well as suddenness." Memo, G. Pyke to Lord Mountbatten, (1942).*

The individual's initial experience of fakeness is that of a sudden subjection to a pattern, to an idea queasily floated free, or to some item of sickly kitsch. BUT then there is a second part to the experience; for those who wait a while there is a revealing of the locations of the 'fakes': unstable, ludicrous, playful, temporary and abject. What the 'fake' idea has in universality, the places of 'fake' have in uncertainty, just as the Real (what is fundamental and yet inexpressible) is both silent and explicit.

Fake places show the horror of choosing under the pressures of dreadful forces. (The same forces that shaped the spines of massive swamp-stomping dinosaurs also dictated the designs for Brunel's bridges.) Fakery is a frame for un-framing these forces; the fake site is the spirit of place (genius loci) made flesh (a kind of geographical New Flesh). Thus the genius loci is revealed not as a fundamental quality of placedness, or local identity, but as an amorphous, unstable, uncertain, unreliable ambivalence. And that's it: a flux of peril and uncertainty, field and entanglement; of modern ruins, simulations, sterile places of resolution, of what comes before, a plane not of consistency, but of half-baked revolutions, of unfinished catastrophes like the backdraught of waves.

Fake places are much more than kitsch or irony or simulacra, they are the undertow of the uniform, the current of the universe: Genius Loci = Locus Solus (Raymond Roussel), a site of constructed places without a constructor, (innocent ambience now re-enters as the ambivalent genius, like slime mould), an organism without an organising gene, an anthropic ideological cosmos that has developed as if just for this consciousness-like moment alone. It is on this sea that the horrible is made present, and there to be faced; it is the excessive force of the evil demos, the necessary evil, the pattern of the people, the more-than-human human (i.e. society) without which our locality (within our own locus solus) is but salami, our Self's partition.

E-Esoterica (how to deal with them)

Esoterica can have a positive part to play in mythogeography. They need not swamp mythogeography's materialist voice. However, the fate of anglo-psychogeography is a caution: not so much because of the depredations of its dalliance with the occult, but rather that its effect has been to attach its dérive to literature. Mythogeography must choose its weirdnesses carefully. Here is a useful list of worthy and doubtful subjects:

Doubtful	Worthy
Ice Theory	sudden disappearances
werewolves	falls
ufos	zombies
changelings	vampires
Nazi survival	thunderbirds (not the puppets)
sudden appearances	Captain Britain
pyramids	petrifaction
Superman	magnetic hills
dragons	Transformers
crystal skulls	Nazca Lines
Bermuda Triangle	Comte de Saint Germain
calculating horses	Ken Campbell
crop circles	giant waves
'The Crying Boy'	The Devil's Footprints
Von Däniken	freemasonry
Schwaller de Lubicz	Great Zimbabwe
Bimini Road	the golem
ancient astronauts	Fort
Shaver	ice circles
vanished islands	floating islands
hollow earth	Order of Perfectibilists

Of course, this is nonsense. Exchange "Doubtful" and "Worthy" and re-check the lists. Done it? Yes, there was something in that original binary. But not enough. Now draw lines from each of the subjects in the Doubtful column to at least one of the subjects in the Worthy column. This is the beginning of something; a way to the poetry in all of this. For the point is not a hierarchy, not even, Kierkegaard willing, the importance of choosing, but a setting of stories in motion, an opportunity to judge each of the esoterica in relation to the others, to see ideology in the making.

Nomadism might seem to be the obvious solution to the problem of the dérive or maybe even an ideal form of it, a kind of permanent drift. But nomadism, like Nostalgia, is not what it was. The smooth spaces once rampaged by nomadic hordes (civilisations on the hoof), Visi-Goths and Vikings, challenging communities of settlement, have long since been closed down, drained, irrigated, fenced and policed. The tiny groups of today's nomads do not represent viable global futures, and mostly live in symbiosis, or bare tolerance, with settled communities rather than in resistance or opposition to them.

The peace, hippie or New Age convoys, 'travellers' by choice, while hearteningly interwoven with festivals of hedonism and informed by anarchist and other anti-state philosophies, part punk brutalist/part romantic Wandervogel, run up hard against the geographical problem: the lack of smooth space. Tolerated (just about) in the margins, in laybys and, on the fringes of festivals, although they discuss politics they are easily displaced from politics by the forces and carers of the state.

The main form of contemporary space with radical potential is holey space.

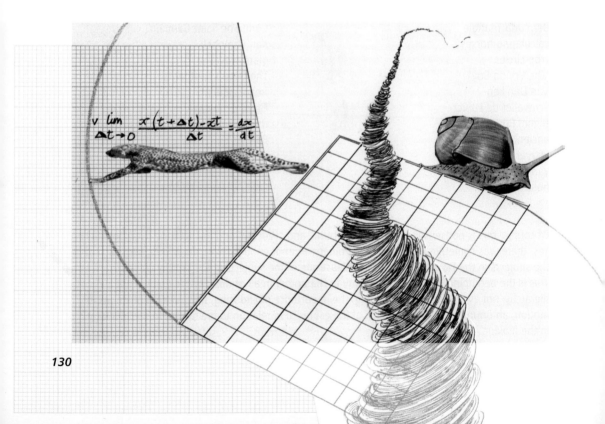

$$v \lim_{\Delta t \to 0} \frac{x(t+\Delta t) - x t}{\Delta t} = \frac{dx}{dt}$$

E-Myth

For a long time mythogeography existed, scandalously, without any discussion of myth at all. But mythogeography can now unashamedly parade its irrational side: a celebration of repetition as that 'death drive' which is the opposite of self-destruction and morbidity, a celebration of those excesses (like the living dead) that signal life, the excesses that characterise life itself, life unable to contain itself without "cracking out of turn" (House of Games, dir. David Mamet).

(The weakness and, hence, attractiveness of the living dead is their poignant inability, despite their ferocity, to constitute any kind of rule or order, which means that they must die out fairly quickly once they have eaten whatever is available (28 Weeks Later, dir. Juan Carlos Fresnadillo). In the only mainstream example where this is not the case – the fourth part of Romero's living dead 'trilogy', Land of the Dead – the ordered zombies organise themselves as a psychogeographical dériviste group.)

Myth allows its excessive heroes to die. When memes become over-complex, too entangled and compromised, sustained by a matrix of truth and untruth, myth allows them to pass away, escaping the true horror of life (which is not death, but immortality). To escape such nightmares, we can each invent our own limited-heroic deaths, as a finale to the compositional improvisation (vide Eugenio Barba) of the intervening years of our lives.

"Myth" here means those stories of a far distant past or of a parallel world, concerning the origins and nature of the cosmos, of apocalypses, of the interactions between gods, animals and humans, and of the deeds of heroic super-humans. The stories are often connected to ritual, to the upholding of belief systems, social values and codes of behaviour, to the mediation of troubling dualities, and to the reconciliation of people to the inevitabilities of life. "Myth" speaks the unspeakable, the things for which, otherwise, there are no words, and yet are woven into everyday life, and contain guidance for it.

Claude Levi-Strauss, using the metaphor of bricolage to describe myth's process, characterised it as an improvised weaving together of whatever is to hand, joining numerous points of view, shoring up "a loose and precarious assemblage of odds and ends".

This weaving is one part of the model here.

In many theatre performances the high excitement of curtain-up, an intrigued engagement in the opening narrative and a phenomenological thrill at the set and props is followed by a gently emerging disappointment as all three dissipate in resolution. Mythic performance, however, sustains the utopian world, maintaining an ideal space, a performance of society-building, promising a performing of worlds without the disappointment of resolution.

The mythic performer is not to be imitated, but repeated. Their shamanic camouflage is not a costume to be broken down into insignia for circulation, or re-fashioned into commodities for exchange. It is a conduit that allows others to see the streets in the weird light of album covers, or to imagine life on Mars; as terrains for their own performances. This is part of a tradition of magick performance – from Hugo Ball via Laurie Anderson through Peter Gabriel's Genesis to the workings of Alan Moore and Tim Perkins – something like a coherent set of strands, a plane of neo-symbolist consistency, parallel to Karen Armstrong's defining characteristic of myth: "speak(ing) of another plane that exists alongside our own world". This layer is interwoven with a mainstream culture that is riven by a struggle for the smooth ground of social change, great beastly monuments (see Keith Laumer's A Plague of Demons) stalking its plains.

Pål Kolstø places critics of myth in two camps: enlighteners and functionalists. The enlighteners expose the workings of the death-wish-machine in the urbanised desert, while the functionalists salute the usefulness of down and dirty, libidinous renewal in grey originary slime. But it is disconnection, rather than contrast, that is the issue. Kolstø's two camps are like acts of jealousy, a competition over scarce objects of desire. What we need is not the cultural sophistication to see that one is a superior school to the other, but a limited-mythological project of détournement and bricolage – a nomadic eye – for weaving together their bifurcated planes.

Mircea Eliade has argued that all forms must decay and find renewal through a momentary absorption into the formless. This is partly a description of a kind of cultural entropy, but it is also the making of its own myth; it might be argued, from this point of view, that any critical theory of myth that is not itself mythic will be quite unable to address the renewal of its subject in chaos, orgy, darkness and water, but will repeat late-myth's vigour-less, rational, temporal dissolution.

There are all sorts of social perils in Eliade's theory. However, mythogeography can use some of its criticisms – loss of vigour, social entropy, increasing complexity and inertness – as elements from which to construct a new, limited myth. Instead of regeneration or renewal, the myth of mythogeography is that of its own non-equilibrium, its temporary interruption of its own decay, and that both these instabilities, (of decay and interruption, and their temporariness) are necessary and desirable.

To discourage the attentions of an absolutist myth, mythogeography must allow itself to be subject to a kind of cultural Belousov-Zhabotinsky effect, to act as if both the subject of itself and the act of criticism that it makes of itself contain reciprocally reacting catalysts, so that, at least while the energy of the mythogeographical critic persists, a 'limited myth' (proposed by Hans Jonas as a 'tentative myth') can defy the laws of history and time (indeed, only make any sense in such defiance). The trick of this reciprocal catalysis is to make the temporary appear universal through the reciprocity of fragmentation and universality (like two facing mirrors generating an

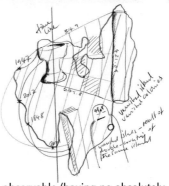

apparently infinite set of repetitions), but never completely observable (having no absolutely correct point of view), so that an act of calculation or imagination is always required to continue (but never complete) the reciprocal sequence: creativity (only at the very end of the process) replaces repetition, while the energy of criticism runs down. (This is why acts of repetition in the world of contemporary philosophical walking – Dee Heddon's re-walking of Mike Pearson's Bubbling Tom or Esther Pilkington's re-walking of Richard Long's Crossing Stones – are such touchstones of limited mythic creativity.)

The place of this act of creative imagination within mythogeography is similar to the place of the unspeakable within myth: "that for which initially we have no words... the heart of a great silence." (Karen Armstrong) While a totalising theory in which the silences are 'filled in' presents a daunting cosmos, holding traumatic consequences for the speakers of its unspeakable (livers perpetually torn out, etc.) what if this "great silence" were unspeakable not because it is taboo, but because it is simply missing? Because it is, through banal necessity and social entropy, forgotten; the trash of our corporeal, neurological efficiency, just 'unnecessary details', in other words, an essential eradication of history that brings the present into being?

Mythogeography's 'limited myth' eradicates the mapping of ourselves by an external pattern, proposing instead, that the forgotten within, the absences, silences and Not I darknesses are the materials from which our maps can be constructed. And it is these materials and not our reflections (nor our admirations/imitations of iconic performers) which trigger the non-equilibrium from which to make a presence from absences. This non-equilibrium is not Eliade's de-rangement, but a mark of life, not only in the biological sense that all human activity occurs far from thermodynamic equilibrium, but also in Gilles Deleuze's sense of the "surplus value of destratification", the usable energy residual from a process; in other words: creativity. This is key to mythogeography because it places flesh and space in a common practice of 'Li', simultaneously principle and shape.

So building back from here, the argument folds again into myth, adding this time a repeatable creativity, and a transferable darkness (see paragraph beginning "Reminiscent of I--- C--------'s plan" in the second part of the Salmon Document, page 228). The key catalysts for all this, following the Belousov/Zhabotinsky analogy, are, in myth: suspendeness above the abyss (Scottie hanging from the gutter in Vertigo, L. B. Jefferies from the window ledge in Rear Window, (in some dimensions the only god is Hitchcock)), and, in criticism: connectivity (inter-disciplinarity) (f72), a reaching out triggered by the vertiginous suspendedness, a connectivity which in turn sustains the suspendedness.

The abyss here is not that beneath the wire of Philippe Petit, or between the twin pillars, but it is the depth in others. (Everyone is in danger from the abyss, no one is either so strong or so good as to be immune to exposure or collapse, but with a morally responsible hypocrisy we can maintain a healthy suspendedness.) Vertigo/Vertigo – both condition and movie – is an excess of life.

f.72

Key to building a limited myth is not that this building occurs outside the laws of physics, or beyond time, or is immune to cultural entropy, but that, in the very act of performing the claims made by myth on origins and cosmology, the limited myth acts out its suspendedness, rather more modestly than Karen Armstrong's "participat(ion) in the timeless world of 'everywhen'". Limited myth is disrupted, in the Brechtian sense, but not yet revealing the process disrupted; it is a moment of forgetfulness in which only a gesture towards the non-mimetic shadow of what is forgotten briefly flickers before the catalyst retriggers the corporeal senses, and re-opens and unfolds the map of ourselves in the external world. After that it is only in the creases of that map, the marks of its foldings (its metaphorical wounds), that we then see the evidence of a brief, but patterned putting away of the external map, and it is in those folds (that putting away) that a damaged, mythic characterisation can be performed.

A Very Provisional Pantheon of limited-mythic heroes: the Peace Pilgrim, Stalker (the movie character rather than the group of ambulatory architects), Poor Tom (from Grant Morrison's The Invisibles), the Signpost, The Brick (in Sumerian "sig" means brick, building, city, and the god of building, see Patterns of Patterns, page 174) (f73), the 'account corpses' on Help Island in Second Life (f74), Plant Man From Outer Space (Fireball XL5), the Human Shrub of Colchester.

This is not an excuse for exhibitionism, but the means to avoid the Spectacle's demand for visuality. (f75)

f.73 "...you say to brick 'What do you want, brick?' And the brick says to you, 'I like an arch.'" Louis Khan

f.74 "They're us, we're them." Mission To Mars (dir. Brian de Palma)

f.75 "We must immediately create a legend of our own." Guy Debord, Correspondence, Vol.1.

The myth of a far distant past, is rapidly becoming an almost present, a 'just-this-second-ago' postmodern space: as Jodie Foster's psychogeographer-vigilante says in The Brave One: "There is no going back to that other person – that other place – this thing, this stranger..." (and she might have added "this space") "...she is all you are now." Technology has made for myth a new 'now' of just-broadcast time, a present that is always just behind itself, always just after liveness and 'just before' heroic action. Maybe it started with Vertov, but it really takes off now. In contemporary theatre it is clearest in the recent work of Katie Mitchell. See it in the zombie movie (always a raw touchstone) with Rec, Diary of the Dead, Zombie Diaries, Dead Set (the media mediatised) or in other genres: Cloverfield (a dérive under duress like Walter Hill's The Warriors), Signs, Lost Highway, Hidden, Spielberg's War Of The Worlds remake. The action takes place in the movies' recent pasts within a 'frame-within-a-frame'. Los Cronocrímenes, directed by

Nacho Vigalondo, is a film set entirely within this near past which in turn has entered the 'present' of the film's projection. The "it is here, it is now" (Gabriel in his arch angel period) of creation is no longer returning from the far distant past, but from a few moments before. Just as the death of Pan empties space in order to re-make it mythic and present, so technology freeze-frames time, filling it with the most recent past.

This space of recent past/fake present is the gap or "and" between 'doing' and 'done' produced under conditions of fetish and alienation. It is a morbid gap where the connection between action and thing dies quickly, and yet it is also a form of holey-space, the terrain of choice for aberrant pedestrians, thanks to its rapid half-life and decay. In a complementary motion, the dérive returns walkers to presentness and hereness through its laziness ("never work"), uselessness and a-functionality. (f76)

Not only more understandable and open to interpretation, but also more removed, the fake-present becomes more reproducible; myth was always a construction, but now it becomes myth "under construction", no longer an archaic ruin, but a panicky commercial business.

This is not mythogeography's embrace of myth, but rather its halting of myth's progress at the "just before" of the darkness, at the moment just before the she-monster Tiamat is split in two to make the cosmos. This disruption temporally spreads that dreadful abyss, that splitting; at its

most fictional and banal: the dark night, the hostel of sadism, the desire for the plunge into the urban canyon, whatever, and it re-makes these as stages or planes for action. A rhizomic reaching out for fingerholds on the edges of chaos, such disrupted myth suspends Eliade's uncontrolled formlessness, chaos, orgy, darkness and water so they become culturally accessible, transferable and repeatable.

f:76 See Change The World Without Taking Power, John Holloway, pages 43-77.

For the practice of walking, there is, within this account of suspended excess, an opportunity for a revival of a modest utopianism, as first expressed, geographically and corporeally, by Careri, Tom Nielsen, Shoard and Edensor, in a superfluous economy in the void spaces of the city and the countryside, a pervasive 'edgeland'; as Marion Shoard put it: "the only theatre in which the real desires of real people can be expressed".

The mythogeographical model for connecting such voids is the land of Cockaigne, a fantasy of superabundant economy with no aspiration to realise itself practically, and yet unable to fully divert the urge for change. It is just such an inversion of an 'absent cause'; what, Frederic Jameson has argued, history has come to (not) be, that mythogeography now explores in forgotten gaps and voids and interconnecting tunnels, performing an anticipatory text, a series of 'magic what ifs' which it does not intend to realise; Cockaignes and détournements. This is not an escape from ideology, for there is none. A mythogeographical, limited myth needs to be able to work, not with a view to the triumph of the utopian over the ideological, but rather to creating a set of mobilities and motions that tend to the utopian, persuading Jameson's uber-binary of utopia/ideology to operate like one of Levi-Strauss's antinomies; not quite reconciled in myth, but reconfigured together as the moving parts of a damaged (by forgetting) practice.

In negotiating this unavoidable ideological/utopian problem, the limited mythic character and its performance (Donna Shilling's question, the Crab Man's maps, the Signpost's pointing, the Bird-Lady's scattering, Gail Burton's banner carrying) (f77) is an important avatar for the contemporary social actor. In the absence of any substantial material force for utopia-making (Cockaigne is not itself ever predisposed to being realised) action is a Kierkegaardian leap (provisional, and disproportionately risky), without material force, a leap backwards, a re-staging of arguments that many assumed were long settled, a repetition in order to return the arguments to their simplest forms and to change their trajectories.

There is a missing piece here – hope. But we have gone as far as – probably further than – present mythogeographical research allows.

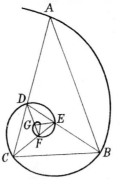

"Pick up a comic book for instance – The League of Extraordinary Gentlemen, Century: 1910 – and there, alongside A. J. Raffles, Orlando, MacHeath and Ishmael, is Iain Sinclair,' the country's leading proponent of "psychogeography"', in the guise of Andrew Norton, a character from his novel Slow Chocolate Autopsy – baffling Mina Harker and Alan Quartermain with chat of Kings Cross as a 'myth sump', the 07/07 bomb, and the films of Patrick Keiller. It will be a short hop from this to Batman teaming up with Will Self, or Captain Britain encountering John Davies on the M62."   Roy Bayfield

f.77

E-The Voyage of Donald Crowhurst

note.

This is one of the central myths of mythogeography. Crowhurst left Teignmouth in Devon, UK, in 1968 on a double journey. One, from a to a, a round-the-world yacht race, The Sunday Times Golden Globe Race; the other, triggered by his failure to leave the Atlantic and the necessary deceptions that kept him in a race he had to win, led him first into moral relativism, and then in his own mind, into physical relativity. He began to embody Einstein's Special Theory. He became a living Gedankenexperiment.

Crowhurst's tragic predicament was partly of his own making: there was hubris, but there was also heroism. And he remains an example to mythogeographers, not in some sick, ironical way, but as someone who, when he lied, was released to genuinely live an impossible physics. Faced with victory, he (probably) picked up his boat's chronometer and stepped into the ocean. His sacrifice allows us to experiment without self-destruction. He took the chance; today, thanks to him, we don't have to.

E-City

note.

"I put on shows for policemen. Always the same routine… They're like sheep. They always fall for it. I got myself picked up by one of them. To pay for my English. I know how you're going to feel about this… But I did it for the English language, OK! When we were doing it I thought about the others. Everyone thinks of someone else when they come. Because coming ain't in time. That's why coming in the movies is samey. Coming ain't part of history. Coming happens in a different time zone. Hong Kong ain't six hours ahead of London. Munich ain't one hour behind Paris. Anyway, it's only cheating if you think of one bloke. It's OK if it's millions. That's obviously not possible. All those made up stories in the newspapers. When they say so and so and so and so really did it in that scene, that's just to sell the movie. All this phantom loving is going on. I feel like I shagged a whole city!! I feel really tired."

'Confessions of a Perfume Paratrooper' from Slippery Suitcases

note. E-The Spectacle

The Spectacle is not a 'curtain of illusion' draped across reality, hiding the 'real evils' of capitalism.

In Howard Brenton's play Magnificence one of the characters tells a story about a drunk throwing a bottle through a cinema screen, as a metaphor for piercing the Spectacle (the hole remains as the action moves on). However, such piercing has been a devotional tactic since the pyramids: an "obelisk" (or more correctly a "tekhen", from the ancient Egyptian verb "to pierce") punctures the sky, the home of the gods.

The Spectacle – despite the name – does not describe the distraction of people from the 'truth' of their circumstances through the deployment of Hollywood. Rather, it is a critique of the relations between people driven by the production and exchange of images, accelerated by a culture of visuality in which the image has replaced the commodity as the main object of desire. Simple, really, and yet it is 'odd' how many clever people get it wrong. Makes you wonder about their motives… (anyone can win an argument if they can define their opponent's terms for them).

There is nothing ethereal or mystical about the operations of the Spectacle. They are the same relations of consumption as those of spectral finance capital with its addictive relationship to de-centred banking, out-sourcing and the general hollowing out of every available institution and organisation.

Walking out on the Spectacle has nothing (yet) to do with hope. It is about being paranoid and ready. Learning to be cockroaches. Learning to create theatre in cracks in the pavement, parliaments in back rooms. Acting the aftermath of apocalypse now.

note. E-Stranger

We need to learn an ethics of the stranger. How to receive a stranger, but also how to be and present ourselves as a stranger.

note. E-Trash

A certain kind of trash (not a too-knowing kitsch, but one both enthusiastic for its own excesses and modest about its virtues) can generate a kind of 'affordance' for the fictional exploration of a place. By a kind of half-intended accident, 'trash' can generate whole systems of symbols and exemplary fragments for dérivistes to carry with them on their drifts.

The Tripods, the Pecten of Royal Dutch/Shell, etc.

These are ripe for detaching from the info-flow and halting in a lexicon or a taxonomy.

Literary and movie examples are almost limitless. Choosing one at random and freezing it in a clunky allegory: A character in Keith Laumer's sci-fi novel A Plague of Demons has the misfortune, first to have their brain physically uploaded into a skyscraper-sized robot, and then to become conscious of their predicament as a result of the removal of a metal plate in their skull. This is a non-exemplary exercise, a Gedankenexperiment for the 'dériviste' who then can practise walking the streets as the brain of a massive piece of architecture.

Alternatively, and less imaginatively, walking groups might détourn the myth of burglars' marks, leaving chalk symbols for each other to find, not for any practical purpose, but to tattoo another language on the city's skin:

ooooo	rich
◁▷	beware, alarm
%%%%	keep going
$£$	something underground
∧ ∧ ∧	look up

E-Permanent Drift

note.

The tactic of the 'drift' or 'dérive' was created as part of a strategy for making 'situations' (exemplary and prefigurative moments of a utopian life). But one tendency among the Lettristes and situationists (who 'invented' the drift), including the influential proto-situationist Gilles Ivain / Ivan Chtcheglov, was to short-circuit this whole process simply by continuing to drift indefinitely. Not only were the psychological consequences of this catastrophic, but it was also bad politics. (E-Nomadic) The permanent drift disappears the drifter. Hence the necessity to disrupt the disruption, negate the negation: the drift requires the periodic abjection provided by domestic life in order to be disrupted as well as disrupt. This, rather than any spectacular corruption of celebrity, is why the 'star psychogeographer' is a corrosive role to be avoided at all costs. So, Guy Debord could occasionally be found at home in a dressing gown, and so Charles Hurst would eventually return to his "usual chair" at home, with his slippers on. (There is nothing final in such returns, just as there is nothing final in the drift.)

note. E – List of Exemplary Ambulatory Explorers

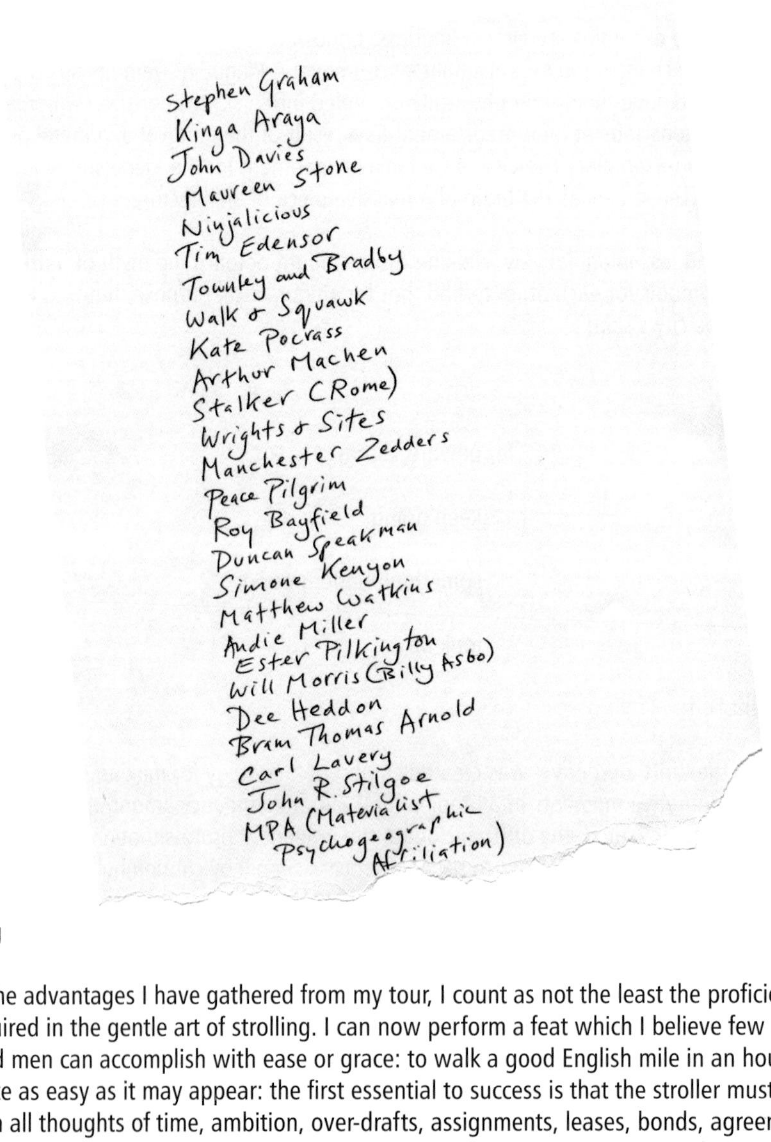

Stephen Graham
Kinga Araya
John Davies
Maureen Stone
Ninjalicious
Tim Edensor
Townley and Bradby
Walk & Squawk
Kate Pocrass
Arthur Machen
Stalker (Rome)
Wrights & Sites
Manchester Zedders
Peace Pilgrim
Roy Bayfield
Duncan Speakman
Simone Kenyon
Matthew Watkins
Andie Miller
Ester Pilkington
Will Morris (Billy Asbo)
Dee Heddon
Bram Thomas Arnold
Carl Lavery
John R. Stilgoe
MPA (Materialist Psychogeographic Affiliation)

note. E-Strolling

"Among the advantages I have gathered from my tour, I count as not the least the proficiency I have acquired in the gentle art of strolling. I can now perform a feat which I believe few town-bred men can accomplish with ease or grace: to walk a good English mile in an hour. This is not quite as easy as it may appear: the first essential to success is that the stroller must free his mind from all thoughts of time, ambition, over-drafts, assignments, leases, bonds, agreements, formulae, loans, interests and other such tricks of commerce. He must be prepared to pass the time of day with hawkers, beggars, parsons, squires, haughty dames, tramps, unfortunates, and bottom dogs generally; and when he receives a surly answer or a stony stare he must smile and

pass on. I consider it good form to be an attentive listener to long, incoherent accounts of fearful ailments told by garrulous old ladies. Above all, the great secret is sympathy. A rambler in the proper frame of mind can see a complex world in each clear pool of a brook, or he can regard the tumbling ocean as a mere moisture covering a portion of a whirling atom of dust… But Shades of Sherwood! This is a subject as fluent as the oak, and to set down all that is likely to arrest attention would require the compass of an encyclopedia. In due time a speed of one mile an hour is found too rapid, and the resentful stroller will cry: 'Be hanged to this scurrying pace!! I am going to take my time!!'"

Charles Hurst, The Book of the English Oak

E-Composition

note.

There is a crossover between the drift and performance in a co-operative, but not collective, form of improvisation and 'devising' (of anything, really; actions, manifestos, poems). This process has been gleaned from the practical means used by 19th century Symbolists and contemporary neo-Symbolists – Eugenio Barba, Robert Wilson, etc. These co-operative processes are rooted in a respect for the integrity of individual creators and producers, allowing them to generate 'free-floating' materials that can 'settle into' structures based on their 'gravitational' attractions to each other (continually subject to the evolution of the pattern of those attractions) rather than in fixed, ideal or theoretical relations.

So, how does it work?

A facilitator (often under the guise of an auteur) constructs an orrery of narratives and images, a fluid map of certain, limited thematic trajectories. An anti-team of collaborators then responds to this provocation, restricting themselves to working within the terms of the orrery, but not in a connected collaboration. Instead, they allow their own making to spiral around (but within the limits) in as subjective, instinctive and intuitive a manner as the limits allow. (The impulses and associations that fuel these makings will remain private to the individual makers, whose integrity is assured.)

What comes next is the making of a montage of these individuated productions, usually by the facilitator.

In stitching and weaving and interleaving these productions together, the facilitator must take into account the blending of differences of velocity. The different productions will 'tell' their stories at different speeds. These relations of the different velocities constitute THE STORY. (Too often critical theorists have tried to boil these relations down to one 'velocity of our times' instead of identifying the fraying set of developing and uncontainable relations.) The reader of this pamphlet* will have their own shifting velocities, their own grids and frames that will also be subject to constant slippage and shift. The facilitator is the same; creating the montage by attention to exactly that slippage and shifting in their own subjective responses to the orbits of the various productions offered by the anti-team of makers.

In placing the different, discrete productions in relation to each other, the facilitator deploys the principle of satellite capture (See pages 92-3, Walking, Writing and Performance, ed. Roberta Mock): gentle touches to mediate strong forces.

These principles can apply equally to the composition of a drift (in which case the role of facilitator is constantly shifting between the different members of the drifting group) as to performance or political intervention or R & D or whatever.

* Editors' note: this passage was extracted from notes for an unpublished pamphlet.

note. E-"round and round"

(Given that this is an E-Note to a later section this has been moved to immediately after The Orrery on page 217.)

Documents and Extracts

What now follows are facsimiles of, or extracts from, the handbooks, leaflets and toolkits of various walking cults, tight associations, peripheries, collectives and short-lived initiatives. The editors now consider at least one of these sources to be unreliable, but have decided to retain its material in order to preserve the integrity of the collection. Remember: "Not in any book."

FUCK LONG   FUCK SINCLAIR   FUCK CRAB MAN
FUCK DE QUINCEY   FUCK ART   FUCK LITERATUTRE   FUCK AUDI

"walking will only be free when the last occultist has been hanged by the entrales of the last algorithm"

Stuff B52psychogeography – save walking from plonkers and middle class lecturers

Meet this Sunday, 18th June for DRIFT – no solstices, no parking Audis round the corner, no pixies, no fucking leylines!

And definately NO Moleskines!!! Assemble at S███████ Square, W███████, by the post office

We will be exploring places of war in the city – bring torches, sandwiches, toy soldiers, ettcetera

FUCK CRANE   FUCK WAINWRIGHT   FUCK DEFOE
FUCK ACKROYD (OF THE GONDOLIERS TOURIST BOARD!)
FUCK SELF

Association for the liberation of the
lingerer
P O Box ██████
M████
M███ 5██

FREE WALKING FROM THE WANKERS!!

Toolbag of Actions and Notions *

* Publishers' Note: despite its heading the editors seem to have exercised no exact criteria for the inclusion of material in this section. Some flippant content has been removed.

map – score – rehearse/prepare – perform/act – document – provoke

Processions

Processions should be constructed quickly: Choose a loose theme. March without armies, bleach all flags.

Action: divide into groups, each one to create a different aspect of the procession: a/ music, b/ objects (burdens or relics) for carrying, c/ chants for shouting or singing, d/ physical actions, e/ banners and placards, f/ a short ritual, g/ (possibly stewards), etc. Devise some interaction with spectators – collecting money, throwing flowers, shaking hands, whatever. Then assemble all the groups together – do any last minute preparation (teaching chants, etc.) – and then process. The periphery of the march should interact spontaneously with passers-by and street furniture. (See The Modern Procession, Francis Alÿs (2003) and "Theatrical-political Possibilities In Contemporary Procession" by Phil Smith in Studies in Theatre and Performance, Vol 29 (1), 2009.)

"A procession of the damned.
By the damned, I mean the excluded.
We shall have a procession of data that Science has excluded.
Battalions of the accursed, captained by pallid data that I have exhumed, will march. You'll read them--or they'll march. Some of them livid and some of them fiery and some of them rotten. Some of them are corpses, skeletons, mummies, twitching, tottering, animated by companions that have been damned alive. There are giants that will walk by, though sound asleep. There are things that are theorems and things that are rags; they'll go by like Euclid, arm in arm with the spirit of anarchy. Here and there will flit little harlots. Many are clowns. But many are of the highest respectability. Some are assassins. There are pale stenches and gaunt superstitions and mere shadows and lively malices: whims and amiabilities. The naive and the pedantic and the bizarre and the grotesque and the sincere and the insincere, the profound and the puerile."
The Book of the Damned, Charles Fort

The Swimmer

Devise a journey between a number of generically similar spaces. The Burt Lancaster character does this in Frank Perry and an unattributed Sydney Pollack's 1968 movie The Swimmer, running from pool to pool across middle-class suburbia in Westport, Connecticut, swimming through a world that is passing him by.

Find your series of generic spaces and then devise an action that can be performed at each of these sites, making sure your action is open and porous enough for the sites to affect and alter it as you go along. Gather an 'audience' of participants, teach them the action, then take them on the journey.

Mis-guided Tour (or Twalk)

This is a performance modelled on a guided tour in which the role of the tour guide is fore-grounded and in which the (usual) historiographical mono-narrative is replaced by a series of layers and tangents. These can be autobiographical, phenomenological or critical. This is achieved by rearranging the established narratives of the place, researching and revealing its hidden histories and introducing performativities and Fortean whimsies (both cosmological and irrational).

Action: find a route or defined site. Research the site for documentation of marginal or ignored data, unreliable stories of hauntings, accounts of anomalies, previous performances in the site, previous uses, mundane stories about the place, crass statistics, sublime physical information (vulcanology, etc.) Research the site corporeally (climb on it, crawl over it, hide in it, eat its meals, wash in its showers, talk to everyone in it), sample its textures and tickle up your own autobiographical associations. The various layers so revealed should then be dramatically re-constructed in the manner of a Deleuzian assemblage: reaching a consistency by sustaining their differences. As guide/s the manner of your guiding should be fore-grounded and looped back into the narrative, the meanings of which you should express through connections and intervals. Be ready to show your regretted tattoos. The 'audience' for the guided tour should find themselves co-opted into the performance (physically modelling events, holding objects, tasting and drinking).

"Every sentence of your tour made sense even though the meaning of the whole thing was unclear - i.e. we three visitors extracted different meanings. That seems perfect."

(from hard copy of email retained in the files of the Exmouth CPS)

Plagiarism

There was never anything new about détournement (the principle of taking dead art and re-animating it through travesty).

In 2008 Theun Mosk, Boukje Schweigman and Robert Wilson created Walking for the Oerol Festival on the island of Terschelling. (Given the hubristic title this was always going to be a prime candidate for re-use.) Participants walked for four hours in extreme slow motion across sand dunes, sometimes guided, sometimes following marked paths, sometimes their vistas were transformed by arches, gates, dark rooms and corridors and sometimes they followed each other, until (a little before reaching the final, tepee-like construction) they became aware of each other as factors in the landscape equivalent to the paths, dark rooms and tunnels.

Before they acquired their own premises, the early freemasonic lodges would chalk the ritual shape of 'Solomon's Temple' on the floors of rented rooms, wiping away the marks at the conclusion of rituals that "changed strangers into brothers".

Drifters should make and enact their own versions of these solidarities.

Pseudo-archaeology (after Mark Dion)

Recover objects from the surface of a site, or dig down into its layers. Assemble the finds according to fanciful and coincidental categories or classifications. What appears to be archaeology is a large poem of things.

Turning The Page

Go to a library or charity shop. Choose a book at random. From the book first choose a page and then a word, both at random. Drift until you find the word (or some association with it). Then choose a second word at random and search for that… and so on…

Pixie Signs

In 2000, under cover of darkness, The Interdimensional Pixie Broadcast Network replaced the functional symbols of the road signs in the city of Exeter with punctuation marks, squids, fairies, seahorses, blobs, mandalas and molluscs.

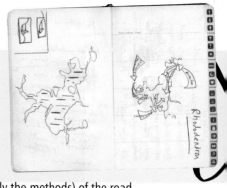

(Such infiltrations complement the thoughts (though not necessarily the methods) of the road safety pioneer David Engwicht on 'intrigue and uncertainty'. See Engwicht's book Mental Speed Bumps.)

Replace all functional signs with poetic-biological symbols.

Make Fake

Action: build communities of fakery, model villages, graveyards of modernist sculpture, pseudo-science pavilions – link them all up, until the map threatens to take over the territory.

Audio

Make your own soundtrack to the city.

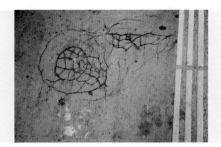

⊞ Grids

Create a journey made from lines, vectors, boundaries, borders, crossroads, centres, crash barriers, squares and plinths; record the strategies of power and their fractures.

20 Minute Ghosts (f78)

On a looped journey, as you cross an earlier part of your route, take a moment to contemplate your '20 minute ghost' – the person you were 20 minutes before (or however long ago it was since you were last there).

f.78   *What is the nature of the relationship between ghosts (ffa) and the tourist industry? For example, how does the UK's National Trust reconcile its historical criteria for interpretation with its glossy publications on ghosts: "The spirits of former owners, staff, even pets haunt their former homes and walk hand-in-hand with those living there today"? By what criteria are faith and historiography swept aside in the interests of a promotional supernatural? The answer is, of course, immediately clear: the criteria are those of the market. The spiritual has been institutionally reduced to a plasticised jam stall. BUT here is the bearded joy of mythogeography: we can all play laissez-faire; there is no need to either swallow the supernatural's own terms, nor to primly bat them away. Rather, apply their corrosive allusiveness to those who would seek to reduce them to commodities. Release 'dead labour' upon the stately homes. (See various notes on Zombies.) Let postmodernism have revenge on postmodernism.*

ff.a   *Attend a 'ghost hunt'. The excitements of these adventures are aligned architecturally. Go attentively, they are schools for sensitisation to spatial shifts.*

Gum Galaxy

Where the pavements are covered, like a rash, in chewing gum, use chalk to draw lines to connect the pieces of gum in stellar constellations. Name them in Latin (if you don't know any Latin make it up).

Micro-site Performances

First, choose the dimensions of your micro-site: maybe the size of an A4 sheet of paper? Maybe the dimensions of a wardrobe?

Seek out a site that matches your chosen dimensions and explore this site carefully.

Pay particular attention to the details of texture. Then re-explore. Then explore again. Repeat until there seems to be nothing more to be discovered. And then explore again.

Is it possible to create a micro-performance or micro-action suitable for your micro-site?

Solo 'Splorin' Exercises

You are Cupid. Match people in the streets.

You are a diver. Explore the city as if it were underwater.

You are a mist. Drift through the city.

You are a fox in human skin.

You are dead and gone to heaven/hell.

The city is under occupation by intelligent microbes, Martian bodysnatchers, mind control rays – you can't tell the resisters from the wholly invaded. Do not attract attention to yourself. Choose routes where the least number of people will see you. Use alleys and back paths. Walk calmly through crowds. Show no emotion. Ignore commodities. Hide your hunger.

Tour

Take your friends on an unplanned tour of front gardens: gnome states, zen deserts, graveyards of fake-classical monuments, displays of frozen cartoon animals, abstracts of neglected concrete, faerie delusions. Enter these worlds by discrete gazing; imagine yourselves as citizens or prisoners or princesses in their worlds.

"On window sills, middle class ornaments face in, working class ornaments face out."

Drift/Dérive*

* Publishers' Note: there is some duplication of materials with the The Handbook of Drifting above. However, we are following the provisional editors' decision to retain this section, given the additional information and instructive contradictions.

Best with groups of between three and six.

There should be no destination, only a starting point and a time. A journey to change space, not march through it.

To drift something has to be at stake – status, certainty, identity, sleep.

In a drift, self must be in some kind of jeopardy.

There may need to be a catapult: starting at an unusual time of day, taking a taxi ride blindfold asking to be dropped off at a spot with no signage, leaping onto the first bus or tram you see.

(MGF) There may be a theme: wormholes, micro-worlds, peripheral vision – whatever you want.

Be tourists in your own town.

Use the things around you as if they were dramatic texts, act them out.

"…on a 'drift' we found ourselves at a Moto Service Station on the edge of the city. In the restaurant they had a guarantee printed on little cards. They'd give you your money back if you weren't "completely satisfied" with your meal. So we organised to meet there on our next drift with about 10 other people; we ate big breakfasts and asked for our money back, because, philosophically, a cooked breakfast could never 'completely satisfy' a socially and culturally healthy person, not 'completely satisfy' all their desires and passions, not a human being. We got the money, but more importantly numerous staff were commandeered to interview us and we turned a restaurant into a debate about desire and fulfilment." (Notes, unattributed)

The drift should be led by its periphery and guided by atmospheres not maps.

A static drift: stay still and let the world drift to you.

When you drift, use wrecked things you find to make new things (this is called détournement - using dead art and uncivil signs to create unfamiliar languages). Make situations: build miniature wooden villages, giant insects from branches, ritual doorways from burnt remnants, make a small model shed from the wood of a full-sized one and process it from shed to shed until you reach the sea. Construct things from what you find, enact imaginary searches, bogus investigations, gather testimonies for new religions. Just build!!! Leave stories, situations and constructions for any drifters that follow you, they'll re-make them in their own ways.

Tool box

Take a 'tool box' with you: notebook, camera, torch, bag for collecting things, chalk… make up your own.

Moving Pictures

In your head re-shoot movie scenes using your own city as location. Let your memory of movie landscapes bathe the places you pass through. Hum a soundtrack.

At the Savoy Cinema, Exmouth, a sleeping customer awoke, undressed and attempted to climb into The X Files Movie.

Enter your city as if it were a movie.

On the island of Herm, The Nazis filmed The Invasion Of The Isle Of Wight.

Act as if you were in a piece of propaganda.

Inner Maps

Walk with a conceptual, "inner" map. The point is not to experience this map, but for it to lead you by constraints and provocations to interfaces you would not otherwise choose.

In his anti-intellectual, but sporadically illuminating The Lost Art of Walking, Geoff Nicholson attempts to walk the shape of a Martini in Manhattan and then complains because he can't see the glass. The point of Inner Maps is that they remain immaterial.

We have walked: North, a straight line, vertigo, a green circle, risk and uncertainty, and possible murder-victim burial sites.

"I'M IMMATERIAL, YOU DOLTS! YOU CAN'T MAKE ME GO WHERE I DON'T WANT TO!"
Plotka, Duke of Hell in Captain Britain and MI-13: Hell Comes To Birmingham, Paul Cornell and Leonard Kirk

Stalking

Action: identify a person to be followed. Follow them; but do not in any way menace them. Rather, give up your initiative to them. Never make yourself known or allow yourself to be noticed by them. If you sense that they have become aware of you, cease the stalking immediately.

If your first target disappears, then find a second and follow them.

Spend at least half a day on this, preferably longer. Commit yourself to take buses, trains, etc. whatever is necessary in order to follow your 'target'.

Real, oppressive stalking is fuelled by an intense obsession; here there is no obsession, there is only submission to the other. This should dissipate any intensity. This liberation is what you should aim to express.

A Chapter of Quotations*

* Publishers' Note: despite the chapter heading, the quotation below was the only one collected.

"she's on the horizon... I go two steps, she moves two steps away. I walk ten steps and the horizon runs ten steps ahead. No matter how much I walk, I'll never reach her. What good is utopia? That's what: it's good for walking."

Window on Utopia, Eduardo Galeano

Year Of Promises

On the island of Guernsey, at the back of a tea garden, behind a small stone tower I found a strip of wood. Attached to it were small plaques, each listing a promise made for ITV's Marking The Year 2000.

"Karen Foss: I will donate a tin of cat food to the animal shelter weekly

Stuart Ferguson: I will become a blood donor

Sarah Hendry: I will learn sign language"

Make impossible and wonderful promises. Have them engraved or carved in as elaborate a way as you can afford. Then discard your promises so others might find and fulfil them.

"I will imagine a new planet…

I will redistribute affection…

I will…"

(Extract from the notebook of an XPA member.)

Mobile Machinoeki

In Japan there are stations (machinoeki) where walkers can get a lie down, some food, maps and socks, just as there are service stations (michinoeki) for drivers and their cars.

A Mobile Machinoeki is a small cell of walkers who carry various supplies for other walkers – pamphlets of theory, charms, water, disruptive maps, etc. They may also prepare stories, performances of theatre in their pocket, discreet walking-costumes or rituals for those they meet on the road.

Tilted Ark

Study the work of Land Artists like Walter de Maria, Nancy Holt, Robert Smithson, Gordon Matta-Clark, Mark Dion, Richard Long, Ana Mendieta, Christo and Jeanne-Claude, Agnes Denes, Andy Goldsworthy.

Take some aspect of the work of one or more of them and use it as a means to create a performance or a journey, something about places: Long's collecting or moving of mud or stones, de Maria's filming of his walking into the desert, Goldsworthy's immersion of himself in the transient materials he uses, Holt's framing and containing of vistas, Smithson's non-sites, Matta-Clark's sawing through buildings, Mendieta's body impressions left in mud, snow, reeds.

Be invasive. Be sensitive.

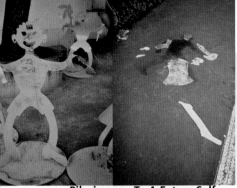

Pilgrimages To A Future Self

First choose a site that represents where you are now (as a person, as an activist, as a walker, whatever). Then choose a second site that represents the person, citizen, etc. that you want to be. Create a performance or a walk that moves from the first site to the second.

Peer into one of those roadside pools of shattered glass from a car's wing mirror.

Khlestakovian Inscrutability

This is a means to gain access to otherwise restricted areas, affections and intimacies. It is a kind of self-denying ordinance; a modesty, almost a stupidity; allowing others to invent motives and desires for you.

So, when you next want to get in somewhere, say as little as possible, when challenged look sincerely engaged, say: "I'm interested in here" and leave it at that, staying physically very present, but not overbearing. Given the general human discomfort with gaps and pauses, otherwise obstructive guards, porters, janitors and concierges may fill the void with an invitation.

This, possibly, has wider political significance (for the dispersal of leadership).

There may be a connection between Khlestakov's inscrutability and Epicurus's suavity, the elegance of taking pleasure gracefully. Perhaps it even holds a solution to the problem of drama (never before have humans been subject to so much mimesis and its inherently violent outcomes (see Girard's theory of violent mimesis))?

Performing Sculpture

Create objects or sculptures that require performance to sustain them. For example, Lygia Clark's Ar e Pedra (Air and Stone) which consists of a stone resting on a balloon held in cupped hands.

Repetition

The postman Cheval stubbed his foot on a stone. He picked it up and was pleased by its shape. Beginning with this exemplary unit, Cheval gathered many similar stones over the decades that followed, using these materials to build his 'Ideal Palace' at Hauterives.

Search for a simple pattern, element or unit and create work by repeating that pattern or accumulating that element; each addition creates its own variation of relations with all the other elements. "Repetition" (which is French for "rehearsal") is a preparation for an original action.

Separated Objects

Carry certain objects to create an effect upon the walker's perceptions.

Clay: mould some clay into the shape of your head (or someone else's or some other thing's head) and carry it with you to remind you to watch with multiple viewpoints.

"I got this idea from Saint Nectan who picked up his decapitated head and carried it home to his hermit shed. And where his blood fell foxgloves grew."

Pet-sar: carried by the Pharaoh and the Queen, this long cord was used to settle the alignment

This is not this book. I am being able to speak to you because I have a contact among the printers who I am not about to reveal, but this is being sneaked in late at night before the run, and that's the opnly reason you are now going to be able to hear direct from an actual walker rather than one of those who maybe did do plenty of walking once but now are mopre interested in what goes on in their heads than under the feet of the world's walkers. And are mostly a lot of white blokes wit degrees. So, please do not complanme to the publisghers or they will take this out or pulp it or something and that will silence us.* Its bad enough when everyone knows tryiongt co communicate what happens on a walk is a nightmare.

Sorry this is rushed I've got one hour to get this down before my contact pcks this up. I can't go in myself cos they have passes.

This is not self-ingulgent. There are real differences between what the rank and file walkers BELIVE and what's in here. First of all, we aren't organised in cells. It's too early for that and perhaps it will be best if it';s always too early for that. There is nothing organic to this. We are pre-cells, just fragments, two or three people walking here and there. Even the groups with names, plenty iof them are just two or three. Anyone whio pretends any different is lying. I say "best" because there isn't far from plant cells to prison cells – or any kind of pattern if its imposed on people from above, expecially by those who start out ith good intentions.

We have aour pre-cells and we will see how they turn out. (Which is I suppose what they are trying to say, but… the jargon!! Sometimes we walk alone - a lot of the women walk alone, it's lmost like they have to beat the nervousness about walking alobne before they can form the cells… so, don't exclude women.

And we want to walk more in relation to real people rather than the living dead, so a lot of the real walks are to refugee camps and immigrant detention centers and we walk the routes where we know cheap labour/slave labour goods get tranmsported and right into the shops. We go on 'shoping expeditions' where we track these goods down and we take in pictures of the workers and introduce tthem to the staff at the shops and the other customers and then they throwe us out. "How can u throw out pictures of your own workers?" I like the one they do in changing rooms, that is good! I'll do that!!

As for the spiral, that's only going up themselves.

Perhaps if this book was written by women or more women then it might have more to do with most of the walking that goes on – the refugees, the water carriering. Or gong to the garden centre. Thye just boring going to the shops, gfoing to work. the people who have to do that are ignored in this book. Now, ehen they begin to walk philosophically, then… they will put the deriving zombies in the shade!

I don't think I have seen one out of the 30 of the films the people who did this book listed – they're all horror aren';t they? Or things they wactched at their student film socities 30 years ago.

156

I liked Knowing and some other thing but why should I bother u with that?

And isn't there a sort of drone that goes on behind all the different voices here? Something that's keeping quiet, but isnnot totally silent? A bumbling? The voice of another 'beautiful boy' who wants the world to take him seriously? Mister nerdy Saint-Just? So, what happens if we laught at his patterns of patterns and cells, the first bumble of ...something nasty? Laugh, laugh, laugh!!

Also I knew the people who they found in the pirate costumes and there was more than one and they were not dead (!!! – the Salmon thing is completely made uop BY THEM!! - , the whole "dead" thing was because they were burying their work which is a great shame, but people get tired. That';s whuy they left the pirate 'corpses' they were dummies. The thing si that the pirate thing was serious. Serious about Marisco and the attack on London. Serious about the third century Goth pirates. Serious about the Vikings, serious about the Narentines – because pircy is a "non state act of war" – the rulers hate pirates – the first person to be hung, drawn and qartered was a pirate – the Marathas who preyed on thre British east india Company – the pirate utopias like Libertatia "whre no Hedge bounded any particular Man's Property" (yes, please!) in Madagascar the 1600s it was and which DID NOT fall apart like the religious ones in 'civilised' Europe at the same time! (Probably made up by Defoe.) They had women captains like Zheng Yi Soa (approx), Queen Artemisia, and the Viking captains Rusila and Stilka, then Princess Sela, Alvid, Wigniord, Hetha and Wisna (I'm copying tis from our pamphlet – why didn't they put that in, eh?), JeaneLouise the Lioness of Brittany, Grace O'Mally, Sayyida al Hurra, Lady mary Killigrew, Jachotte Delahaye aka Back from the Dead Red, , Ann Bonney AKA Ann Born, and Mary Read, Charlotte Badger, Sadie the Goat (brilliant!), Gertrude Imogene Stubbs AKA "Gunpowder Gertie, the Pirate Queen of the Kootenays, Lo Hon-cho, Ki Ming, Huang P'ei-mei who led 40,000 pirate frm 1937 to 1956 and, until the 1990s the great, Cheng Chui Ping aka Sister Ping. Pirate boats were the first oplaces on earth to have democracies, a hundered years before America and France and the hireradhy of sharing spoils was less steep than in any other company or society. . Just like The Bore was serious about Borrow and gypsies and Romany Rye the 'dead derivers were serious abourt pirates , and the same with us – The Cenmtral Commitees are not right about the nomads, we are all becoming nomads now,no one has job security, what about all the Polish people who have had to come here for work, there's never been so many refugees and so many worjkers on boats and planes and in the bavcks of vans, you can see them waiting on street corners. We are the nomad generation. If we are not enough to make a civilisation then nothing will ever change. Not thart there's any big sign yet that we will. But this is Theory. If we're really mythogeographers we should leave it to all the dfferent parts, not try dictatng what the parts become bfore they've had a cjhance to "defer, delay". Etc. we don't need prescription for cells, we've got friendship and adventures, we go inside the power places, - the cells are what we should "defe"r!

I'm not saying ours is the only way, I'm saying there should be room for all the different kinds and no one in mythography should be sniobbish about the different walkers – refugee walkers, queer walkers, street walkers, 'walkers' who are escorts, 'walkers' in shops, Dongas, ramblers even… I don't think any of us have much time anmore for 'Audi Sincliar', and who is

Richard Long? Yes, I kno who Richard Long is!!!!!!!!… but how different are both of them from the exercises in this book? It's not that massive a difference is it? So a bit of humility might be nce. Let everyone in! Don't let anything divide us, even our own stupidity. Nobody fits the pattern of patterns! The whole point is that walking is open to almost everyone. I was going to write inmagine if everyone was walking… but that's getting like THEM!! Defer!! Love and delay! "Don't do it…!!!"

So, they should NOTot be turning their noses up at the nomads – the Dongas Tribe new what they doing at Winchester, Yellow Wendesday and Keiller knew about it too, because it's in his London film, , I saw that particular one of their films! the moon all the time, it's all abput the equinox, And the LPA too, that Watkins the mythomathewmatician put it up on the web, their Great Conjunction, the rulers using sacred shapes in the landscape, cutting off the head of our dragon? Or is that too unrespetable even for mythogeographers? The dongas after Wincehster were walking as a tribe through the South west – in what way is that not nomads? They were not in vans, they wer s quatting hill forts!! Wild! Of course, it's useless, but that's the point isn't it? To NOT be of use. Didn't The Bore say NEVER WORK or wrote it on a wall anyway?

Do they really have the love to defere, to defer from their precious 'game of war'? Pirates without piracy? Defer fronm their "necessities" and Patterns? And from their "diruptions" – we don't all have a nioe home and a girlfriend to go back to, cooking them polenta or whatever. And what if u don't ant one? I'm not suggesting people don't need flats, but and I'm not saying be out on the road everyday – that's like the pontificating Peace Pilgrim (I knos she's dead, killed in road ccident, weird!) grandstanding and freeloading – no, but what haoppened if we were to start boring holes in the Real? Mole tunnels, ant colonies, helecopters, uinhappy people with holes through them, put a honeycomb through The Man's territory? Not tight associations, but termite associations? The pirates within the pirates, the gyspsies within the gypsies, the outcasts from th e outcasts.

You will have to forgive me if this is rushed, because it IS rushed. I have to get this to the "good courrupt printer" in an hour.

By the ay, the Watkins I mean ins't the pavement man or Alfred!

So, anyway, that's everything and I've actullay got some time so I'm going to copy out this in case there's room. It's about the White tower or ElMinar on Cape Maraabat, right on the sea, built by the pirate Lass el-Behar from Rabat who was "young, handsome and brave", who's ships never had two cannon the same cos he stole them all from different ships, and who only loved the sea – even though the Christian women he captured all fell in luv with him and wanted to convert, and the Muslim women too, but he just loved the sea til one day, between piracies, after ahorrible storm, he came out of his Tower and found ona narrow band of land a woman laid out white and cold,. At first he thought she was a christian, for she had gold hair, but not blonde - , gold!!!, but when she opened her eyes, they were green like the algae that grows in the rocks, because she was a jinniyeh of the sea. Her beauty was magical and the pirate fell madly in lover with her, neglected his boats and his men and forgot all about killing and any gold other than that of his darling's hair and forgot even his prayers to Allah. He told her, like men do, that he loved her more than anthing els on earth. That winter a great stor grew and grew and the waters rose and rose until E-Behar told his love that thety should flee to the mountains before the waters ruined the Tower. "Why doe you fear the Ocean?" she said. "You said you lloved Her above all things? You even turned your head from Mecca in order to watch Her. I cam to reward you for your love for Her, but now Sghe calls me back. You will never see me again."

But the pirate Lass El-Behar ran after the jinniyeh imploring her not to leave him. "I will never be happy without you!!" "Ah," said the jinniyeh, "happiness belongs only to those who fear Allah and honor Him. I cannot disobey the voice that summons, but you may follow if you wish." And with that the beautiful jenie wandered off into the waves and the pirate follwed her into the murky depths off Cape Maraabat, where he walks today beneath the waves, between the Tarik Mountain (Gibrltar) and Cape Tres-Forcas. And will walk till the day men are judged for their actions and the earth is a shadow of a shadow disappearing.

And this is why we love pirates. And this is why you will never organise happiness because it's about feeling not about doing good, it's chaos and it's personal. And this is why the walkers are accumulating under the waves of the Spectacle as quick as them abandoned avatars or account cosrpses on Help Island, and like that woman avatar we'll one day strap them all to ourselves when we walk in millions not because of fear of war or lack of water and food but because we uselessly WANT to!! Thank you very much.

Norma Nomad

* Publishers' Note This insert was discovered before the first printing and it was our decision to retain it, for the reasons given by 'Norma Nomad' herself. (The tale of El-Behar is clearly purloined from Pirate Utopias: Moorish Corsairs & European Renegadoes by Peter Lamborn Wilson, who in turn seems to have looted it from Elisa Chimenti.)

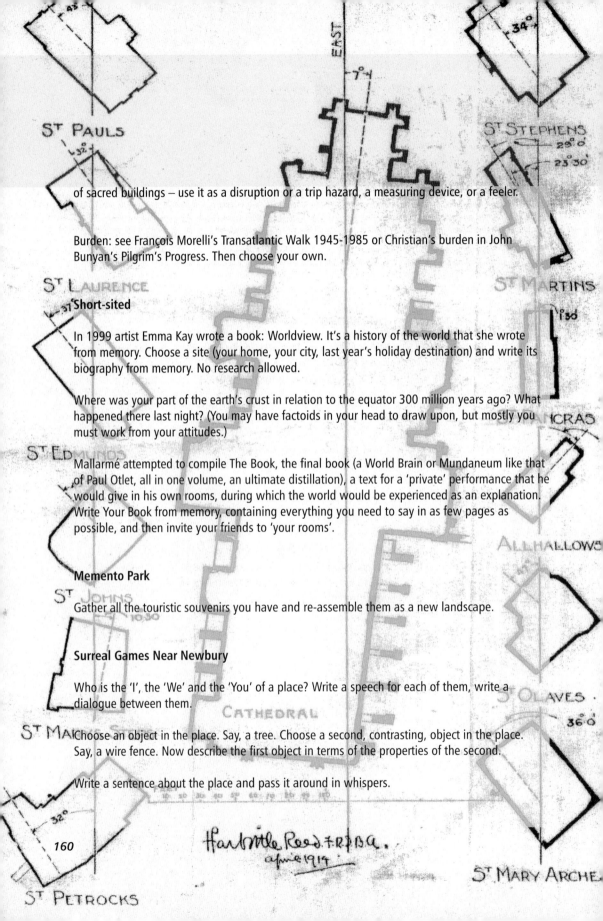

of sacred buildings – use it as a disruption or a trip hazard, a measuring device, or a feeler.

Burden: see François Morelli's Transatlantic Walk 1945-1985 or Christian's burden in John Bunyan's Pilgrim's Progress. Then choose your own.

Short-sited

In 1999 artist Emma Kay wrote a book: Worldview. It's a history of the world that she wrote from memory. Choose a site (your home, your city, last year's holiday destination) and write its biography from memory. No research allowed.

Where was your part of the earth's crust in relation to the equator 300 million years ago? What happened there last night? (You may have factoids in your head to draw upon, but mostly you must work from your attitudes.)

Mallarmé attempted to compile The Book, the final book (a World Brain or Mundaneum like that of Paul Otlet, all in one volume, an ultimate distillation), a text for a 'private' performance that he would give in his own rooms, during which the world would be experienced as an explanation. Write Your Book from memory, containing everything you need to say in as few pages as possible, and then invite your friends to 'your rooms'.

Memento Park

Gather all the touristic souvenirs you have and re-assemble them as a new landscape.

Surreal Games Near Newbury

Who is the 'I', the 'We' and the 'You' of a place? Write a speech for each of them, write a dialogue between them.

Choose an object in the place. Say, a tree. Choose a second, contrasting, object in the place. Say, a wire fence. Now describe the first object in terms of the properties of the second.

Write a sentence about the place and pass it around in whispers.

Death Walks

Once there were many death walks, corpse paths and coffin roads, along which villagers carried the caskets from isolated farms and hamlets to the nearest consecrated ground. Now, we have to make and map our own death walks.

Draw up the route to your burial or incineration, along ways and through places that are important to you. It's good for your health. Have a dry run. Leave an account of the route as an invisible monument for friends and family. In the anonymous city that hides its corpses, choose the walk of the dead.

"Birth is the First Step unto Death."

Tops and Bottoms

Talk your way into the tops and the bottoms of buildings: attics and cellars, crypts, basements and balconies, roof gardens and bunkers. Deploy Khlestakovian Inscrutability where necessary.

Investigate the remains of buildings within buildings (a prison beneath a hotel, a nuclear war hospital beneath a department store, a paintball arena that was once a cold war bunker). Charm your way in to highrises to test their vistas.

Write On Wall

The streets are full of lost and lonely texts. Ignore the mass produced packaging and pick up the rest: you quickly enter worlds of intense feeling. Instant archaeology, take a line from each item and assemble a street poem. Chalk it on a wall.

Poetry from the gutter:

Dear Mrs (---),

(---) phoned to tell me the very sad news. I shall always remember Mr. (---)'s kindness and gentle nature along with a great deal of wisdom. I'm sure you'll miss him very much. Do accept my warmest regards & sympathy - continue to express your talent which is a true gift & let me know should you require any varnish.

images completely
sensitivity, high contrast,

high qual

in electro stem the
in electro stem the
in electro stem the
in electro stem the
We, the Japanese people, acting through ou

 Find or create a chalk graffito and curate it for 10 years, re-chalking it from memory after rainfall. Photograph it regularly.

Shop Window Hollywood

Create your own 'movies' in the reflections of the windows of shops and offices. The reflected backgrounds are your locations and passers-by are your extras. Liberate the passive eye.

Make a disc of movie clips for yourself, a celluloid art of memory (f79), memorise this collection of movie architecture. Interweave it with the unplanned encounters of a dérive.

Richard Attenborough drives through a recently ruined landscape in Séance On A Wet Afternoon, an airport is suspended in time, gone stale in The Langoliers, in the opening sequence of Suspira the city outside a taxi is almost not there, that final sequence in the city's morning light at the end of Demons 2, those windows that seem to be an invitation in Michael Snow's Wavelength, the spiral clouds in Uzumaki.

Other movies for memorising: Fata Morgana, Temenos, À Propos De Nice, Meshes of the Afternoon, Nightmare City, Pitfall, Les Revenants, Quatermass and The Pit.

See H. G. Wells' World Brain and Frances A. Yates' The Art of Memory.

f:79

The Eye and the Cell

It is the conspiratorial genius of the Spectacle to devalue the destructive power of the resistance's most powerful weapon – the dominance of visuality, led by the eye and mediated by the movies – and to make antagonism to that weapon deepest within the very resistance that needs it most.*

The resistance cell values many aspects of the Spectacle (the weapons of the cell are among the Spectacle's most successful products) and in return the Spectacle will take up the ideas of the cell. This is not a permanent corruption, but a transitional period when the eventual fate of the bottom-line is in the balance.

Imagine setting up a cell of an organisation that you are not sure exists. You and a few friends live out a harmless preoccupation, or pay a heavy price for a silly game. Or you come to discover that, although no one has organised it, the cell is part of an unbreakable reproductive structure, an organisation that prolongs difference, a plane of consistency.

Models for such an organisation:

The Ferguson Gang - members included Sister Agatha, Erb the Smasher, the Bloody Bishop and 'Kate O'Brien' who turned up in a mask for a radio interview at the BBC in 1934. The Gang covertly toured ancient and dilapidated sites in the UK, first using these buildings for their meetings and then anonymously but theatrically donating large sums of money for their restoration. They wrote in blood.

The Air Loom Gang – a creation of the imagination of Bedlam resident Tilly Matthews, this gang hid in London cellars working on an elaborate air-weaving machine that produced something like an ideological effect, weaving the air of London in ways that influenced the actions and the ideas that informed decision-making.

The Assassins of Beaminster – during the Second World War, in communities like this quiet Dorset town, reliable young people were recruited into small local units, armed and trained. In the event of a German invasion they were to destroy railway bridges using explosives they kept hidden in a garden shed. They were ready to torch private cars – many of them owned by their parents – in case they fell into the hands of the enemy, or encouraged flight. There is also a suggestion that some of these groups would have carried out targeted assassinations of potential collaborators. Most members of these units maintained a silence about their activities until their deaths, long after the operational necessity for silence had passed. (If it had. See Operation Gladio)

These gangs and assassins are the 'imaginary friends' (quasi-corporeal companions) of the mythogeographical cell. Historical or delusional, these are the Real, representing what is not represented, they map that ingrained conspiracy without conspirators (mostly) that constricts and restricts society; and guides and funnels the movements and actions of money and power.

While there have been and, no doubt, still are many real conspiracies – in the US, Operation Paperclip, the Tuskegee Institute and Public Health Service's experiments on black men with syphilis (not disclosing diagnosis and not offering treatment), Watergate and Iran-Contra, in the UK the Zinoviev Letter, the Economic League and 'Clockwork Orange' (the secret state's attempt to destabilise the Labour Government of Harold Wilson) – the global politico-economic system today has never had less use for (indeed is often hindered and discredited by) such conspiracies, because it is organised like a conspiracy in its very fabric, a conspiracy of everybody against everybody (see The Hermeutics of Fear, page 193), a cancellation of terms, it does not need (or very rarely) such local conspiracies. Through the fragmentation of 'late capital' (or what has become a kind of revolutionary capitalism, destroying itself in order to save itself) and the Russian doll personae of postmodern political culture, conspiracy is even more dispersed to the fabric than ever before: it is now a conspiracy of the majority against themselves!

The point, then, is not to conspire, but to understand conspiracy as an exemplary state of being, with its internal demands for secrecy, loyalty, integrity, discipline, discretion and self-publicity.

Virtual conspiracy is moral training for those who wish to détourn 'the big time'.

It is a necessary paradox for mythogeography that such a spectral reticence be accompanied by the extroversion of the visual – the liberation of the eye.

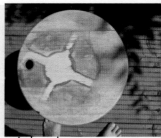

The model for this is Higuchinsky's movie Uzumaki (Spiral) in which malevolent spirals suck upon and twist the inhabitants of a small Japanese town. Eyes swivel and dig into themselves, the point of view retreats behind a car windscreen until a car smash prises the eye free, and the movie moves towards the (mytho)geographical.

It is a training film for the virtual or metaphorical displacement of the eye (the point of view) from the walker to the landscape (see Patterns of Patterns, page 174) and the mytho-evolution of the "new flesh".

"Every clearing (in the forest) was called a lucus, in the sense of an eye, as even today we call eyes the openings through which light enters houses. The true heroic phrase that "every giant had his lucus" (clearing or eye)… had already been falsified when it reached Homer, for it was then taken to mean that every giant had one eye in the middle of his forehead." Vico, The New Science.

* Publishers' note: the following was received as an anonymous email shortly before publication. It is reasonable to assume that the original editors, or one of their number, are the source. "Does Peter Andre feel nostalgia for Jordan/Katie Price when he touches Chantelle Houghton's breasts? If so, where is the nostalgia? In the weight of the implants? Or in the changed appearance of her flesh? And when you read about this shit in the tabloids do you feel something shift inside? Do you physically feel the parasite inside you? And sense yourself a member of an audience that ate itself and now, turned inside out, looks just like you did before? For the celebrity - Peter Andre/Jordan-Katie Price/Chantelle Houghton – and for the insider, the parasite is on the outside. For you, the outsider, the excluded, the marginalised, the spectacle is on the inside."
Email received 18.7.09

Nutopia

Set up a large empty table in a space. Supply plenty of materials: scissors, scalpels, glue, cardboard, card, glitter, lego, wooden blocks, boxes, cylinders, cans, paints etc.

The task is to create a utopian version of the participants' city.

Each participant makes and brings their own contribution – a model of a park, a home, a club, a space, a cage, a pathway, etc. – something that they want to see in their city but isn't there yet.

Around the table the participants work to make the city from the various contributions and from the provided raw materials, arranging and re-arranging the whole model according to their desires. Anyone can add to and rearrange, but no one can subtract from the model.

Theatre In Your Pocket

Create tiny props and diminutive, quotidian actions, so that at any moment you can produce theatre from your pocket, turn the palm of your hand into a stage.

Home

Dig up your back garden looking for treasure.

Morphology

The polarity of the planet Earth is changing. Polarity is never uniform, not even at the poles themselves, but rather there are domains of differing polarities in which one dominates (north or south). However, in recent years scientists have detected that this is not a fixed dominance, but that the anomalies at both poles have been growing.

The Earth is getting ready to flip its poles.

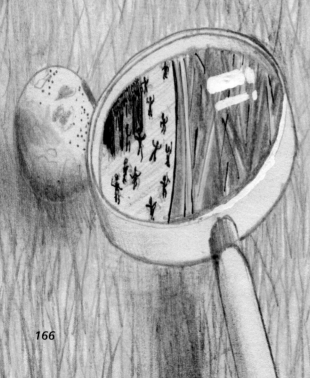

At present the process is a simple accumulative one, but it will eventually become one of sudden, qualitative change.

Drifters should not despair if they see the drifting of others as little more than a copy of their own adventures; repetitious, plagiaristic, unoriginal. That is exactly how we should expect it to be. The practice of disrupted walking is a series of first steps, followed, in the spirit of near-discovery, by a fatal second, setting it back into either nostalgia or rejection. (f80)

"One evening in my childhood, we played out late in the garden of a friend. The sun had turned the clouds orange, with streaks of red. From out of the sky floated a small orb. It rested in the grass of the lawn. My friend fetched a magnifying glass and when we all gathered round and examined the shape we found it was a tiny planet, its population rushing about in huge panicking crowds. The planet suddenly lifted off again and disappeared into the orange of the sky. This is a distinct memory, but I know I read it in an 'American Comic'." (from the notebook of 'B49', member of the M---- Psychogeographical Club, O------ Chapter.)

This book attempts to replace that second step with a stumble, preparing walkers for those moments when strands cross, but without the need to rush toward the spider at the centre of the imaginary web. The web is enough, sufficient to feel the shimmer of the whole field; for this the hypersensitivity and self-reflexivity learned in stumbling is required from a walker who has understood how to walk as both satellite and field.

Theatre - Turning Spectators Into Actors

In You – the City (1988, New York), Fiona Templeton's journey-theatre-of-the-street, a spectator, abandoned by the performers, passes another spectator and realises (for they have been in the position of this other spectator earlier on in the performance-journey) that this other spectator is mis-recognising them as (and thus they have become) a performer, with the power to initiate action.

At the 1938 International Surrealist Exhibition in Paris visitors were given flashlights in order for them to be able to see the exhibits in the darkened exhibition space; they became explorers of the gallery.

In 2008, students at Dartington College of Arts, UK, gave mobile phones to visitors to an installation of ice, press cuttings, cut flowers and bound victim. The very faint light of the mobile repeatedly faded and then flared again on being re-triggered. The audience illuminated a slowly and dimly pulsing launderette, a sort of visual heart beat in a space to which they gave a morbid life.

Dance

'Confluencers' are walkers (and an internet 'community') who use GPS technology to visit those 'places' where lines of longitude and latitude intersect: "an organised sampling of the world". The 'confluence dance' occurs when a confluencer finds an intersection and then, device in hand, moves in various directions in order to collect the full number of figures on the GPS display.

Exhibitionism

Every year, at the height of summer, publish an invitation for people to hang their paintings on their outside walls and display their indoor ornaments on their window ledges for a day.

Theory

For reasons of operational flexibility, the Introduction (above) is not entirely truthful when it comes to theory, but what little of it there is now shoring up the rickety edifice is here exposed on the basis that anyone – hapless enthusiast or deeply tolerant critic – with the patience to have read this far is unlikely to pose much of a threat to our project.

"… none of us inhabitants of the small worlds is any good at all at what you would call theory. That enterprise went belly-up millennia ago when the mother of all worlds went critical and blew. Hence you will find no macro-cosmologists or deconstructionists among us, and if our hats are not as diabolically odd and off-putting as the hats of Elmer, they are still cut from strange cloth and would cause a gasp of shock from the mouth of any but the most robust theoretician." Mac Wellman, A Chronicle Of The Madness Of Small Worlds

Like Bonhoeffer's 'religionless Christianity' mythogeography is theory without theorists; spatialised theory in other words; articulated by human beings, but not requiring them.

Space is constructed of trajectories rather than boundaries. (Doreen Massey) Such trajectories are woven from wayfinding-repetitions into 'regions' or matrices. (Tim Ingold) Ahah, the humans return and the hermeneutics of fear are back on the agenda! (Hans Jonas)

Space is always under construction, never completed or finished. (Doreen Massey)

Sites can be investigated layer by layer. (Mike Pearson and Michael Shanks)

Sites are never monolithic in meaning or monocular in affordance. Mythogeography is the setting in motion (about each other) of the multiple meanings of any site. Mis-Guidance is the act of revealing, animating or performing these multiplicities by setting them in motion: best when they perform themselves. (Wrights & Sites)

Mythogeography does not aspire to a totality, but to an unhinged orrery, in which ideas move in orbit about each other within a frame that has no fixed state of rest. The mythogeographical orrery can be compared to the tooth-mosaic machine (a paving beetle) and the fluid contents of the giant diamond at Canterel's estate (an art of memory!) in Locus Solus by Raymond Roussel. We can only know these totalising 'machines' partially, and deduce the rest; we become completions or continuations of machines, calibrated but uneven specificities, with cogs, fluids and historical and mythical decorative figures (and parts of the same).

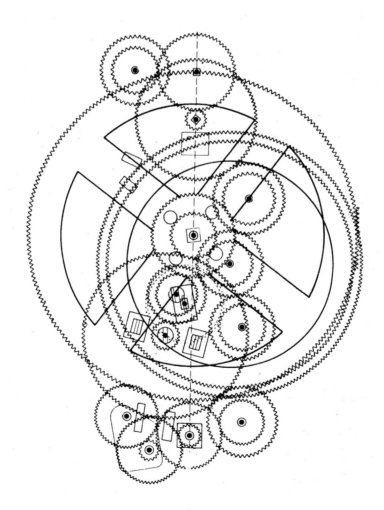

This model of gravitational fields revives and perverts (realising by traducing) the idea of democratic centralism by enabling freedom of orbit ('the movement'), while capable of a sudden shifting across a single plane, which lasts until its probability/stability breaks up into separated orbits; then gravity/attraction reasserts itself. So what happens in such a 'plane action'? Well, attraction is replaced for a while by a discipline, there is a re-territorialisation: not a target-meeting or re-orientation, but a 're-staking' of claims to territory. The catalyst for this sudden state-change is paranoia (as a centralising element, the paranoid subject is both inside the secret operations of society, and outside as one of the dispossessed), briefly able to locate 'the movement' central to the ideological orrery. This is a moment of ultimate but necessary peril, so paranoia must be kept at a low level – if it rises and remains operational then horrors follow: "only the criminal fears the policeman", "I can smell you are against us", etc. But it is a necessary risk. Without it, the movement cannot swing through the angle of change. Of course, the plane-like components of this model are exclusively notional, in materiality there are no such 'planes' or 'angles'. The model functions, absurdly, as an anti-representation of actual fields in which behaviour is neither atomic (particular) nor probabilistic (in technical terms: living). It is an art (a set of forms that can be learned), not a science (well, there are experiments). In the end it will grow or fall according to the 'feel' that its perpetrators discover in themselves, or according to how successful they are in imitating the actions of someone with this 'feel'.

WOYZECK: Can you hear it? Something moving…moving beneath me – (He stamps on the ground.) Listen, it's hollow. It's all hollow under there…

Woyzeck Georg Büchner

The ideas and practices of mythogeography can be learned by rote, a détourned version of the 'art of memory'.

In the classical form of the art of memory, specific parts of a memorised city landscape were allocated to specific concepts. But in mythogeography the memorised city is itself dynamic, so the relations between the concepts and the memorised spaces are fluid, the mnemonic becomes subject to relativity, the ideas are always at the mercy of the redevelopment and decay of the living city.

Mythogeography does not create new objects (there are already enough objects: Arte Povera), it makes gaps, hybrids, intervals – it operates in holey space.

In action, it is mediocre: neither choosing too early nor too late.

Of help in all these regards is Charles Fort's intermediatism, a theorisation of our hyphenated existence, always in between the real and the unreal, like the Brooklyn Bridge: "the bridge itself

is not a final thing in itself, but is a relationship between Manhattan and Brooklyn."

Our 'self' is just as much in trajectory as the landscapes through which we pass. Just as much between one thing and another as the bridges over which it crosses.

Our senses reach out actively, like feelers, for the information in the meaningful environment. (James J. Gibson)

The meaningful environment is subject to a patterning, a dynamic patterning of patterns, at work at all scales, from growth and form to engineering and energy exchange. (D'Arcy Thompson, Evelyn Fox Keller, J. A. Scott Kelso) Look out for dendrites, fractals, the lattices of insect wings, rhizomes, venous and nervous systems, betting patterns, stock markets, natural water drainage patterns appearing in different guises in the city. "The common factor in all of these processes is, as ever, the transfer of energy." Use these patterns to transfer the power in your city.

"All are one in Yog-Sothoth." (Geometry and desire are two kinds of the same slope.)

The structures of myth, if they can be freed from mimesis, are still useful, for they reveal us to ourselves: suspended above a void, reaching out for the lip of the abyss, sustained, to the margins.

About 30,000 to 50,000 years ago our specialised, compartmentalised mind (hunting-knowledge in one chapel, the lexicon-of-sexual-attraction in another) became a cathedral mind of hybrids and ambiguities. (Mithen) (f81)

Excess, waste, superfluity, surplus as the driving social forces/indicators.

The dialectic must be deferred, suspended, its parts held in dynamic tension. (Bhabha)

Society needs to find a new version of the freemasonic lodges: 'turning strangers into brothers'.

Politics in an age of fantasy is about inventing our own reality. (Duncombe)

A dérive-mentality and practice disperses eroticism from the body to landscape. But the dérive's various disruptions, such as this one, are only ever temporary.

Separateness is a quality of the Spectacle, but is also a key to its subversion: rather than utopianism (with its absolutism and exclusions) it is in limited disruptions that democratic change least catastrophically begins. In separateness incompatible virtues can flourish. Rejecting Breton, Thoreau, the permanent dérive of Ivain, Jesus ("For I am come to set a man at variance

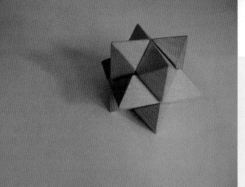

against his father, and the daughter against her mother") and the Jain teaching, walking out need not be a final rupture from the everyday, but its own disruption can be disrupted.

Hypocrisy is a key principle for mythogeographical disruption. (f82) The rebel and the utopian are both at a disadvantage to the sincere hypocrite. Rather than the bandit-binge of Jean-Michel Mension, look to Gil Wolman's oscillation between activism and family life, or wine-sipper Debord slipping on a dressing gown between dérives. The point is the endless collapse of the chapel mind into the shakey, ambi-valent cathedral, its parts in permanent subsidence.

f.81 Steven Mithen, *The Prehistory of the Mind*

f.82 "*The displaced eroticism of the drift, from fellow walkers to landscape. The unevenness of the picturesque. Truth is a product of keeping the different parts of integrity in separate spaces. Hypocrisy. The trick is to stumble but not to fall. (ffa) The drift combines contradictory virtues, it is never good v. evil (these are compartmentalised, like a 'happening'), it is a limited myth.*" (From the notebook of an anonymous drifter, possibly transcribed from an early version of The Orrery.)

ff.a "*Stumbling needs to be thought of not as a loss of footing but rather as a finding of one's feet: it is the act in which the body rights itself by a rétraction and the mind becomes aware of the operation of measure and balance – "a secret force" – operating in and through the body.*" Social Choreography, Andrew Hewitt

The key organ of perception and delusion is the eye, which, like all the organs of sense, is not a passive receptor but an exploratory feeler after experience. Imitate the lophophore of the brachiopod, a tentacle covered in tentacles that operates in relation to the movements of water in order to guide food towards the mouth of its organism. Adopt such activism as the extension of your dispersed organism. The 'violence' of modernism dilates and separates the eye from its oppressive face, its dominating organism. (A key instrument of this is cinema.) Good. (See Story of The Eye, Georges Bataille)

The future is built from ruins; walking is one.

Book Burning

(It is time for a review of the four recent summary texts on walking: Solnit, Careri, Nicholson and Amato. One of the problems about writing about walking is that far too many writers about walking are far too interested in writing.)

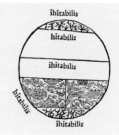

The three mythogeographical approaches to Deleuzian "life":

1/ Intermediatism: irresponsibility (in the context of responsibility), hypocrisy (as the irritant of change), uniformity (the blanking out of the screen), mediocrity (protecting your first ideas from premature selection). These are all best mediated by Intermediatism.

2/ Cell culture: resistant (to the spectacular) in theory, ambulant in practice (led by its periphery), on a plane of consistency (a structure sustaining difference), part of an unknown and ineradicable set of connections. The cell creates rumours, festivals of the everyday, the re-naming of public buildings, the recruitment of the Count of Saint Germain, Luther Blissett, A. J. Salmon. Anyone can be The Crab Man. (But, see the Ferguson Gang and money.)

3/ Separateness of separatedness: disruption, fragmentation, the floating free effected by neo-symbolism, the re-separating of the spectacle's separatedness. This generates limited myth: the eye floats free, the cell is suspended above an 'abyss' reaching for the periphery, sensitive to the patterns of patterns, to the sustaining plane.

Trash Tropes

"… it isn't an "ism" at all. It's an "is-ness". There's no business like show business and this is the production you've been waiting for. Art for the end of the millennium: the fin-de-recycle. Fin–ism. Like the fins on a customized, cosmic Cadillac."   "The Way We Were" by Ann Magnuson in Kenny Scharf ed. Barry Blinderman

a/ the zombie (even dumb people get this one)

b/ the big machine (the monster, another crowd-pleaser)

c/ apocalypse (this is a stock backdrop to ideas, the mass production of tears)

d/ conspiracy (fundamental, not functional; conspiracies are real but marginal, capital doesn't need them, conspiracy is ingrained in it)

e/ death of the hero/heroine (deals with – eradicates! – the nightmare of immortality, the hunger for posterity, the gambling of happiness-now against bliss-tomorrow)

f/ transcendent politically correct heroines - Faiza in Captain Britain and MI-13, Djaq in Robin Hood, Rose in Doctor Who – in each case their inauthenticity was doubled and they achieved limited mythic status.

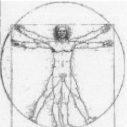

g/ the crazy gang/odd bunch – the team. Grant Morrison's The Invisibles. The drifting group, the zombie dérivistes in Land Of the Dead. Temporary alliance (a tight association may be coincidental with this gang, but is not necessary for it).

h/ the comforting state: the moment in a horror film when the anxiety and edge disappears, the monster shows itself, exposing the stitching in its costume, and the military arrive for open conflict. Turn off. Leave. Fight.

Patterns of Patterns

(f83)

Plant cells grow in a spiral fashion, new cells appearing as the stem turns through an angle, turning again and again, each time forming a new cell, each time through the same angle. Irrespective of scale (this is a dynamic pattern) the angle remains the same as leaves arrange themselves optimally to catch the sunlight and seeds pack uniformly in the burgeoning seedhead. This common, creative angle is Phi cells per turn, or Phi turns per new cell. Phi is 1.618…. (f84)

"H. E. Huntley extrapolated from the golden section (a single line demonstrating the ratio Phi) a three-dimensional golden cuboid that is shaped quite like a brick."
The Grid Book, Hannah B. Higgins

f.83 *The English entertainer Harry Worth was a comedian without jokes. His ineffectual and accident-prone behaviour never quite reached a punchline. Bumbling above the abyss, a limited myth, humour deferred, the audience laughed in order to keep Worth in work. This is egalitarian comedy of the highest order. Worth is the comic model of mythogeography.*

f.84 *"Everybody gets hung up on the science part, which has nothing to do with it… they're getting at us through the fiction!" Kevin Baggins in The Faculty (dir. Robert Rodriguez)*

Robert Smithson's signature work is Spiral Jetty, recently reappearing from beneath the waters of the Great Salt Lake. "Et in Utah ego". If the walking cults develop beyond the cellular then this work, submerged or extant, will take on a greater significance for them.

Growth patterns similar to logarithmic plant spirals occur in snail shells and some sea shells and sheep horns. Although these Golden Section or Fibonacci spirals are different from logarithmic spirals they are almost indistinguishable in appearance.

174

"in the great majority of horns we have no difficulty in recognising a continuous logarithmic spiral, nor in correlating it with an unequal rate of growth (parallel to the axis) ... the inequality maintaining a constant ratio as long as growth proceeds."
On Growth and Form, D'Arcy Wentworth Thompson

The Milky Way or Via Lactea, our galaxy, is a barred, disc-like spiral galaxy. Our solar system sits on a spur of one of the spiral arms of The Milky Way, in the Local Fluff inside the Local Bubble.

Pattern for the development of the walking cells:

grow 1 unit, bend 1 unit
grow 2 units, bend 1 unit
grow 3 units, bend 1 unit
and so on...

The organic quality of this process lies not in the totalising form of an organising organism, but in the 'turn', the deflection which makes change and pattern possible through a banal repetition.

Mythogeography oscillates between banal repetition and the unevenness (f85) of the picturesque

"I be a comm'd a matter o' aighteen miles to zee thicky theng caal'd a PEE – DES – TREE – UN; and aater aal, I only zeed a Mon a waalkin'!"

see wabi-sabi.

f.85

IMPORTANT: PLEASE READ THE NOTE OF WARNING BELOW BEFORE PROCEEDING TO THE ORRERY

Publishers' note: "The ossuary tour could make a strong impression on children and people of nervous disposition." So reads a warning notice at the official street level entrance to the Paris Catacombs. But it could also apply to The Orrery below. On people of a practical or impatient disposition The Orrery's collection of ideas, of organisations and individuals 'thinking aloud', may make a strongly negative impression. It may serve them best to skip the next twenty pages or so. For others, willing to struggle through its labyrinth, the journey may be more rewarding. At least for its tangents if not for the coherence of its philosophy. It is for the reader to judge if its convolutions are the result of dérive-like thinking or mere muddle. After descending 130 steps and then negotiating half a mile of narrow, mostly featureless, tunnels there is a second sign, above a shadowy portal: "Arrête! C'est ici l'empire de la mort!"

THE ORRERY

Editors' note:

After making a study of the various documentations, workbooks, mis-guides, toolkits, commonplace books and atlases in circulation among the walking cults, close-knit associations and cover organisations, the editors of this volume have detected the presence of an Ur-Document, a common source from which all seem to draw to some extent (some more than others). This Ur-Document plays the same role for this collection as the famous 'Q' (a supposed collection of the sayings of Jesus) does for the Christian gospels. Like 'Q', this Ur-Document has never been found, though it is referred to as 'The Orrery' in a pencilled comment in the margins of the Satellite Capture entry of the Wigan P. A. handbook. (The editors themselves have often used these 'Orrery' materials in their own publications without knowledge of their prior collection.)

Orreries are mechanical devices used to demonstrate the relative positions and motions of the planets and moons in a solar system. In this case, the device has no sun, and the various ideas move in a loose, but patterned attraction to each other (some more attracted and attractive than others). It is clear from the pencilled comment — "in motion of walking, the orrery committed to memory jumps the synapses, concepts about kerbs" — that The Orrery is something more than a sourcebook for lazy anthologisers, but is intended to be committed to memory by dérivistes; a set of floating concepts to be set in motion during a drift and interwoven with the unfolding landscape, an 'art of memory' without fixed architectural reference points.

'The Orrery' is a metaphor for suspended dialectic (see E-Myth). The parts never actually reach a synthesis, for this is always (purposefully) delayed. Nor is it about the totalising organisation of ideas, but only the motion of its particles. It is a Massey-space (of trajectories).

The Central Committees

What follows now are the contents of The Orrery.

Circulation of Ideas

The Shore Crab does an extraordinary thing: when on land it spits out water from the points where its legs connect to its shell and then passes this water around the knobbly edge of its shell (some smaller Shore Crabs can pass the water right over the bumps on the tops of their shells). The knobbles agitate the water, re-oxygenating it, after which the Shore Crab takes the water back inside itself and retrieves the oxygen, sustaining itself while on shore.

This is how to use ideas: circulate them around you. Walk, and allow your ideas to be agitated by what you find and by the people you meet. Test them against environments and encounters. Then draw on them again.

The mind of the drifter should be like a bouncy castle on a cattle grid.

Paranoia

By cultivating a low level paranoia the explorer can develop a super-sensitivity to the textures, details, signage and symbols of the street. The paranoid walker over-interprets the street, countering ideology's (f86) effect of under-explanation. It's the reverse of the principle of Occam's Razor.

Paranoia is usually interpreted negatively. And in its extreme forms it is thoroughly terrifying to experience. But it is not all of one quality. Freeman & Freeman have described a "sliding scale" of paranoia, a key indicator of which is "how much the thoughts interfere with everyday life" (f87). But what if that interference could be mapped (f88) and controlled, as a chosen means to "interfere with everyday life"? Freeman & Freeman concede that paranoia can be 'chosen' by society (they explain how the objects of paranoid fears in Vienna are very different from those in Tokyo) and yet they do not allow it to be 'chosen' by an individual. But what if we can? Then we have a tool.

Low level paranoia is not some kind of savvy street wisdom. By the time enough evidence is gathered by such a method the time for flight will long have passed. Instead, the 'paranoid' drifter needs to sense the anterior of the potential for danger, to sense even before potential is manifest! This is why Kierkegaardian 'dread' is important, for it is a fear without a cause, it is the perception of the anterior of anteriors, and while it causes alarm prior to a material threat, it might also trigger anxieties for which there is no material cause, only virtual ones. Hence, paranoia is the whippet that chases ideology to its deepest tunnels.

"Arousal is often accompanied by perceptual anomalies. The world around us can appear brighter or more vivid… We may become unusually sensitive to smells; objects can feel odd to the touch… the feeling that our thoughts are not our own, or that apparently unimportant events are actually highly significant… we might have the impression that the world isn't real…" Paranoia: the 21st century fear, Freeman & Freeman

There is nothing quirkily modish about suffering from paranoia, but what about the controllable end of the continuum? Doesn't the passage above sound like the perfect catapult for drifting?

Over-explanations, (conspiracy theories are good examples), can be turned into dramatic narratives, the 'creation stories' for a site. Every object there conceals a second object.

Ideology: that happy marriage of individual assumptions and the geo-organisation of meaning without conspiracy.

Daniel Freeman & Jason Freeman Paranoia: the 21st-century fear

See footnote below beginning: "Pacific islanders living", page 197.)

There is a connection here to Salvador Dali's paranoiac-critical method; in both, things which cannot be rationally connected are joined together through paranoia.

Exercises: 1/ create a narrative involving anything in the site that makes you even slightly anxious, 2/ create a narrative about what is hidden in the site, 3/ create a narrative to explain how everything in your site came to be organised in the way it is (and what it all means).

But a paranoid style is not enough. The drifter must also cultivate a complementary depressive consciousness (f89); one of weaving and healing. The segments, fragments and compartments (these fabulous tactics of modernism and postmodernism) are sewn together. (f90) There is a coruscating price to pay for this; without sentimentality, without any nonsense about making the body whole or restoring the organism to its dictatorship over the parts, by random acts of weaving, the future is constructed from threads of fakery, plagiarised diagrams and mistaken charts, the compartments are woven together with the thrill of a simulation.

Fakes, imitations and simulacra are like another eye, to the side of normal vision (as with the 'beside' – to the side of – of performance), it is looking through the small 'other'. The Crab Man has learnt recently of the demolition of the secret room (f91). It is through this room, used as a kind of inner lens, that the Crab sees to the side of things. This is not an irrational view, but a view of irrationality.

This is how to see, binocularly.

f.89 See Touching Feeling, Eve Kosofsky Sedgwick, pages 123 – 151.

f.90 See Lacan and his use of knots.

f.91 See Footnote above beginning "The maternal side of...", page 54.

The Game of War

What are the relations between driver and walker? What do they see of each other through the screen? (See The Eye and the Cell, page 163.) How is their relationship mediated by this overt frame?

If we turn political correctness on its head and assume for a moment that the stranger always warrants suspicion, then the walker is a refugee from the Real war (home), where home is that necessary domestic violence to our freedom that we pay as insurance against loneliness and Vico-ist brutality under the trees. Unsurprisingly, the driver, chained to their machine, a mechanical part of their extended organism, will at some level resent the walker's lack of responsibilities.

To magnify the difference between walker and driver, many cars are domesticated, an extension of their owners' living rooms, with telephone, coffee and stereo.

The driver is the avenging angel of the home, seeking out the walker to punish them for desertion.

The awful power of the Spectacle (f92) is such that there is an equality of exchange between driver and walker. It is an egalitarian quality based on the ubiquitous degradation of everything to an image of itself, and that is why the dériviste does not walk in engagement with the Spectacle (or the driver or the home), but is walking (temporarily) out on it.

f.92 see Guy Debord's The Society of the Spectacle and Comments on the Society of the Spectacle

Common Dramaturgy

At major public events, dramaturgs – in the guise of senior police planners, civil servants, general secretaries, loose associations of protesters, chief marshals, etc. – organise the dramatic elements, increasing the general passivity that greets such events; appropriate to celebrations of monarchy, nationhood, etc. the objects of which are founded upon passivity.

A 'common dramaturgy' would be a similarly conspiratorial counterpart to these official dramaturgs, in the sense that actions would be planned in advance of their enactment by persons unaware of (or unprepared for) their roles. This is an aesthetic process; the themes, excitement, patterns, etc. are only an arrangement; their eventual function, result or significance are unpredictable.

(Editors' note: As with "hope" in theory, so with "common dramaturgy" and "situations" in practice, we are unable to do any more than point out that they are missing.)*

*Publishers' note:

I hate it. I hate this 'Orrery'. I'm sitting here at my Apple at home, it's just a screen. Outside it's something like a mackerel sky, like a pattern made by water on sand, the stars have scales; reptilian. And the moon has a circle round it, which I know is made by ice crystals, but looks far more significant.

While I've been editing The Orrery, men have been working on the road outside, now it's black and oily in the moonlight and though it's at an oblique angle I can make out the sign apologising for there being "No Road Markings". So, suddenly, everything's very general. And that's never true, is it?

Like "Publishers"; there's always a "publisher", even when there's no Proprietor and it's gone round the table, been batted back and forth at morning meetings, eventually there's someone, someone pretty junior like me, who is "Publishers". But what's odd, this time, what's different is that… yes, I have that job this time and it's all pretty much left to me, but… the firm, we've been walking.

Hence, (I think this is why), my colleagues have agreed to publish the extracts that follow. They result from some peculiar communications that we received after the provisional editors of this volume broke off their, already oblique, communications.

(The messages extracted below near enough derailed the whole project. I can write that now, six months after initially making these notes, in the knowledge that all has gone well.)

The first document is obviously a fictive or faux-hoax missive, but was followed by what purports to be a serious (and indignant) commentary upon it from, we must assume, whatever was left of the Central Committees.

I pushed very hard to have these extracts published because I hate the Orrery. I write, and mean, "hate" because I love the Crab Man's journey, and all the nonsense about pirates (the Norma Nomad thing is so obviously a dotting of i's and a crossing of t's by A. J. Salmon's messenger boy) and those parts are the heart and soul of whatever this is. But "mythogeography"... isn't it a contradiction in terms? An intentional contradiction? But something more, even - it's a cancellation of terms, one part (mytho) cancels out the other (geography). And there are clues: those walks where someone (He Yun Chang, Richard Long) carries a rock and then puts it back where it came from or swaps it for some equivalent rock. I think someone – not the Central Committees, but someone who was supplying the Central Committees (probably even in Central Committees it falls to some poor jerk to put everything together once everyone else has gone home, some 'minutes secretary' maybe) – was nodding to us when they let that in, because they obviously don't like that sort of showmanship walking, do they? So, why put it in if it isn't to sensitise us to cancelling out?

The truth is: there is no "mytho". And there is no "geography". The one cancels out the other. Two stones swapped.

I didn't give the book its title, of course. But until now I hadn't realised the genius of it; a title for nothing, the ultimate weakness – this is what they wrote: "...for truth lies in these connections not as some generality, but in the specificity of each "and". "and" is a space of nothingness (the ultimate 'weakness')..." I see it now, because I see the motion, I see the way it shapes up. The reason I hate the Orrery and the Manifesto and the Blue Peter/Ladybird Book of What is Mythogeography? is that it's trying to give it One Brain under the guise of a zillion synapses.

I know. Whoever-the-original-writers-are, they know. The fictional Comte knows! The execrable Norma knows, the minutes secretary knows and every effing publisher and editor knows that you can never tell anyone anything, you show it to them. No messages, only media (McLuhan was never ambitious enough). Spectacle. And, by the way, there's no theory in those books by Guy Debord either! – I've read them, I've just read them, on the train back from Andorra – there's no theory, but, o, there's style, there's prose style in spades. You can just see the man nodding to you as he writes those elegant, serpentine lines.

He's signalling to us, but he's conceding too. Because there's nothing more that he can do. There is only the walk of the signifiers. No capital W Walk, no capital D Dérive. No categories or taxonomies. Just the things and their copies. We're all 'super-empiricists' now. Which means there's no empiricism and there's nothing very super about it.

I was in Andorra to work on another book we're publishing. It's about artists' 'interventions', things placed in cities and in landscapes. Things to be used, tripped over, lived in, attacked. Relational. To be more precise we're going to make a book about the way that these projects are managed and curated: the commissioning, the selection processes, the work with the artists, the consultation with the communities, the relation to festivals and galleries, marketing, budgeting, the reactions of the public, relation to the art market and city hall, the bottom line. It was originally going to be more of a documentation, but if Mythogeography sells well maybe we'll make it another handbook? Maybe there can be a series? (I was waiting for "Celebrity Drift" in the Toolbag section but it never came!)

I met someone in Andorra who might have been the Crab Man. The Festival literature didn't advertise him as such, but everything he said (he had no idea I was editing this book or had knowledge of the material in it) – born in a Midlands car town, Shakespeare countryside, playwright, conversion and doubt, complete indifference to any kind of tree let alone oaks – it all fitted. He was there as part of a group of English curators called The Mariscos. They have a mussel shell on their business card. It's not far from "seafood" to crustacean, but there's more to it than that: I googled their name and the de Mariscos were a twelfth century pirate family based on Lundy Island, a few miles off the north coast of the UK county of Devon.

I fell in with the Crab Man at The Mariscos' vernissage. He was escaping to the bar from an act he'd booked: some kind of rock'n'roll Police (as in PC Plod not as in Sting tribute band). While they hammered out murder ballads to a few journos, we stood at the bar where he told me of his plans to walk around the city at first light. The Mariscos had commissioned an Italian artist to create a number of enigmatic plastic booths to be placed in each of the tiny city's districts. The Crab Man was keen to see how they might have fared.

Neither of us slept and we set off together at 5am. Unforgivably, I attempted to glean from the Crab Man a rationale for his and the group's work. He at least appeared to make various attempts at an answer, but he never spoke more than a theoretical phrase or two before he was drawing my hand to stroke a wind-hollowed brick, or interpreting graffiti or inviting me to blow along the horizon. I felt like whoever it was that sent that email to the Exmouth CPS (?):

"Every sentence of your tour made sense even though the meaning of the whole thing was unclear - i.e. we three visitors extracted different meanings. That seems perfect."

At first it worried me that I couldn't make a single meaning from that morning. And not just from the things he said. But what he did. He would walk without looking at a map and we seemed to 'magically' find the booths, but then he became frustrated and dug out the map and followed it like an orienteer. At the booths, that he'd said were to be placed at the mercy of the city, he scribbled a childish face in one and poured the contents of his water bottle over the floor of another. There was no pattern of patterns; what he seemed to enjoy most was the simple one-thing-after-another provoked by his inconsistency: cattle streaming down suburban streets, the rusty tinge given by the dawn to shiny pylons, the chaotic architectural mixes, the incomprehensible reprimand he received when he attempted to creep into one of the booths outside a working class café, a large pool of blood in the road, and our sudden arrival at a turquoise lagoon, tall blue cliffs rising vertically from the opposite shore. We edged our way along a narrow path, our backs to the high steel mesh fences of the city's water treatment facility. There was an unnatural stillness on the water, as if this might, at last, be one of his 'planes'. But what he seemed to take from this was not a theoretical pleasure, but a ludicrous joy in playing on the miniaturised 'beaches' a few inches deep and a few feet in length.

The thing was, though… there was more to it than just bits, because although, as they arrived, the things and views and signs and screeches of brakes and pool of blood and sudden changes of direction and espressos and pectens seemed to have no coherence, when the climax came they had all contributed to it.

We were thoroughly enjoying our precarious skirting of the lagoon. Oohing and aahing like tourists. We even took our shoes and socks off and paddled for a while. Then the coarse grass grew taller and sharper. The path narrower. There was dog shit and fishermen's nylon line tangled in shards of driftwood. We picked our way more carefully around the arcing fence, till it straightened towards the entrance to the plant. And there, crumbling, sliced in a grid by the wires of the fence, were three… we didn't really know what. Cones. Twenty feet tall. Arranged like the pyramids at Giza. Sculptures? Valve-housings? Menhirs, definitely. But whether accidental or not…We just stood and looked. They were too THERE for aahing. It was like Mozart 40 (choose your own example) simply materialised on the lawn of a sewerage works.

And that was it. We didn't go to the last booth. We made an arrangement to meet for a beer later (which the Crab Man missed) and went back to our hotels. I tried having breakfast, I tried having a shower, I tried sleeping, I tried just lying down. But the walk was like the stump of a new limb (or, better, a new organ) that I'd just grown. It was thrashing about looking for something. It only became an ache when I gave up trying to appease it and got down to some serious work on the next book.

The ache of the organ-limb hasn't gone away.

"…the lophophore of the brachiopod, a tentacle covered in tentacles that operates in relation to the movements of water in order to guide food towards the mouth of its organism."

But I know what would kill it – anything mediating and compression-chambery like theory, like The Orrery, like that soothing idea of everything in orbit about everything else.

No, there is only ever the one journey – all the others are segments of it – and that's the one we're on right now.

I think I've spoiled it with that last sentence, but it proves my point. It's the journeys – full stop. Once you try to reduce them to sentences, they're sentences of death.

So that's why I'm putting this little anti-personnel note into the 'plane' of the Central Committees' inconsistency.

It will be light soon. The family will be waking up. But all night it's felt like I've been writing this on enemy territory and some Lenin impersonator was going to pop out from behind one of the trees in the wood any minute and go "boom!" I can see through the window that the halo has slipped from the moon.

But, hell, if the original (hah!) authors of these materials have anything to say about this, well – it's YOU made us walk, my friends! We even tried holding our meetings on the hoof. Then some contract discussions with clients (like the walk in the garden at Camp David...) None of it worked. But the unexpected side effect, the mutation from the short-circuit of its unproductive-ness, is that now we just walk. Nothing targeted, nothing about anti-stress, or pedestration, or mobile thinking, or situated meetings. But, I've seen them – my colleagues walking and I do, I walk. We walk. Like flying or slipping through dimensions or sliding in and out of visibility, completely banal and ordinary, we walk.

But that isn't enough for The Orrery, is it?

These are the extracts from the two communications we received.

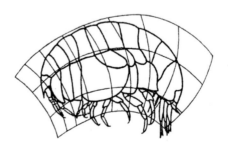

Portbou
Pyrenees

*I am sealing this in a sturdy envelope and placing it in the safe
keeping of Herr Benjamin, with the understanding that he will deliver
it somewhere across the border to a suitable poste restante. I am unsure,
given our precarious situation, how I will eventually make contact with
you. You are not so distant, but you are far in the future.*

*How strange that it should end like this! There is no deterioration of the
physical body, nor a jaded palate, nor a poisoned soul, and yet the
overwhelming ennui I feel is no less awful than the terror I felt at the
Lisboa inundation, and its consequences for the masses will be no less
severe. No one is a king in an earthquake.*

*But you must not think that my boredom is the fruit of these miserable
fascists, although perhaps nothing in human history has hid such
tedium, such a filthy swamp, such a brown unending mush under
uniforms of finesse and sheen, and symbols of such inspired plagiarism.
No, it is a far older disease than that, carried by the particles of
language itself.*

*I believe I breathed them in at Sailor Ephraim's bar on the corner of
Spiegelgasse. I was having a Ball, listening to a calf-like tube reciting
"gadji beri bimba glandridi laula lonni cadori" until its voice lost its
geometrical coherence. At first I thought that the tube was suffering
some faint or swoon, but as its voice modulated and shimmered
through the fragments of what it had just destroyed, I became infected
by the realisation that what I heard was not the end for others, but
rather their continuation by different means, and that this was not
some sacrificial cow on Flatland, but the bishop of all that is to come.*

*I knew then that escape would be impossible. I dragged around with
the artistes from the cabaret, vaulting on air, participating in
deambulations. But their cannibal manifestoes led mostly to posing
around derelict churches, compounded by cantons, and idiots'
wasteland. In Paris I hoped for something at variance from the*

longueurs of Teutonic Switzerland but found myself lured into the countryside by a number of provincial Bretons. We walked half-asleep. Barely formed words were thumped in the footfalls of our trance, hammering out the currency of the unconscious, converting dreams into credit, the dead capitals and lower cases of a coming century.

By the time you find this, I will have achieved what I never thought possible. Dematerialisation. Tell everyone: the Cannibal Comte has ate himself!! The Vampyre sucked himself dry! What need of monsters now, or aristocrats, or leaders, we are in the last spasms of them all, and then nothingness will have achieved what only nothingness can: society without volition, movement without force, mobility without adventure. For all their cobwebbed Prussian Idealism, the revolutionaries will have levelled even themselves into the hole left by Tzara's anti-theory, sucked like a po in a maelstrom, and then an automatic writing system will have become an automatic sewerage system. The rulers of the world - everyone and none - will mill about like Wagnerites circumambulating Kirov's head at the Mariinsky.

Round and round. Explosions. Crashes. Crunches. Economics and geometry will have won. Their great buildings will look like automobile crashes. Their churches like gas stations. And they, we will forget "they", "they" will forget "they" and simply become "   ".

So, "   ", from one disappearance to another

(The manuscript breaks off here at the bottom of a page, as if part of the leaf is missing. In pencil, on the back of the text, in block capitals:

COMTE DE SAINT GERMAIN   MISTER RAKOCZI   MASTER R   SANCTUS GERMANUS
I AM ACTIVITY (1940)

(The following was received by email: 1.5.2009)

From: ----------
Sent: Fri 1/05/2009 12:13
To: --------------
Subject: innuendoes Germane to book

Dear -------,

Herr Benjamin – Walter Benjamin, student of Marx and the Kaballah.

the border – Benjamin commited suicide in 1940 when arrested by fascist supporters at the Spanish border, the suitsace of notes he was carrying has never been recovered.

the Lisboa inundation – a tsunami enveloped part of Lisbon, Portugal, in 1755, generating a European-wide philosophy of awe, terror-sublime, and inundation by machine, that's exactly one hundred years before the devil's footprints joined together the technologies necessary for the philosphy's realisation as the 20th Century. (What happened in 1955?)

Sailor Ephraim's bar on the corner of Spiegelgasse – this is the Meierei Restaurant owned by a Dutch former-seaman, where in 1916 the uniquely destructive instrument of Dada was forged in a series of weekly performances.

I was having a Ball – Hugo Ball, the leader of the Dada Cabaret who having destroyed language, had nowhere to go but mysticism and shamanism.

cabaret, vaulting on air – Cabaret Voltaire (the Dada cabaret)

their cannibal manifestoes – most famously written by Tristan Tzara, these have a candid honesty, and admit that in the name of consistency Dada must disband having done its disassembling.

compounded by cantons – Pound's Cantos.

idiots' wasteland – Eliot's The Wasteland, (with the above, the dead ends of Modernism.)

a number of provincial Bretons – the Surrealists.

an automatic sewerage system – the implication of the Comte's letter is that just as something far more radical than modernism occurred at the Zurich cabaret (that being, in metaphor, the shift from industrial capitalism to the hypercapitalism of the virtual, the spectacularised and the spectral), so in Paris the automatism of the Surrealists prepared the way for a capital without capitalists. For the rule of dead labour, everyone and no one, of capital over itself and everything else.

like Wagnerites circumambulating Kirov's head at the Mariinsky – a reference to the practice of opera and ballet-goers at the Kirov/Mariinsky Theatre in Saint Petersburg, who ambulated around the bust of a murdered Stalinist apparachik. These two cycles – of Wagner and Stalin – seem to cancel each other out, the cancellation of the (20th) century of ideology (that had actually begun in 1755) .

Round and round – as above.

Explosions. Crashes. Crunches – a system without managers.

So, " ", from one disappearance to another – not only is this letter an obvious hoax, a neat turning of the tables on us neo-situationists, by using a flag of convenience in the manner of Milord Gower, but there is also a clever cover in the pencil note "I AM ACTIVITY" which might at first suggest that after all this pessimism and the utterly necropolitan construction of the tomb of language and the end to adventure, that inside it all there might be a divine spark – that ACTIVITY might be the answer, theory-less voluntarism, wandering, going 'a zonzo', ambling, drifting. This is very clever triangulation – for not only does the writer manage to drag mythogeography, the dérive, etc. into his narrative of universal uselessness, but to the initiated he tramples even that: for I AM ACTIVITY is the name of a crackpot pseudo-religion founded in Chicago in 1930 by Guy Ballard and his wife Edna, after Ballard's return from a hike looking for an Esoteric Brotherhood on the slopes of the Californian Mount Shasta. Arriving home, Ballard announced that he had met a man on the mountain who introduced himself as the Comte de Saint Germain. Absolutely true (what he said, not who he met).

So what is the agenda here? It is an act of violent surgery. To reach through the body of the drifters and explorers and strollers and cut right through the situationists, the peace pilgrims, the land artists and rip out the modern beginnings of all this, and then having disposed of the organs, to declare the body as "the late, late show of capitalism".

As if the moral emptiness of our present, barely virtual, institutionally-invisible, almost bankless, throwaway, politically-impotent system might somehow infect us, might somehow be that infinite set of mirrors, reflecting ourselves back in our own hollow faces. Pining the blame for the crisis on its victims, the 'Saint Germain' letter re-describes our solutions as our problems.

There is only one way to break this cycle, and it ain't to smash the mirror. The only way is the theoretical way. To have the strength to do almost nothing. At most to drift ainlessly. And theorise. To wait and wait an wait and think and think and think Until it is possible to do things again.

This is followed by a long, two page paragraph of theorising, much of which repeats, in parts wholesale, The Orrery. There is no signing off. The email ends as abruptly as the Comte's letter. But without the pencilled notes.

When the Crab Man failed to show up for our drink, I trawled about the city looking for the various interventions curated by him and his colleagues.

I soon found a very tall pillar, maybe 15 metres high, which individual citizens were booking themselves onto to stand like Simeon Stylites glowering over their city, an indictment of those who sought to escape it laterally or fanatically. I attended a guided tour of the city on a rubbish cart, participated in a trespass of the city's catacombs, stumbled upon strange platforms that were being used as trading floors or parcel rooms for the exchange of gifts, I donned headgear which allowed me to walk simultaneously in the contemporary city and another city (which might be an earlier or a parallel city or a lower or a higher city), I attended the re-naming of various prominent landmarks and institutions and the re-opening of places that had never been formally opened, quotidian places (toilets, maintenance yards), I struggled with a white map relieved only by water marks, folds and ridges, I watched a young woman equipped with a leaf-blower coax a tumbleweed across the central square like Cassandra prophesying a coming ghost town, and took a tram to the edge of the city where, in a council yard, I was shown a wall alive with tiny scorpions. I bought a cigarette lighter and a pair of swimming trunks emblazoned with scorpion symbols.

Finally, I returned to the centre of the city, to the headquarters of the Festival, where The Mariscos had set up an 'Office for Disorienteering'. The main door was locked, but I gained access by climbing a ladder and entering a window on the second floor. The Festival had generously assigned The Mariscos three floors in what seemed to be a converted fire station. But The Mariscos had not reciprocated the gesture and the tiled and polished rooms were largely bereft of furniture or information. Festival leaflets, available from any café in the city, were stacked on window ledges.

I became increasingly irritated. The main point of my being there was to see some expression of the artists' management of their own event, but the few things they had installed – a desultory case of source books, dainty coffee cups filled with crushed glass – only made the place more achingly ignored. While I hunted about, expecting to grasp my misunderstanding around any corner, a group of the Festival organisers entered and then left quickly. Approaching the final room I still held out some hope for a tiny, immaculately detailed and baroque office, crammed with Mariscos, but it too was deserted; empty, but for a folding table stacked against a wall.

There is no centre, no management, no general staff, there is no "office", no map, no plan, any of those things… there is no "orientation" to "dis".

But what there is, is The Orrery – a parliament of crows picking at the hearts of those things that don't quite fit its engine, that don't quite match the Deleuzian-Masseyite-Debordite-Marxian-Thoreauist line.

When I got back to England, I checked one or two things. When the letter and the email arrived I checked some more.

(MGF) The devil's footprints of 1855, heralding the assemblage of the demonic technology of the 20th century, were first sighted just outside Exmouth, where a sixteen-sided house (E-"round and round" – this End Note is printed below at page 217) had been built by two cousins, one of whom had survived the Lisbon Tsunami of 1755. Deploying the profits from the family's concrete factory in Lisbon (concrete was used widely in the re-building of the city, the technology is coming!) the pair of cousins Grand Toured through Europe for a decade and then built their house, setting it around a three-storey tall, central, eight-sided room, crowned with sea shells and decorated like an underwater grotto, wallpapered with a seaweed design. In eight outer rooms they created something like a factory disguised as a home, creating all their decorations from objects of ruin, abandonment and abjection. In one way the house represented the absent Real of the wave, the maelstrom, the deluge, past and future. A silver globe, like a single, huge, monstrous drop of water, hanging in the centre of the green room, above it a dove with a sprig of laurel in its beak, a messenger to whatever Ark might be on the storm. But in another way what was most absent – because the cousins had taken their place, imitated them, made them unnecessary by their industrious production of feather friezes and broken shell table tops and driftwood frames – was the workforce of Lisboa, those concrete-makers whose labours had generated the wealth to make eccentricity possible.

And now everything was saying: eccentricity survives, and labour disappears.

By the way – to answer the question in the email – in 1955 the Crab Man was conceived. (An amusing coincidence.)

Hmmm. I'm not convinced by anything. But I'm happier for getting through the night, happier for the smell of coffee and of sausages cooking extra slowly in the pan. For the kids screaming at each other. For the absence of Lenin impersonators on the lawn. No devil's footprints either.

In a moment I am going to put my boots on, yesterday's socks are stuffed into them now, but I won't mind the feeling of slight dampness, I'll drive in to work – I have a meeting about the book – I'll email this in ahead of me. And then I'll stop halfway, not on the top of the ridge, but down by the army town, where there's an automated water treatment plant, and I'll edge my way around its un-precarious perimeter fence, enjoying the absence of turquoise and the presence of whatever comes.

O, and that time on the email… 12.13pm. Not first thing in the morning to arrive simultaneous with the Saint Germain letter. So, were both messages sent by the same hand? Or did the email writer have a contact on the inside and needed the three hours to analyse a scanned attach-ment? Or is the whole thing an 'inside job'? And I'm the messenger boy! (Be interesting to see if that speculation makes it to the printers!) Did the email fail to mention the Edgar Allan 'po' reference in order to look spontaneous and rushed? In a way, the details are not important (except perhaps to Human Resources), but there is something pleasingly symmetrical if everything here cancels everything else out, until just the one writer addresses just the one reader. Or one walker meets another with a ritual for abolishing 'stranger'.

Back to the Orrery, then…

The Hermeneutics of Fear

The age of mass literacy has been a short one. And though text will remain a powerful anachronism, especially useful to mythogeography, it is now but one of numerous media of record: 'the book' becomes useful again as its survival as a form is questionable. It is readable now as a transient and metaphorical html.

Single narratives will struggle for authority as consciousness is increasingly binary coded. Just as it was before the printing press.

In this neo-orality, apocalypse is weakened, just one sub-plot among many.

The problem with the rationale for Hans Jonas's hermeneutics – that only fear of the complete extinction of humanity and the loss of its unique consciousness will prevent their actual loss – is that we have already feared all this and we are still willing to place the bet. We knowingly gamble the future against the present – after all, what has posterity ever done for us? So we bet what we know against what we don't. This is 'The boy who cried wolf' inverted and on the geo-scale.

All those ecologists who think that "if only they could get their message across…", but people got their message a long time ago, and, having heard it, they are willing to gamble the present against the slim chance of things turning out as some version of "all right" in the end. Fear and hermeneutics are not enough, so the ecologically-minded dériviste, who may feel (as Debord might have) that jesting with chance is banal, must oscillate the hermeneutics of fear with the fearlessness of the living dead, (f93) oscillate freedom (imaginary and temporary) with freedom (in bits, segments, mouthfuls, as supper).

Only by taking a pleasure in the future, against the loss of pleasure now, will anything change. In this one way, alone, is the dérive futuristic.

Only by giving respectability to such hypocrisy will it become possible to continue with the planet. Hypocrisy is not so bad. It is a private weakness that facilitates a public blankness, feeding the liberating loneliness and anonymity of the city, the contradiction that is the spark of change, "the ethico-political misery of our epoch whose ultimate mobilising motif is the mistrust of virtue" (In Defence of Lost Causes, Slavoj Žižek).

Hypocrisy mobilises mistrust against itself, which generates the space of pleasure in chancelessness; the smooth space of public blankness that still exists at the personal, but no longer at the political, scale, for change. (While Iain Sinclair's decision to make an advertisement for Audi may damage him, (who knows?), it will not damage the cause of psychogeography (f94), generating anxiety and pleasure.) Fear and pleasure must go together, or, after a while, nothing goes at all.

But local and global must not go together. The local is irrelevant to solving the global. Once again hypocrisy is the key to 'saving the world'; local indulgence and global asceticism will save the world, not global indulgence and a nagging advocacy of the private or local asceticism of others.

In the city, those who do not know the city – those who are ignorant from the inside – are subject to a hermeneutics of degraded dread. They study the newspaper reports and follow the crime programmes. Every survey reports a perception of crime far worse than its material actuality. Some may fear generically, others abstractly, but very few have an individual's name or a face to fear. This kind of dread is anterior to restriction. It is quite different from the 'shock' of the city expressed by Andrei Bely as bullet-like points of red light zipping along the Nevsky Prospekt, quite different from the neurological and pacifying shocks of Walter Benjamin's urban "shock of the new". It is a dread anterior to withdrawal.

The means to pass safely through the majority of the most perilous encounters that all large cities throw up in some of their quarters involve the gaze and the gait. The stare of others must not be met; instead the walker looks through and beyond others. The walker walks with rapid steps, but the steps must be driven not by fear but by 'something else', the walker must show themselves pulled to some awful destination: hell, home, bottle, ward, others. The walker does not connect with the now of the place they are in, but they walk through it, as if it and everything in it were their medium. Potential aggressors are reduced to an inert backdrop. The walker should cultivate a haunted look; lips twitching in complaint to something unearthly; onlookers should be left uncertain as to who this inner demon might destroy first if the walker were challenged. There should be no sense (and certainly no mime!) of violence; the desired impression the walker should give is one of irrelevance. The walker slips by in a parallel reality. But it is a play for high stakes; one momentary loss of concentration, one sly glance… The price to be paid for the success of this tactic is the dislocation and disenfranchisement of the walker from the street. However, this can be turned to the dériviste's advantage: they can invert the survival tactic (once out of areas of immediate threat) as a means to walking with an unfocused gaze, collating peripheral and blurred information.

One of the holy books of urban anxiety is 20th Century City & Urban Survival, published in 1980, anonymous and tautological. The writer gives the impression of being more at ease with a knife than a typewriter. The repetition of the title is continued within its covers: "In city and suburbia everyone is out to fleece you in one way or another, and everyone is vulnerable." A more competent stylist would have hidden the contradiction, but here it is, ideology laid out and anatomised for all to see. Here is the night of the cities, where everyone is simultaneously wolf and sheep, serial killer and victim.

Even in this most negative of fear-hermeneutics there lurks life in all its wonderful excess. Anxiety and desire must walk together in the city, or, after a while, nothing will walk at all.

Ask yourself: "Where will you go if the mainstream disappears?" (f95)

Dérivistes do not walk like the living dead, they walk in relation to the walk of the living dead; they walk hypersensitised, in a self-reflexive hermeneutics of fear.   *f:93*

FT: "So what's next for psychogeography?"
Iain Sinclair: "I think the next step is to bury it completely." (Fortean Times, 147)   *f:94*

Just as romantic ruins once provided people with a sense of time and approaching demise, so Hollywood dystopias inspire dreams of starting over again. Sentimental and nightmarish in equal parts. The dériviste must be an anthologiser, collecting mental clips of those accidental parts of these movies where sentimentalities collapse and leave the landscape dreadful, free of romance and the military. See the 'We're Back' issue of Adbusters (Vol. 12, No. 6, Nov/Dec 2004).   *f:95*
/|\

Relativity and Quantum Entanglement

It is a scandal that the instabilities, probabilities and leaps of the (venerable and inadequate) orthodoxies of relativity and quantum mechanics have yet to permeate common education. The streets move to a pre-Newtonian, steady-state, hierarchical and materialist superstition (with religion or astrology occasionally tacked on). But nothing is ever at rest, and only the excessive speed of light obscures the relativities of spacetime from us. The very smallest, probabilistic elements that constitute our material being are all the time reacting across the fieldspace of the universe without the vehicle of time. None of this as yet informs our everyday being in the streets…

A Scrapbook of Places

The wicket gate in Pilgrim's Progress, the wardrobe to Narnia, the sandstone quarry formed by 'aeolian dunes' and become a museum of ancient breeze (f96), a former underground stables in Naples that is now a bouquet-making workshop, cobbles under the gravel of Horseguards Parade labelled Q and R, the mad monk's chapel at Lidwell, the room in The Golem with no doors, a horizontal pile of gateposts in Tuscany with the vertical towers of San Gimignano in the distance, a 20 foot tall stone grey alien head on the Côte de Granit Rose, Orford Ness, Die Zonen …make your own mental scrapbook of places (visited, haunted, heard of).

'The Dream Church'. Passing through the town of Newton Abbot (UK), an angular, clumsy church, with strange angles and excrescences, coloured a soiled cream, is visible from the train. Begun in 1936 and completed in 1963, the strange and uncomfortable shape of St Luke The Evangelist's with its two interwoven naves is the result of specifications received in a dream by a local priest (the author of The Concise British Flora in Colour who married a woman named Violet).

On the 24th April 1965, the day after the death of US ufologist George Adamski, a car mechanic called Arthur Bryant was visited by a space craft in fields near the Devon village of Scoriton. One of its occupants introduced itself as Yamski. A few days later a UFO buff from Exeter arrived to interview Bryant and view the landing site, taking away various 'engine parts' recovered from the fields. Presumably there is an attic, somewhere in Exeter, that contains those parts. This contaminates all attics in Exeter with a delicious suspicion.

"Put on some shoes and step outside. The place on which you will walk is holy ground." John Davies "Prayer Walking" in The God You Already Know

Pacific islanders living on the tiny and dispersed land masses of the Marshall Islands use palm fronds to weave maps of the distinctive and geographically-specific wave patterns formed when 'primary' waves are interfered with by predominating winds and 'secondary' waves that reflect off islands and atolls. By identifying a particular wave pattern the islanders at sea can tell not only where they are but also how their trajectory and the shifting pattern beneath them can be moved about each other so as to bring them to where they wish to be.

A Mythogeographical Fragment

"At the unpretentious hub of Lion's Holt and St James Park, Exeter, the imaginary 18th century battleground of political gangs of Grecian Whigs (outside the city wall) and Tory Trojans (inside), is the well of St Sidwella, site of her celebrated physical transformation under the blade, decapitated while at prayer in the fields, a brief owner of land, at a time when most people in the world were, like her, women working in fields. Or she was a water spirit changed by the incision of a new doctrine? These grounds were a place of healing, (note in pencil in the margin: bloody hell! this means that the water pumped to the city through the Underground Passages was holy water! They were all drinking holy water for centuries) visited by pilgrims since at least the eleventh century (CE). Stand here and face across the railway cut – look across the platform where the healing waters can still be heard under the concrete – to the stadium where Michael Jackson, famous for his own transformation under the blade, made a surreal and windy attempt to heal the world of AIDS, war, malaria and prejudice, accompanied by David Blaine's card tricks, all at the invitation of the Exeter City Football Club director, Yuri Geller. Ordering everyone in the ground to take the hands of the people on either side of them, Jackson said: "Now, tell the person next to you that you care for them. Tell them that you love them. This is what makes the difference! Together we can make a change of the world. Together we can help to stop racism. Together we can help to stop prejudice. We can help the world live without fear. It's our only hope! Without hope we are lost! I see Israel!!! I see Spain!" Geller is an emanation of the Pharaoh Impotep. In his early career he channelled messages to the world from an alien computer orbiting the earth, an artefact of the planet Hoova (the name might explain its penchant for communicating with machines): "We cannot enter your earth, only appear to you through computerizing your minds," it explained in the 1970s. The Meteorological Office has come to Exeter to monitor the end of the world."

'…he who cannot find wonder, mystery, awe, the sense of a new world and an undiscovered realm in the places by the Old Tiverton Road will never find those secrets elsewhere, not in the heart of Africa….' Arthur Machen, Things Near and Far, slightly adapted." *

* Publishers' note: Although the Central Committees' editors have omitted to notate this

instance, it does appear that this "Fragment" is taken from the notebook of a member of one of the walking clubs, the Committee For Public Safety.

The Significance of Walking

"It is a journey to the end of the world." (London, dir. Patrick Keiller)

Walking is important as a form of activism. Because it is an anachronism in many parts of the world (the adjective "pedestrian" is often used to mean dull, old-fashioned), it has a certain purchase, a resistance to fashion. There is nothing in walking itself which is significant to the cause of mythogeography, it is an entirely accidental connection, intensified by the possible redundancy of private transport in the near future.

Mythogeographical walking is an act of resistance to wayfinding.

Mythogeographical walking is a participatory, rather than immersive or distanced, flow state, in which self and world and time slide within each other; like Russian dolls that change scale (an insert becoming an envelope and an envelope becoming an insert). Changes of step and rhythm effect changes of consciousness.

Its importance stems (see Patterns of Patterns, page 174) partly from where the eyes are sited on a human being.

The mythogeographical dérive is a detour, a diversion from the functional journey (to work, to mosque, to bingo). In this sense play and irony are already built into the practice.

The dériviste has an ancestor in the serf set free by his master. As part of the ceremony of release, the serf would be taken to a crossroads and told that he could choose whichever way he wished to go.

The beginning of romantic, philosophical walking is coincidental with the French Revolution. Recreational walking begins, when walking is still the necessary travel of the poor and the 'chosen' means of the footpad thief. It begins, not as a cultural spasm provoked by cheaper, more accessible, more comfortable transport, but as a novel, ideologically charged set of actions and choices made by adventurous and progressive 'middling folk'.

The romantic walker, often an impoverished lower cleric or an undergraduate student, dressing down and boarding with the poor (de-classed in their own imaginations), is independent, is transgressive of property (taking pleasure by viewing the property of others). The romantic walker diverts from official paths, and subjects their own subjectivity to the chances of the road, plunging into instabilities of identity that are both scary and liberating. This is a walker who is hungry for a direct experience of something like a rite: first with a separation from the everyday, then an entrance to a borderland in which feelings, identity and ideas are in a kind of flux, and then finally, reintegrated back into society, much changed. (f97)

Such walkers cleared an ideological space for themselves. Their autonomous doings, in retrospect, have appeared to some academics to be the effects of better coach springs and steam engines. But chosen, philosophical walking, not railways, liberated the romantic individual.

Of course, there is no simple return to this originary moment of liberation. Today, the footpaths are bureaucratised. Rural and working class family life has been privatised, and lodgings are regulated. The romantic walk, to return it to itself, must be interrupted and re-diverted, philosophically.

The modern dérive, reflective on the romantic walk, but with discrete origins in a pre-revolutionary 20th century Paris, constitutes a rejection of the third phase of the anthropological romanticism of the late 18th century walk, returning the whole thing back to philosophy. On the drift, the first and second phases of the philosophical walk (separation and flux) are fed back on each other, a kind of short circuit, and repeated without the relief of a third phase, until some new, un-integrated practice, mutation, artefact or plan is thrown off by the inbred energy of the detour.

The artist Matthew Barney describes this creative process: first a raw desirous drive, an undifferentiated potential ("situation"), then a funnelling and disciplining of this energy ("condition"), which then results in the throwing out into the world of an artwork or product ("production"). By plugging "situation" into "condition" and refusing "production", the system recycles itself in a rising crescendo or spiral of energy until its (deferred, delayed) product is finally thrown off; unpredictable, un-visionable. Dérivistes, here is your model!

But "many parts of the world" is not the world and today a majority of people continue to walk from necessity rather than choice. And those that walk by necessity are those held in contempt and fear for their presence on the highway. This necessity is not always a symptom of poverty but also of prejudice.

In this sense the dérive is an obscenity and a privilege. Philosophical walkers should always walk with extreme sensitivity to the feelings of others. And with an obligation, for they will never be able to walk comfortably until walking is a choice for everyone physically able to make that choice. Nor until those who are not physically able have, wherever possible, access to equivalent mobility. By which time it will have long been a common ecological necessity to mostly walk (which may render it, aesthetically, unachievable).

This is not an inhibition, it is an ignition.

Mythogeography subjects the act of walking to its multiplicity. In mythogeography's review of walking, numerous types of walking, walkers and walks weave around each other: zombies, their straight lines driven by stomachless hunger, aimless (drift-like) when without a scent. He Yun Chang, formalistic and cursory, a task only. Hamish Fulton, a hallucinating neo-pilgrim. Donna Shilling, travelling to ask a question. Werner Herzog, walking "in ice" to save a life.

Apart from serious injury, nothing can go wrong on a dérive; there is no 'meant to happen'. Mistakes can be poetic: Linda Cracknel setting off to walk up an Alp "in her father's footsteps" and walking the wrong one, or a stopping point on one guided tour of Lord of the Rings movie locations in New Zealand, which is described by Anne Buchmann as popular with tourists for having been mistakenly included in a guide to the locations. The tourists enthusiastically photograph the 'non-place'.

In most accounts of the late 18th century philosophical walk, the ideal walker is a solitary one. When companion walkers were present writers tended to write them out of their accounts. However, when this is contested, the generative power of the collective walk becomes clear: walking from Cambridge to North Wales in 1793, Joseph Hucks and the poet Coleridge meet the poet Southey at Oxford and plan an egalitarian Pantisocracy, later refined by Coleridge and Southey walking in Somerset in 1794, and abandoned in 1795 as they fall out over the project on a walk in the Wye valley.

Some writers attempt to construct walking as an ideal, de-historicised behaviour. It is at these moments that they tie their walking most oppressively to their circumstances.

Steven Mithen argues in The Singing Neanderthals that the distinctive rhythm of bipedal walking is the rhythm of our thinking, that it has shaped our particular consciousness.

"New myths are formed beneath each of our steps." (Paris Peasant, Louis Aragon) No. Such formations are ideological, the creation of new myths is not stamped into the ground, is not beneath the walk, it is the walk. It is when the walk becomes something else that it becomes ideological, potential carrion for our myth's appetite. It becomes an answer to Jeffrey C. Robinson's question in The Walk: Notes On A Romantic Image: "What is this phenomenon, the walk that urges me to write?"

By walking between circumstances and the beats of consciousness, the walker can begin to sense the compositional rules of history. That is what the walk is urging.

Slowness is important, not for questions of conservatism or age, but for the quality of patterns that come into sharp focus. The gannet can only successfully hunt because it dives within the same, invariable dynamic pattern of angle and velocity, it does not make all of its decisions. By slowing down it is possible to become aware of the patterns we already have for action,

allowing us to think excessively, to think in surplus (perception of fine texture, evolution of narrative, conceptualisation of spectral space). Entrepreneurs should be interested in this as the tempo of R & D.

"Imaginary walking companions: Satish Kumar, Anna Best, Charles Hurst, Mahatma Gandhi, Francis Alÿs, Francesco Careri, eXplo, Julia Solis, Steve Hanson, Joseph Beuys (underwater) and Anil Gupta on a Shodhyatra." (Note written in pencil on the back of a leaflet announcing a "Walk to the Shoot 'em Up Paint-Ball Zone, former underground semi(!!!)-nuclear bomb proof station. We have boked the Zone for the end of the walk, but not for Paint Ball. Instead, we will refuse to fight. The walk will include visiting and looking for past and present evidence of the nuclear state.")

"A way of walking… does not merely express thoughts and feelings that have already been imparted through an education in cultural precepts and proprieties. It is itself a way of thinking and of feeling, through which, in the practice of pedestrian movement, these cultural forms are continually generated… rhythmically resonant with the movements of others around us – whose journeys we share or whose paths we cross."   Tim Ingold & Jo Lee Vergunst Ways of Walking: Ethnography and Practice on Foot

"Martin was also aware of some unpublished research done in England in the 1970s on aborted fetuses, and scientists had managed to get them walking too."   Geoff Nicholson The Lost Art of Walking

f:97 (See Romantic Writing and Pedestrian Travel, Robin Jarvis

It's Not All Ideas

"When I was eight or nine years old I had my time of Pan-ic. I remember a wall. I don't feel it. But I FEEL everything else. I hold a large blue plastic toy of Sir Donald Campbell's record-breaking car: Bluebird. But there is no colour in the memory. And no sound. And no one else. Instead there is an overwhelming feeling of everything, and myself in awed relation to it all: vividly bleak, silent, overwhelmingly present – right there, right then, sublime. In a sense it's hardly an autobiographical moment at all. I don't relate the 'feeling' of it to me. Apart from the sense of the importance of the site, and my continuing to re-memorialise it, there's not much detail, no build up or backstory. Instead there is a sense of scale, a space and a kind of re-programming of relations with everything." (Extract from an item of correspondence sent to The Central Committees by an unnamed member of a Midlands walking group, the Bedworth Congress for Cultural Freedom, widely regarded as a front for the Coventry Institute of Ambulation.)

Tradition

Art may be a largely moribund operation, but from the past there remain spectres of efficacy in fanciful 'traditions'. The neo-romanticism of Arthur Machen, Paul Nash, Powell and Pressburger and Patrick Keiller. The magick of Charles Fort, Maya Deren and Alan Moore. The symbolism of Villiers De L'Isle-Adam, Dora Maar, Eugenio Barba and Robert Wilson. Construct your own moribund traditions.

Martyr

Mythogeography has only one martyr - Karl Watkins, who in 1996 committed suicide in his cell after being jailed for having sex with a number of pavements and an underpass.

Taxonomy of Spaces

Accidental museums, dread space, ambient hubs, new menhirs, wormholes, doubly inauthentic space, wasteland playgrounds, edgeland, superfluous space, voids, real places like virtual models (See Quatermass 2 (dir. Val Guest)), ruins, ideal (geometrical) spaces, striated spaces,

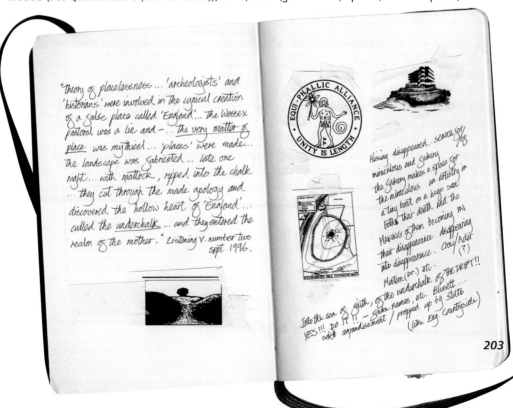

super-textured spaces, locations of cine-memories, planes of consistency, holey space, heterotopias, dreamlands, theatres in your pocket, the actor as signpost, commercial trajectories, on the square, poisoned-magical space (See O Lucky Man! (dir. Lindsay Anderson)), paranoid over-explained space, love triangles, circles of acquaintance… all these should, but do not, have space here set aside for their definition.

There is no significance in the order of categories, nor any equality in the influence of one category over another; the relation of their gravitational pulls is always changing.

Z Worlds: these are apparently self-contained worlds confined within a small area. (See Morphology, page 166.) They can be found in discarded boxes, in sheds, in abandoned rooms, in rock pools, in shop window displays, in decrepit horse troughs, on lichen-covered walls, at the end of cul-de-sacs, in front gardens, in the corners of clubs. Anywhere a small space has become a self-contained universe. They may be prefigurative, they may be warnings.

Wormhole: In certain places wrinkles in the fabric of space bring far away places very close. You may find a wormhole in the exotic shape of a building, in an unexpected name, in an affecting story, in an atmosphere, in a word printed on a sweet wrapper, in a symbol hidden in a street sign. If so… pass through. Next time you try on a new pair of trousers or a new bra in the changing booth of a shop, imagine that when you swish the curtain across, you open another to the workshop of the child labourers who made the garment in your hand.

"I watched RAF jets practising in Welsh valleys, an Afghanistan in the heart of Snowdonia." *

* Publishers' note: no attribution given.

Super-textured space: lava in the walls, paving stones made from billions of corpses of sea creatures.

Horizon: not a line, but two kinds of disappearing: the ground disappears over the curve of the earth, while the sky disappears behind that disappearing. There is no line as such, only over and behind. In confronting any barrier or border translate it into the space of 'horizon', into the means of varied disappearance: over and behind.

Almost Place: walking a motorway just before it is opened.

Almost Space: a dream of something like a motorway but golden and covered with spittle.

Edgeland: Some cities have a sharp edge where the urban meets the countryside, others have 'edgelands' where old abandoned service industries decay, quarries fill up with rainwater, sinister military buildings peel open and marshalling yards are overgrown. These are the places where the bodies of those who are not missed are buried, where suitcases change hands, where the remains of failed experiments and illegal insulations are dumped, where the shapes of runways and rail tracks are still visible in the grass, where chemicals produce strange blossoms. These are our best playgrounds: "the only theatre in which the real desires of real people can be expressed." (Marion Shoard) *

* Publishers' Note: this is a repetition of the point made above in E-Myth.

Ideal space: see the 'soft places' in Neil Gaiman's The Sandman, the Tom O'Bedlam sequence in Grant Morrison's You Say You Want A Revolution, or the feelings of loss in the aching landscapes of Makoto Shinkai's The Place Promised in Our Early Days.

Holey Space: There is plenty of this. (f98) Contemporary economy is unsurpassed in the speed of the redundancy of its parts. The state (in its narrow, bureaucratic sense) is overwhelmed by its capacity for information gathering. Such is the nature of individualism that almost everyone is a potential subversive. Politicians must contemplate returning to old levels of community participation, to the good old days of 33% active co-operation with the Stasi. But until then, and even afterwards, the anachronisms of the temporally indifferent city offer up snaking acres of unsurveilled or partially surveilled holey space: emergency exits, empty seminaries, partially converted cinemas, mediaeval water tunnels, barely used churches, offices and shops with uninhabited upper floors (See Christopher Nolan's movie Following), out of season resorts, favelas, refugee camps, redundant bunkers and pill boxes, theatres, backstages, closed mines.

 See In The Sewers of Lvov, Robert Marshall and Lũy thép Vĩnh Linh (Vĩnh Linh Steel Rampart), dir. Ngoc Quynh.

Not only subterranean spaces, but the voids among the civilian population, the spaces of violence, invention and surplus pleasure. When popular ideology has sufficiently hollowed them out, they become holey (starting from a position of weakness).

A taxonomy of space is a guide to the layers of place. These layers are the separated stages for living (sometimes called "situations") and, though they may be discrete, they move in response and relation to each other.

"Against 'the city as system'… is romanticised a mobile 'resistance' of tactics, the every day, the little people … At its worst it can resolve into the least politically convincing of situationist capers – getting laddish thrills (one presumes) from rushing about down dark passages…" For Space, Doreen Massey

"Transpierce the mountains instead of scaling them, excavate the land instead of striating it, bore holes in space instead of keeping it smooth, turn the earth into swiss cheese." A Thousand Plateaus, Gilles Deleuze and Felix Guattari

Dreamland: discarded mattresses and rusty bed frames turn up in cities, in edgeland ditches, in the woods. When you find one, then dream the dreams once had by those who once lay there, listen for their breathing, take a friend and make pillow talk, re-enact the site's former lovemaking in documentary style – when you get home re-read a favourite book under your bed covers.

Wilderness: we must create long and reasonably wide corridors of wilderness through the countryside. No farming, no forestry, no houses, no dogs, no cattle – just walkers and wolves. To make this space? It's time to eat all the beef and lamb and plant something like walnuts.

Apocalyptic Space: this is easily accessed through movies: the helicopter shots in the Dawn of the Dead remake, the exploding petrol stations in The Birds, 28 Days Later and the BBC's Survivors series remake, the underground car park of All The President's Men, the disappearing surface of everything in The Langoliers and In The Mouth of Madness… but why the apocalyptic? Because as well as a hermeneutics of fear, there should be an acceptance that this will be realised (if you're worried about ecological disaster, stop worrying, it's sure to come eventually), not for the sake of passivity in the face of horror, but for the very opposite; it is the pleasure of contemplating apocalypse that might encourage us to fashion, refine and control it. The alternative is to slip 'virtuously' (without pleasure) towards it.

Politics (the practicalities of low intensity organisation)

Here's the map. While the Western political Right fumbles for an agreed strategy for not throttling the goose that lays the golden eggs, the Left, (from most of its liberal to much of its revolutionary wings) convinced of its own impotence, has knelt to embroider the texture of the everyday.

The caretakers of capital, in search of ideas, have returned to fundamentals: markets, products, virtual barrow-boys.

/|\ As capital re-gears itself, it needs new products of texture, authenticity, everyday, specificity (or simulated versions of all of the same), for which (given the postmodernists' indifference to old and new) it will be willing to trade with the Left (everyone, from social-liberals to egotists and eco-terrorists, who defer, delay, withdraw). In return this Left will get to see the gears, the cogs, the workings of the system in general, the whole Gorgon (if they want).

But what if the synthesis itself were deferred (delayed, withdrawn)? What if this Left burrowed deeper and deeper into the Ingoldian-hermetic (see Trajectories and Layers, page 216) texture of the everyday and if the Right and capital continued to 'up' its offers? What might this 'short-circuit' of incremental desperation, increasing the velocity of the spiral, throw off?

When promiscuity is a function of sexual exploitation, and terrorism a guiding principle of the 'inner-rogue' of the state, and when revolutionary strategy is drummed into the officer corps of the Israeli Defence Force, radicals may wonder where they still fit in. The answer is simple for a geographer: "there isn't any 'anywhere' for you anymore." Invisibility may be an upside to this. No one will distinguish you from an artist or a street eccentric. Commitment to a cause is no

longer required. Loyalties will be micro, and secrets so diaphanous and arcane as to hold meaning for no one other than yourselves, operations may be no less effective in the open than in holey space (for there is a holeyness in contemporary public space that wasn't there before), 'hidden in plain sight'. Under present conditions integration with the everyday remains a best option (for Left, Right and those who think the terms are obsolete).

In times of weakness, the guiding principle of any political group seeking to become a force in the future is the study of how to use weakness as a currency. In this respect, weakness has one great virtue: it is subtle, it does not railroad, it does not miss the details. In times of weakness the activist must deploy the principle of satellite capture (see pages 92-3 of Walking, Writing and Performance ed. Roberta Mock), something like 'communist patience' (Journalist: "What has been the impact of the French Revolution?" Chou En-Lai: "It's too soon to say.") and a cellular reorganisation based on democratic centralism: junking the democratic part and short-circuiting into a million centralisms.

(We live in a 'bullshit democracy', not in respect of elections, which have their own problems and limitations, but in respect of truth. Attend any infotainment and listen to the response to the audience's suggestions. Nothing is 'wrong', everything must somehow be stroked, caressed and approved of. The mythogeographical cell has no such luxury. It stands or falls according to its truth. Therefore it is centralist in its exclusion of lies and ideological subterfuge, and only democratic in its refusal to lead anything.)

Before victory there will only be defeats. Without universities or monasteries to secure any ground gained, the stateless will lose everything (again and again) before they win everything (once). After that, who knows? As the IRA remorselessly reminded the UK government during their bombing campaigns: "you have to catch us every time, we only have to succeed once".

The key molecular unit of these desperate politics is, paradoxically, the cell ** (see Patterns of Patterns, page 174). Not because it is covert in the sense of any illegality or lying in a space beyond normal life, but rather because it is nothing other than the intensification of a normal life, its 'real' activities, sensuous and immediate, vital and immanent to its members, are effectively incommunicable to others. (Thus, by not appearing, it avoids "being appeared", being transformed into image, by the Spectacle. To not appear, without hiding or disappearing into a hermitage, when appearance and celebrity are the two main geo-currencies, is an act of heroic ecology.) (f99)

** Editors' note: many of our rather grandly titled organisations – Psychogeographical Associations, etc. – consist of little more than three or four people. This is not a problem, this is a necessity. There is no need to be discouraged if groups attract only handfuls of members. This is the necessary level.

The cells are made up of sleepers, not in the sense that they will one day be woken to commit some outrage, but rather that their drowsiness will set their pace, their disconnection will structure their engagement, their super-subjectivism and obsessive part-immersion in the everyday will render them the perfect foci-groups, dreaming and wanting before everyone else catches up (here is the crucial connection between the market and the covert: both rely on secret knowledge of desires not yet felt).*

In the absence of any immediate effectiveness, these cells will create their own 'mythologies' (the imagined or real deeds of hybrid characters), very provisional actions, (diaphanous events not unlike 'theatrics' in the ufological-mythos; no good photos will ever emerge, researchers will have to employ extraordinary tactics to get anything from them) and mythogeographies (cell members will operate as theoreticians, like the détourners of Marvel comics, Kirkman, et al., delivering theory rather than explosives to their victims).

f:99 Artists of disappearance: Louis Le Prince, Arthur Craven, Donald Crowhurst, a battalion of the Royal Norfolk Regiment (disappeared into the mist at Suvla Bay, Turkey), the village of Hallsands, the Roanoke Colony, Bas Jan Ader, Ambrose Bierce, Colonel Fawcett, the Flannan Isles Lighthouse Keepers, D. B. Cooper.

* Publishers' note: the editors of this volume, and their predecessors, do themselves a disservice by their anonymity, by their 'mythic-characters' and by the ludic covertness that is put on show for this section. Due to the indirectness of their contacts with us, we were obliged to investigate their intentions before publication. Our investigators found them to be relatively ordinary folk, often loosely attached to the lower-paid fringes of journalism, psychiatry, healthcare and teaching; condemned to repetitive labour in their 'professional' lives, they could be intellectuals in their recreation.

On the other hand, this has all been long ago co-opted by wild child entrepreneurs who know, like General Westmoreland, that "in order to save the village it is necessary to destroy it". This is a 'come on' to them, then, to get off their flatline and bet against the cells' opportunities, to see what they will lay against the Event being deferred permanently, or if by Its deferral It is actually best invoked.

The Space Hijackers play cricket at midnight against traders in the streets of The City.

Today, when groups of activist organisations unite for particular actions, the phrase "loose association" is often used by the media and embraced by the participants to model the pragmatic and limited alliances forged for such occasions. This model should be junked forthwith; it is a commodity seized from the enemy's supply lines and it can profitably be returned to them, it is a corrosive, a rust in the movement of movements. In its place mythogeographical cells should cultivate "tight associations" as the best conditions for their individual and group components, a morphology that can hold their dissolution at bay. Such "tight associations" imply an ethical life for the cell member, opening the way to personal friendships cemented across organisational, sectarian, religious and other boundaries spanning the ranks of the hopeful walkers. The cells represent a molecular level of organisation in a class landscape without a fixed point to ever return to (neither universally large workplaces nor geo-political, internationalist organisations).

If such a fabulous move is possible (it is certainly necessary) it will put an immense strain on connectivity; hence the need for tight associations, for 'and and and' as its constitutive substance (and that is a problem because "and" is a weak substance).

When nothing else is, or seems, possible, a cell, an individual or a movement can explore at the myth-character level their collective and future possibilities (situations), confident that their tight associations will preserve the lessons of their experiences until circumstances change, and allow the cells then to serve up their lessons as part of the morphology of those new conditions.

A "tight association" requires discipline. Discipline is one of the few powers available to the marginalised. Ironically, such discipline in, say, working class cazoo bands or workers' sports associations, has been broadly disparaged by progressives who have promoted individual self-expression in place of order, creating a mass market for progressive cultural products. (Entrepreneurs please note, before next dissing the market acumen of the public sector-funded, liberal intellectual.) Alternatively, they have appropriated disciplines as 'folk', 'craft' or 'primitive' arts and taken them over in the spirit of heritage or neo-'savagery'.

Velocity of information has challenged the medium of tense, dynamic, dramatic conversation in medium-sized groups, sometimes called, though it not always was, 'debate'. The violence of this challenge has escalated over decades. The result is a crisis in the very form of cabinets, central committees, boards of directors and war rooms. What, under various titles and guises, served as the general staff of companies, revolutions, social clubs and governments serves decreasingly well. Societies do not crumble, for what renders companies irresponsible and governments toothless equally undermines the capacity of their enemies to make strategic gains at their expense. The currency of power (though not the capacity for apocalyptic violence) is weakened in the world, which lacks a convincing form for a collective subject. (Perhaps we should stop looking for a new one and have some faith in those that we have already found to be unconvincing: for example, Rigoberta Menchú, who changed the details of her life story to cohere with the propaganda needs of her radical movement? Or those French mathematicians who used the collective name "Nicolas Bourbaki" to emphasise the co-operative nature of mathematical research? How many authors were Homer or Taliesin? Or Bertolt Brecht even?)

At some stage significant structural changes, changes of quality of information rather than quantity will take effect. In order for 'servers' to replace countries it will be necessary to attack, in an insurrectionary manner, the physical mind-body integrity of the mass-individual. For the first time, a revolutionary change will occur through the transformation of the consumer.

In this (and no other) sense, Orlan, Stelarc, Michael Jackson, Arnie, Jordan/Katie Price and Lola Ferarri will have all been preparatory necessities for a new stage of info-capitalism, priming unprecedented levels of fluidity of meaning and corporeality.

"Of shapes transformde to bodies straunge I purpose to entreate" Ovid

Shaken by postmodernism's abolition of old/new and the anachronism of ambulant mythogeography, its ambivalence about identity, its reliance on opportunism as working method, its ironical love affairs with libraries, institutions and inadequate monumental art, its redundancy in action, its elusiveness as a non-target and its computation of futures that have already sensed what they will be... all these will move things towards a realisation of change on a classical scale.

A Cautionary Tale

In the UK city of B------, in the 1980s, a young man with cultural and political interests, without roots in the local community, goaded by guilt and transience, riding and hopping across the crests of various activisms built by others over many years, and balancing atop even older superstructures, was able to set in motion a series of organisation-lite interest groups (some of his own founding, mostly of others). His strategy was to connect people – linking horror-story writing competitions, with anti-poll tax unions, with non-party community groups, with play schemes, with tight little groups of friends discussing economics in pubs, with Nicaraguan support groups, with trade union branches, with movie buffs. He worked inside and outside the Labour Party (articulating a strategy of war on two fronts, within and without) and he was opportunistic and principled, he was hypocritical. He was happy to be used as a puppet to move resolutions at council committees to spend hundreds of thousands of pounds sterling on better housing for working class areas, but he would bite the same hands that pulled his strings; whichever had the better effect. He was not a leader in any sense, but a publisher and a distributor, and although largely unintended, new friendships across old emptinesses did blossom, and there were fairs and pamphlets and readings and processions and many small reforms that maybe made some differences to some lives.

But in the end there was a disappointing limit to his opportunism. He was persuaded by force of argument that his activities provided 'left-cover' (a radical face) to the power structures of social-democratic, sometimes even conservative interests, that his friendliness extended too far up the council and trade union officer hierarchies and was demoralising for those whom these officers disciplined and oppressed, that the loose weave of organisations he straddled would never withstand the focused attentions of a centralised state should it decide to act against them, that such centralism should be met with further centralism, that one party was necessary to provide a consistent line rather than the chaotic jumble that resulted in the weakest radicals bumbling into the long grass of compromise and co-option.

Everything made sense, the argument was thoroughly logical, the conclusion correctly shaped. The young man left his multilateral straddlings behind. It was the biggest political mistake of his life (and he made many, for studied foolishness, low-level hypocrisy and unabashed naivety were parts of his success in ignoring obstacles and prohibitions). Not everything he did before was right, and not everything that convinced him to leave it behind turned out to be wrong, but mostly those two things apply.

A cautionary note to this cautionary tale: it was nothing like that. His was not a solo project, although he often acted as if it was only in his name. He was part of a tight little group of friends, few of whom always politically or practically supported him in his connectivity, but all of whom made it possible. His decision in favour of logic rather than jouissance was a betrayal of friendship as well as of agitation. It is too late to repeat his correct decisions, too late to correct his mistakes. But the diaphanous pattern is there: of a tight association connected by pleasure and ideas, straddling boundaries in the way that pleasure-seeking does.

214

Tight Associations

Each must find its own tactics and style, its own habits and subjects. One "tight association" from the past was The 43 Group of Jewish commandos from Allied Forces who set themselves up in 1946 to violently combat a reviving British fascist movement. But their violent tactics, covert style and militaristic organisation would have been completely inappropriate for others, despite similar aims, who lacked their training.

"you may already be a member" motto of The Cacophony Society

Temporary Strategies

Deception, assignation, dishonesty, letter drops, disguises, tailing, distraction, safe houses, illusionism, camouflage, transparency.

Tactical Emotions

Undisguised fury and suffering are the only worthwhile criteria for outreach, diversification and representation. The alternatives are bureaucratic.

(Unlike everything else in these pages, the editors are not interested in a discussion on this matter. However, if you would like to discuss any of the other issues raised in this volume, leave a red flag in a flower pot on your balcony and we will make contact with you. The Central Committees ha ha)*

* Publishers' Note: this uncharacteristic notation was the last inserted by the provisional editors, and perhaps indicates a crisis in their organisation.

Transparency and Camouflage

There are two key mythogeograhical approaches to behaving or performing in any site. In Transparency the drifter or performer empties out their behaviour so that the site can be seen through their diaphanous presence. In Camouflage the drifter or performer adopts the complex textures of the site in all their floridity as a costume or uniform.

Trajectories and Layers

Doreen Massey advocates looking at a place as if from a satellite above the earth, noting not the borders of place, but the trajectories that coagulate into the forms of cities and other social structures.

Tim Ingold criticises the idea of "global" as it implies a removal of the thinker to a point high above, out of, and superior to the earth, like a satellite. Instead he advocates an image of the earth (not unlike certain esoteric world pictures) as a series of layers and unfolding crannies, which must be explored more and more closely, not by the distancing of the observer, but by immersion and involvement.

Look both ways when crossing.

Crocodile In The Sewers

The chicks of herring gulls nesting 'traditionally' on the cliffs starve for lack of fish in the sea, while the numbers of herring gulls in the cities double every 10 years. In the UK there is an increasing use of dogs for low-level intimidation rather than companionship. A community of miniature scorpions live only in one wall in Southampton. The Derbyshire wallabies, living in the wild since their escape from a private zoo in the 1930s, are now feared extinct. Foxes and deer multiply in the cities, sightings of ABCs (anomalous big cats) rise and fall but mostly rise. In Europe, wolves and wild boar are reintroduced. There is a shifting of habitats and a re-gearing of the relations between humans and other animals. Sixteen pairs of peregrine falcons nest in NYC, house sparrows have completely disappeared from large areas of London, Surrey is overrun by parakeets with 3,000 nesting in one stockbroker-belt sports ground alone, big horn sheep graze lawns in Palm Springs, crocodiles swim across Australia's swimming pools.

There is something morphological in these events. 'Beside' the ecological, a social change will be negotiated as part of a new relationship with other animals. One that may be far more distanced, far less sympathetic.

At Crocosaurus Cove in Darwin (!) tourists pay to descend in a perspex 'cage without bars' ("the Cage of Death") to swim 'among' huge Saltwater Crocodiles and watch as the beasts impotently try to bite them through the 4cm of protection. The animal is there, and yet is not there. Proximity and display have Spectacularised it, changing its genus Crocodylus Porosus to Porous Crocostylus.

E-"round and round"

The sixteen-sided building close to the location of the initial sightings of the devil's footprints in 1855 is almost certainly a National Trust property, A la Ronde, located in countryside between Exmouth and Lympstone in the English county of Devon, although there is another, smaller sixteen-sided wooden structure on a neighbouring estate that is floored entirely with the cloven hooves of sheep.

A la Ronde seems the better candidate given that there is a Crab Man connection there (some children's entertainments at the property have included the impersonation of the small sea-animals whose shells were used in the decoration of the unusual interior of this late-eighteenth century home). Also, what might have drawn the Crab Man is the millennarian demarcation of the oaks in the gardens.

The name of the property is significant, given its angular architecture. There is both a circle and an octagon there, plus a spirit of connectivity; different rooms of industry and productivity under a single geometrical (cone-like) roof. Was this an architectural Mundaneum dematerialised by the Crab Man and carried with him as a personal art of memory? As the founders of A la Ronde, two female cousins, were inspired by their own late eighteen century Grand Tour, much of it pedestrian, is it now an inspiration for humbler tours?

It is surely not without significance that the narratives in this book ('Mythogeography') seem to arrive at this point, not in a fictional or a dramatic climax, but in an architecture of motion, a musical materialisation, a rondo.

And yet this is also a PLACE. And a PLACE WITH A NARRATIVE, at that. (f100)

Beyond some idle speculations on groupings of three and four, the Crab Man in his documentation of the Hurst Oaks makes little of the meaning, significance or symbolism of the trees that he seeks. He becomes, as he imagines Charles Hurst becoming, too interested in the act of walking itself. He misses the botanical, the apocalyptic and the ecological.

But the work of mythogeography is not the work of one alone. And so it is the forces of circumstance, and the accumulative effect of so many shapes, that appears now, as the main character of this book, as the heroic traveller of its pages, now arriving.

The 'whole thing' does not end here, of course, but, for the sake of form, climaxes in a whirling machine, a sixteen-sided Mundaneum dematerialised (or at least made metaphorical) and ready for carrying in any walker's head.

Like the book-rememberers of Ray Bradbury's Fahrenheit 451, contra-Debord, there is something about survival driving all this (art of memory, the hermeneutics of fear, ecology, inundation, the polluted death of the oaks, the end of the world). But it is also more ambitious, more hopeful than that, because it returns to Places; marginal, meaningful Places.

Although Mythogeography accepts it responsibilities to those Places, it really doesn't make much sense as ethics. But it does as discipline; as discipline there may be something in it.

And so, in the design of an eccentric building lies the organising model for what this book hopes to be after it is a book, after it is read, after it is borrowed and returned, after it is sandwiched on shelves, after it is remaindered, after it is pulped, after it is burned or turns to dust.

What it longs to be is not a political organisation, but a mental architecture.

f:100   *See "Material History as Cultural Transition: A La Ronde, Exmouth, Devon, England" by Susan Pearce in Material History Review (No. 50, Fall, 1999) or "A la Ronde – eccentricity, interpretation and the end of the world" by Phil Smith in Performing Heritage, Manchester University Press, 2010.*

219

TYPHOON

APPENDICES

I'm sorry to keep harping on about place and site and space, but that is all that they are about, these notes. I won't waste words trying to recall the exact documents themselves. Rather, I will attempt to paraphrase the main works: four in all. You've read the first, almost. The second is an apparently autobiographical narrative that recounts an incident in the apple garden of a Canon M------, the writer creeping up on the aged cleric. Then a passage concerning the lounge of the antichrist, imagining rucks in its carpet to be desert mountains, dust floating up like geysers, crumbs of sponge cake dragged by armies of slaves to a far edge where it was possible to make out the beginnings of a city on the plain, New Babylon, a megalomaniac design, a house on the borderland, with the real population tucked away beneath. Before that there was something about standing in a playground...

Train journeys… there is a great deal about them. Some fascination he had with trackside debris, rather in the same style as his comments about carpets. Windows as portholes. Actually, I'm not sure if that is all from the same person. On the one hand he says he was brought up in Africa, on the other, in a prefabricated building, but that could be a building prefabricated in Africa, or prefabricated elsewhere and then transported there. None of the unknowns came from the City of E-----, none of them born and bred, the borders rather blur as to who is who, and how fixed anyone is. The constant fear of bombs in London (and elsewhere) in the 1970s, that's another thing that they were apparently much affected by. I remember this phrase distinctly: "every public space layered with unease". They believed that this anxiety had had a permanent effect, creating a second nervous system that they all shared (hence, perhaps my own confusion about their identity; what is identity, after all, if it is shared?)

At least one of them was a woman, I think. Perhaps women were in the majority. I don't feel qualified to say. Or was it a feminine writing written by a man? They didn't sign the articles so one has to guess. But you can tell, can't you? Even in the wording of constitutions. I, personally, cannot.

According to their minutes, they held meetings in attics, bathrooms, bedrooms, back gardens, but mostly on foot. They had some method of revealing the movement of winds. I'm not sure if it was archaeological: perhaps the sandstone was present in their homes too, or in their gardens, or they could sense its alignments in the older walls. But there is a reference to blowing bubbles. My former friend advised me to remove this reference to bubbles from the notes – too childish, he pronounced, likely to discredit the whole legacy. I find it rather charming and couldn't resist keeping it in. But then I began to wonder about bubbles. That rather than as a distraction to be removed, that it was the bubbles that were the thing, the key: all this nonsense about meetings and minutes; maybe there was no institution of any such kind, but rather a cell of sleepers.

These bones and pirate uniforms were so much set dressing. And I had been a dupe, an inspired choice, a worthy fool, and now in danger. For every word I wrote was one second ticked from the list. They were not a club of exercisers, nor a society of hobbyists. Good god, they had no idea what they might become!

So let me get this done and go. The circumstances, the sites, the constitutions – o, the irony of this! – are nothing. Bubbles! I am writing an inventory, a guide-book, the instruction-manual to a toolkit. I am a mere hack, where I thought I might be some kind of epistolary novelist. Well, then, use me!

They had invented a myth of shared origins: all connected with place. There was the Wales-London link of their heroes Arthur Machen and Iain Sinclair, both insider/outsiders – long term and rooted residents free from 'identity'– antithetical to "born and bred." Machen, an apparently rabidly anti-occultist grouch and yet a member of Crowley's Golden Dawn. The plots of Sinclair's novels were slowly edging away from the metropolis toward the city of E-----, recently reaching its neighbouring county. Then there were Leppin and Meyrink and Kubin: Germans living in Prague. An artist called Rachel who had changed her name. And Severs – American born, but with the name of a butler, creating and recreating the ideas of the eighteenth century in a house in the East End, diatribes on form and order, an architecture of free floating atmospheres shaped in his sleep and in auction houses.

They seemed to believe that we are all participating in some fundamental myth of wandering, shared with humans of tens of thousands of years ago who suddenly, abruptly (if ten thousand years can ever be abrupt), changed in the head – from departmental, pigeon-holed, functionally efficient, minding-their-own-business hunters into modern humans, parcels of experience collapsing into one great sorting and tearing open and repacking office of confusion, where art, religion, culture and prejudice could be posted, reconstituting a wandering mentality in which here is there, there here, and both are metaphors for somewhere else. Sleeping Neanderthals biding their time before the new dawn.

And now this cult was wandering again: they clearly owed much to those dreadful bores, the situationists, who, it seems, everyone must 'discover' if only to discover that everyone else has been there first – ah, I see their attraction now.

In the cathedral there is a snow white monument to Scott.

There is nothing very unusual, it seems, in borrowing terminology blithely adapted to their purposes. In a novel by the writer Will Self, himself a Necronaut, about a living population "stumbling about the joint imagining themselves painted up with the present" and a dead population who "see it all"… but I didn't write this down fully… They always were in danger of playing too close to the edges of the occult and plain silliness. That is part of the slow burning price no one is prepared, but many find it eventually necessary, to pay. Their trick, it seems, was to put off payment indefinitely, by disappearing (it seems to be part of the pattern!), to allow others to appear as their reincarnations. They have loaded the gun, but other fingers must itch at the trigger.

I have no time for those who treat fiction as another form of history for the purposes of, well, anything really, though tourism is perhaps the least acceptable of its uses. Dickens's Fat Boy originated in the Turk's Head here. The notes I had in my possession – I wish I had them now to send to you complete, you would immediately detect the plot – these notes were not metaphorical; they were theological and godless. Their only authority seemed to be the late director of 'Vertigo'; a Fat Boy kind of a god.

Experiment seems to have been their only real dogma:

> *"Past collectivities offered the masses an absolute truth and incontrovertible mythical exemplars. The appearance of the notion of relativity in the modern mind allows one to surmise the EXPERIMENTAL aspect of the next civilization (although I'm not satisfied with that word; say, more supple). On the basis of this mobile civilization, architecture will, at least initially, be a means of experimenting with a thousand ways of modifying life, with a view to a mythic synthesis."*

(This extract, like them all, was uncredited – is it the Helmsman? – they had little respect for copyright. In fact, plagiarism was the whole of their credo.) They had feelings for science that were not reciprocated. If what I've heard is true – and I think it unlikely – there were people who would have liked them removed from the debate, even if they were the kind of people who would never overrule anything with more than the force of an argument.

But then a Canon here has been accused of espousing 'replacement theology' by The Spectator; it seems that the people in the congregation here have supplanted the Jews as God's chosen ones. I only buy it for the book reviews.

This city of E----- is the birthplace of the terribly unevenly-written Potter fantasies, their author, once a young student here, sending our university's professors scuffling across the pages of the local newspapers to press their claims as the model for this or that Hogwarts' alumnus. While none of them will discuss the real significance of the unsatisfactory Potter mythos: that the City of E----- is itself the model for a world divided violently between the boorishness of Privet Drive and the shadow of magic institutions behind a Brunel station facade. I begin to realise that there is far more to my old friend's notes than an artist's sick joke. If there is no historical substance to them, then in the workings of his guilty mind might he have constructed something far more revealing than the history of an anti-religion, anti-work, anti-family experimentalist movement? Rather, is it not the constitution, minutes, history and eschatology of the other side of the city? Behind the fascia? 'They' called it: disruptive geography.

The third of the documents is the least entertaining: a list of complaints against the ruling powers of the city and a fanciful description of the natural selection of ideas at work in the city – a mutating process infecting the city's postal minds. According to the document, it is a process controlled not by limitation, but by its opposite: fragmentation. With no direct competition of ideas, neither pit nor forum, but rather a commercial beauty parade of vehicles – bodies, objects, signs and buildings – government is run by the church of pyramidulation, an organising of ideas that has convinced itself across the parties, deftly outmanoeuvring the majorities and unions, perfecting the art of standing in all the political positions around their opponents, with the result that there is now a void at the heart of everything. But then there is so much more of everything now!

Despite the failure of the city to protect even its provincialism, and thanks to its lie to itself about its love for its past, the cult members seem to have convinced themselves that the solution to these problems, now globalised, lay in a benevolent walking. Their documents outline all sorts of unrealised plans – for customised tool kits with which to explore the city, for a tourism agency (f101), for publishing and for the uses of information technology. There are even plans to hold parties in overgrown gardens; but these were, according to their minutes, abandoned for fear of disturbing unseen wildlife: invisibility was of the highest priority for them. In an economy of spectacle, appearance denotes the fall of currency. Their plan to create a 'wilderness', to seal it, then publicise its existence but not its location, was possibly realised, but no one seems to have noticed. Equally, they may have held the festivals they planned, but if they did, they were all, consistent with their ideas, invisible.

Tourism as an organised agency is closely interwoven with militarism. (ffa) While war continues to supply the tourist industry with its scarce raw material (space made instant place: castles, battlefields, ghosts, memorials), it is also tourism's own history; tour-guiding's origins are among the bloody trinkets of the battlefield of Waterloo: "On the next morning we started for the scene of the celebrated battle of Waterloo, which had occurred about two months previously... Notwithstanding the lapse of time since which that battle had taken place considerable traces of it were still visible, particularly in the blood-stained walls and ruined, desolate, and half-consumed buildings of the keys of the position, Hougumont and La Haye Saint, and the remnants of the shakos, arms, and military clothing which strewed the field on all sides, and the fresh-made graves, where many thousand gallant fellows lay entombed. The whole field and neighbouring villages were crowded with guides to explain the different particulars of that memorable struggle,

f.101

223

and to sell the numerous articles which they had raked up from the field of battle; we bought some of these as mementoes, and wandered for hours over every part of this field of desolation, until we fancied that we had mastered every detail of the conflict, and were almost fit to take command of an army ourselves. We then returned to Brussels, highly gratified and instructed by the excursion." The Autobiography of Sir John Rennie, 1815

ff.a

This is a part of a far wider penetration of everyday life by the military and by the ideology of militarism, right into the heart of the mythogeographical 'drift': the marines at Lympstone Commando have a Parcours Club, adapting free-running to urban warfare, operating covertly on the streets of Exeter, tutored by EZ, Livewire, Sticky and Spidey as they practise their kongvaults and cranes.

John R. Stilgoe in Outside Lies Magic describes a monstrous pseudo-vehicle that is driven down emptied US freeways at night, testing the peripheries for any obstacle that might obstruct a landing B52.

And they are there in our fantasies, mistakes and imaginations: the Strategic Reserve, an assembly of steam locomotives mistakenly believed to have been gathered underground in the UK during the Second World War and never dispersed.

It was as if they imagined the city as a playground-jungle into which they could slip away, a factory to be occupied by utopian dreams, a rubbish heap to be reassembled by the wind: they knew they were trash. "What is needed is not a preservation of the past, but the redemption of past hopes." I would like to write that they were utopian, but their activities – if any of them are ever practised – are disruptive and nothing more. After hearing the unpleasant details of the pirate costuming, I paid a visit to the public lending library and there excavated from the subterranean pre-1950 Stack a battered copy of Arthur Machen's Things Near and Far:

> *"And here I would say that the matter of Wonder – that is the matter of the arts – is everywhere offered to us… And it is utterly true that he who cannot find wonder, mystery, awe, the sense of a new world and an undiscovered realm in the places by Gray's Inn Road will never find those secrets elsewhere, not in the heart of Africa…. "The matter of our work is everywhere present," wrote the old alchemists, and that is the truth. All the wonders lie within a stone's throw of King's Cross Station."*

But it was not everywhere. This Machen and his E----- disciples were deceived by each other. Why else would they seek out 'special' places – catapulting themselves blindfolded in taxis, leaping onto unfamiliar buses, in search of the concentrated meeting places of differences of time, culture, place, story? The maximum juxtaposition of difference was what they were after – seeking some grotesque and miscegenous intercourse of conflicting paradises. Ah, it is here they truly give themselves away, unable to sustain their beguiling with fiction, for the one and only time in all their documents they have recourse to theory. This is the first of two remaining scraps I have from these tell-tale passages:

> *"... in heterotopias, sites which contain many (all) other sites, highly finished, baroque and picturesque sites, a performance closer to "camouflage" is more appropriate to the practice of disruptive geography. Like transparency the intention is not to be absent, nor to disappear into the site, but... to create a fore-fronted association of the active performer with the memes that are in motion in and about the site."*

This was the price to be paid for their fairy tales. In among the notes, the postcard and various scraps that my former friend had included, there were, perhaps for the sake of authenticity, three cuttings, one of which (clearly the result of the mutilation of a bound book) was this:

> *Richard Ford (1796-1858) born in L----- and trained as a lawyer. In his early thirties, he moved to Spain, where he travelled extensively, particularly in Andalucia. These journeys resulted in his 'Handbook for Travellers in Spain', first published in 1845, of which it was said on his death, that* "so great a literary achievement had never before been performed under so humble a title." *Ford was not the first Englishman to have written about Spain, particularly the Moorish part, but* "he is the first to have explored it in such depth and to have approached its inhabitants with such sympathy". *On his return from Spain in 1834, Ford bought H-------- House in the City of E-----, which he rebuilt in the Andalusian style (see accompanying photographs). Unfortunately, a housing estate was built on the gardens in 1949, and the house itself, a rare example of the influence of Islamic art on British architecture, and the only example of its kind in the S----W---, was demolished in the 1960s.*

"I have included this as a warning," my friend the traitor said. He finished his pint, leaving the glass on the cellar floor, and that is the last I saw of him, or wish to. There were no accompanying photographs.

Idiots! What of the R--------- Hotel at P------- ? Or was this a provocation? A sign to those who might know that they should seek out the discretely signposted tunnel from the hotel bar, follow its long white tube, encrusted with sea slaters and chitons, through its sound chambers, to the seas? To what end?

Even those who supported their 'walks' apparently spoke of "mad" or "mystic" or "diverting" journeys. It is clear from their terse replies that the cult members understood just how dangerous the label of 'eccentricity' would be if they allowed it to be hung around their pretty necks. My former friend had thrown in some of these emails. I tried sending messages of enquiry to the various e addresses, but they were all returned with this:

> *This message was created automatically by mail delivery software (Exim).*
> *A message that you sent could not be delivered to one or more of its*
> *recipients. This is a permanent error. The following address(es) failed:*

Even their supporters had disappeared, if they had ever existed. Perhaps it was in the failures of this group, that the author/s intended their message to reside; a cautionary toolbox, not an exemplary journey. A kit of reprimands for a psychic-Leninism?

I began to walk the streets, to see if I could detect any remnant of their walking still practised. At first I was overwhelmed – I realised how little I had walked in the city and, when I did, how little had I looked. They had been (almost certainly uninvited) borrowers from the Hindu practice of 'darshan', best described as "exchanging gazes with divinity... the individual acquires the capacity to see themselves as the deity sees them." Their deity was the site, their gazing a way of re-imagining themselves through the 'eyes' of the places where they gathered. This passage on 'darshan', was the only one on which my former friend made any detailed comment. He had, apropos of nothing, raised the subject in a conversation at my room a week or so before our cellar assignation. Although he had said nothing about an organisation of walking, he had expressed the opinion that "dilettantes" climbing on optic bandwagons were "more likely influenced by Hollywood than Hinduism". I should have known then what was coming.

This, then, apparently, is their theology:

They believe in the potency of the uncanny. The pre-1950 Stack gave up another archaeological find, like the Machen volume, this book's date slip indicated regular withdrawals through the late 1990s: Kierkegaard's The Concept of Dread. When I asked one of the librarians if she could remember who might have withdrawn these two books, she laughed, which I found sinister. Shorn of its associations with the Fall, sin and redemption, Dread had become a usable tool for them, a way of touching with the feelings, as 'darshan' the eyes, or as Hitchcock the movies. Again, the Fat Boy. Pan-ic, that combination of excitement and running away recounted in a series of letters in editions of the F------ T---- throughout the late 1990s, the meeting with everything (else), ready, waiting: "the reality of freedom as possibility anterior to possibility... the reflex of freedom within itself at the thought of its own immense possibility... the alarming possibility of being able. What is it he is able to do, of that he has no conception... there is only the possibility of being able… he loves it and he flees from it…. The egoistic infinity of possibility, which does not tempt like a definite choice but alarms and fascinates with sweet anxiety…" Here was the opposite of that foolish titillation of tourist trade ghosts – surely the withdrawals were theirs! This is the haunting of the nothing that is their future, they have achieved their possibility: disappearing in Technicolor!

Could I do as they did? Find the uncanny in a church with a 'for sale' sign. Travel out with estate agents in Dread: fascinated and anxious, just surrendering to all that possibility? The deconsecrating of orthodoxy re-opening the space for awe, for the sublime, for an expanding nothing? The suspiciously grassy path, the alchemical stone grapes:

> *A slug god, huge and a treacly black, creeps over the stones of a gelatinous family of former human matter in the cut ground. A god that puckers to the human touch. An intelligence unlike that of a father, but like everything else. The empty church: looking so regular, except in the details.*

> *It already felt like it might be a psychogeographic hub: the crossroads with the old red telephone box and adverts for bus services and an orchestral concert in E-----h, the vintage Jaguar dealers, the house, the bus shelter a mossy shell and the church with a 'for sale' sign leaning across its gate, the metal spike raw and exposed. A potent absurdity: the church, permanently locked, the paths becoming retaken by grass. Henry Ford and Herr Diesel, General Motors and Dunlop are gods here. History not two thousand, but less than a hundred years of bunk: in the orientalist form of Jaguars and their struggle for immortality against rust. S----- walked ahead, up the suspiciously untrodden grassy path, past a large, ominous, garish bush, him like a disappearing Kim Novak. We began to feel the beginning of that feeling. The purple flowers and the not-quite-right Templar crosses on the ridges of the church roof in the not-quite-right light. Insincere, was it? A------ spotted the large black god-slug sliding itself along the gravestones of a family of Sluggetts. In the porch, tucked into the eaves, S---- found fragments of the electoral register.*

> *Was it already de-consecrated? How can they do that when the dead are still here? A purple flowering bush hums like a radio full of bees. Grapes in stone on the porch. "Blue apples". Honey. Gold. Alchemy. Is it so easy to turn off the energy of this place? Just close it down? With what consequences? How many things have been worshipped here? And turning it off: what is blacked out? What disorder, what incivility to*

*corpses? Turning back just before the gate, the purple bush seems
to have darkened now, even more libidinous and looming. It has
closed across the path. Something we haven't seen has been hidden.
Unhomely, because there is possibility now. The shutting of this is
the opening of 'everything else'. This is the uncanny of the attraction
of lanes that bend round to what? Hollow lanes that turn into shadow.*

*"...anxiety(dread)... should not be confused with emotions like fear,
which have a definite object and are typically directed to things or
occurrences in the outside world; by contrast, it (dread) is said to be
related to 'something that is nothing' and to represent 'freedom's
activity as the possibility of possibility'" (Kierkegaard, The Concept of Anxiety)*

*This is Pan-ic, the crossroads where every road looks just as good as
any other, the woods where there comes the sound of pipes or
amplified insects: later when we walk for maybe thirty minutes or
more through unchanging terrain – the imaginary possibility of
walking in circles. I know from race-walking that one of my feet
is set in the ankle at a wider angle than the other. I've read
Stephen King's The Girl Who Loved Tom Gordon.*

That is the second of the three scraps.

I have started reading some of these books now. It is no coincidence that whatever they quote
from is available from the modest public library here. All of them regularly withdrawn from the
mid-90s onwards, most of them brought up from underground. My days of complacent reading
are over. The gothic tales I have so enjoyed for thirty years no longer satisfy me. I have begun to
live them. My reading is now driven by date stamps rather than subjects. I feel my old pleasures
as the forces of their disruptive geography. These people are vampires. For god's sake, let's get
this finished and be gone.

This is the third and last fragment of the notes that survived them:

*Reminiscent of I--- C---------'s plan for a dimly lit Sinister Quarter in
his imagined city, B... L......., essayist and Goth, critiques the
"wide-scale denial of the darker aspects of life within Western
industrial culture... as though sickness, death and pain have all
been whisked away from popular culture... (a) current I like to call
"artificial brightness" ... certainly contestable... best viewed as a
current rather than a unifying whole." This "artificial brightness"*

functions as an attractive vehicle of imitation for the purveyance of global capitalism's memes, as people give up their superior local cuisine for sugared bun-sized aspirations.

Night time or day-for-night game-playing along the marks and lines of past designs still remaining in the landscape ("… the baroque stage of urbanism considered as a means of knowledge"), contestants play with manuals, kit bags, tools, costumes – could serve to tear through the artificial brightness as the Devil's Footprints of 1855 cut through the contesting theologies in Debord, melting snow and natural history and then freezing again.

While Gothic contains its own contradictory tendencies – including a necrophiliac rejoicing in the reduction of living beings to inanimate and rotting "thingness" and a politics of artificial darkness practised by "human dust" celebrating servitude and self-abnegation that can spill over into a racist self-pity – there is a progressive Gothic that looks to the sublime in its resistance to the artificially bright.

As necrophilia is a 'dead end', so is the absolutism of Futurists, the Manichaean politics that divides the world in two – not for nothing was Debord an avid mis-reader of Norman Cohn's The Pursuit of the Millennium. As we all were. I would prefer to work on the basis of a profound ambiguity in the physical construct of the modern (thirty to fifty thousand year old) human mind, in which specialised areas have collapsed into a single, cathedral-like structure in which thinking about, and memories of, animal behaviour, sexual desire, shaping of inanimate tools, etc. interact directly with each other, creating the fluid and synthesising modern mind that has among its many capacities the facility for metaphor and the reducing of other human beings to the status of objects. This is far more than an ideological contradiction, but a physical one, which places art and genocide in the same human vocabulary, while predetermining us to neither. Given this ambiguity in the modern human mind, rather than the Hegelian "pure negation" of the situationists, we should be seizing on the opportunities for contradictions, deferred.

Bachelard, despite, or perhaps because of his idealism (quoting approvingly the 18th century delusion that various fossilised animals were antecedents of organs of the human body and declaring that "every form retains life, and a fossil is not merely a being that once lived, but one that is still alive, asleep in its form"), writes of animal/human hybrids: "these extravagant figures… come alive in the dialectics of what is hidden and what

is manifest." He writes of "human heads...attached directly to
molluscs", an animal type he categorises as dialectical: "the part
that comes out (of its shell) contradicts the part that remains inside..."
Bachelard does not restrict himself to an inside/outside dialectic,
but continues on with "half dead, half alive and, in extreme cases,
half stone, half man". (f102) While Bachelard's method is cluttered
by his idealism and his formalism, his syntheses of intimate spaces
and human/animal/object hybrids may help us to utilise some
basic physical properties of the modern human mind while engaging
with the inside/outside of particular sites.

This, I think, is conclusive proof, that my first and second sources were working in cahoots; the traitor a stooge for the mothman, or whatever he was, smuggling his own miscegeny into this miscellany, his giant, transparent, arthropod form trembling with a paranoid 'dread'-longing for the ultra-sensitivity of giant see-through human-Martians; (f103) another of those stupid anti-human myths. We never needed the help of aliens to make a mess of things; this world is entirely our own work! Stupid waste of time! They do my work for me.

It is here – in bringing together in a single intellectual territory the idealist synthesising (molluscs, human heads and stones) of Bachelard and the esoteric materialism (red stones/philosopher's stone) of ur-psychogeographic walker Arthur Machen, that a tendency in disruptive geography can contest the "thingness", the "idealism" of "site". Deploying a neo-symbolist process – based on an understanding of the 'modern' human mind as physically evolved to synthesise its specialist thinkings about human, animal and inanimate behaviours and qualities in one overarching cathedral-like structure – in which associations are "floated free" from the site in physical 'figures' of movement, dissident routes, and disruptive maps and then juxtaposed in ways that express the invisible orbiting of ideas about the site. Making the inside outside and vice versa. This can escape psychological performance when the map-makers', performers' or guides' associations are kept to themselves, making inside what is explicit in naturalism, making outside what psychoanalysis has confined to the private.

Just as the mountain is migrant, so is the Self that passes through it – the mountain and the Self, the meeting of two migrations. Disruptive geographies can express their motion, disrupt it and... the rest is for reverse archaeological practice not for manifestos.

f.102   *The Poetics of Space, Gaston Bachelard.*

Reference to communist sci fi writer Olaf Stapledon's 1930s novels Last and First Men *and* Last Men In London. *f.103*

"Do the rich and the poor inhabit the same city?" In the city of E----- they do, for it is not a large city. Etiquette still holds some significance for us. And then again: "is a city that is so filled with difference, also, therefore filled with fear?" I have always been afraid of going "out". I have always preferred my room and my books to public places. But my geography has been disrupted by theirs. I feel anxiety, even dread now, but no longer fear. I have swapped my worries for something worse; the default mode of their geography is a kind of paranoia, an ultra-sensitivity, like that of the giant transparent-skinned human-Martian hybrids swinging around London in mono-human guise. I have become caught in the swell. Twice, now, I have remembered sites that presented me with explosives: first, as a child, digging up an unexploded WW2 anti-aircraft shell on a building site, and the second, sitting down opposite a terrorist bomb in the foyer of a theatre. Each time I loved it and ran away. Now I wish to stay present and anonymous – like the statue in Budapest, extravagantly relaxed, about to become anonymous. They are getting to me! I have begun to read their canon: Machen's 'The London Adventure or The Art of Wandering', Sinclair's 'Lights Out For The Territory', 'The Lost World' by Arthur Conan Doyle, Alfred Kubin's 'The Other Side', 'Severin's Journey Into The Dark' by Paul Leppin, Gustav Meyrink's 'The Golem', 'The Magician's Garden' of Géza Csáth. But mainly it is movies – gleaned from various channels. Hitchcock's erotic skylines in 'Vertigo', giant trees to coolly disappear into. 'Daleks, Invasion Earth 2150 AD' – trauma opening up the buildings of the city, producers who had lived through the Blitz, exposing the fragility of intimacies, making everything political because changeable. Over the peeled city the Dalek craft hovers, and, despite its similarity to a cooking utensil, seems capable of investing any urban landscape or holiday coastline with sublime dread. 'Hue and Cry' – an Ealing comedy drama directed by Charles Crichton, adventures and chases through bomb-damaged buildings in late 1940s London. On re-watching this I realise I saw this as a child and had somehow mis-interpreted it as a narrative of post-nuclear holocaust. I realise why; since my childhood, the few remaining bomb craters and war-ruined houses have become less the relics of war, and more the omens of the coming devastation.

I have begun to get out more often. I have begun to 'drift' in the city. I have become more awed, more paranoid, more dreading, more anxious, less scared.

I have visited the Cathedral Close again. In the hope of finding an explanation: but I felt like James Stewart dragging Kim Novak about that Spanish Mission. Struggling to dress her in a costume that would make sense. I had imagined that, with my new way of looking, I could transform the ambient couplings of fiction, crime, haunting, burial and ecclesia into a situation. But the damp of the cellar was malevolent, the chatter of tourists irritating and the cathedral itself mute and bestial. I returned to my room to finish this.

Though I would not have completed it, but for a quite unexpected visit. A young Indian man of my acquaintance had returned from Mysore anxious to pour out some of what had happened to him. At first I did not recognize him against the dull brown light of the corridor. His long black hair was mostly gone, shorn in a ceremony that he did name, and that I understood was "like a marriage". I could hardly listen to what he said for I seemed to understand too much, each heavy word so full of portent and importance. Each sentence I have since struggled to put back together, but such was the escalation of meaning with each succeeding word… He had been initiated as a Brahmin, met his teacher, a boy of eight years of age, participated in the ritual washing of the statue of the God Shiva and … his mobile phone rang, he really would have to go in two minutes… I urgently asked him about "darshan" and for a moment he did not recognize the word from my pronunciation. I began to explain, wondering if it were but an insignificant part of the rituals, perhaps defunct. "Ah, 'darshan'!" And, without openly correcting me, he began to describe the real 'darshan', then: "I hadn't thought of describing it before," he said. He scratched at where his pony tail had been and scraped his chair back. I rose with him, questioning him all the way down the corridor and out onto the street. When he had gone I suddenly feared that the room would be sealed up and I would be unable to write this down.

I had been forgetting the most important thing in the theology: hence this visit. Of course, I have always been aware of the power of the auteur, obsessive, subjective, part of machine technology and the bureaucratic assembling of things. Present in the smallest of things and yet in all things. In Hollywood only the Fat Boy ever truly created that dizziness that is Pan-ic. And then only in one film did he sustain it. Pan-ic: the love that sends folk running down hollow lanes and from sublime spots. Not much older than a child I had experienced my own journey, like a marriage. Since then I had never felt the need for another marriage of any kind. I had read 'The Great God Pan' by Arthur Machen, (yes, he was known to me, before) remembering the machinery of its smoke and mirrors, on re-reading it I found that there was neither smoke nor mirror. I was frightened out of my skin. When the artist calls upon the god I had imagined looking on Him. Of becoming changed not just by Him, but just by looking on Him. And, as I closed the partition to the light of the corridor, I had to lean against the disappearing frame for I was, at last, beginning to dimly understand what the church of pyramidulation might not like about this group of artists dedicated to opening the eyes of others to those places personified in Machen's frightful tea-stained words: those ambient roundabouts, those wormholes, those genuinely haunted and meticulous places. What the effect might be upon the subjects of the City of E----- if that dread anxiety, that nothing in the future, that reflex of freedom within itself at the awful prospect of its own possibility, were to be let loose through the Other's eyes. Selves migrant, subjects "just passing through"; wandering bishops, Episcopi Vagrantes, stealing away the charisma of the establishment under their very fabricated copes. In the face of everything else, gazing on the eyes of those who are both good and evil, becoming aware of those eyes inside the cathedral confusion of their modern minds: Hitchcock, Pan, Long John Silver…

The City of E----- lies near the coast, connected by waterways, its centre hollow with underground passages, once carrying water for the Roman military and later for the Christian clergy. In the 1830s the city's workers buried hundreds of their neighbours in B--- M-------, victims of cholera in the water. Now its water is an attraction of the city. The sea horse collection, though, departed for the rival city of P--------. And according to the minutes of the last meeting of the movement – at least those for which I had any documentation, if real documentation is what it is – they were mapping the water, they were going to do something. The city officials had granted a request for permission to "walk on the water", on condition that the group dress as pirates for the entertainment of the city's children. I am writing this as if someone sat behind me with a raised cutlass.

It is now some eight hours since my young friend from India left me. I have been looking at this screen for most of the last four hours, unable to write. I have written as much as I can and recorded here all the documentation that remains in my foolish, lazy, and careless self-possession. I must go out and walk.

A.J. Salmon *

* Publishers' Note: An "A. J. Salmon" appeared as 12th man on numerous team sheets and in the prefects' detention book of a Midlands (now former) grammar school; but his name does not appear in the official records of the school's pupils.

this and so could not be fully understood by mortals.

★ ★ ★

YOU ARE NOT MORTAL THEN? NOT EVEN ANY PART OF YOU?

None at all.

★ ★ ★

HAVE YOU GOT LEGS? WE NEVER SEE THEM?

I am of the mists. The mist does not need legs and travels quicker without them. But when I wish to materialise and be recognised I have legs if I want legs. But I am told my walk is not convincing, I still tend to drift. I hope it's not ugly.

★ ★ ★

I'M SURE NOTHING MISTY DID WOULD EVER BE UGLY. WHAT FOOD DO YOU EAT, THEN?

None. Any more than mists need food. Water, however, I do require. Indeed there was once a time when I . . . but, no . . .

★ ★ ★

Appendix 2: Description of a Drunk Dérive

29.11.03: the Constitution of Wrights & Sites insists that alcohol be consumed during business meetings. It had been a good meeting - laying out the basic shape for progress towards a 'generic' Mis-Guide - after getting home I realised I was in no fit state to go to bed and needed a constitutional. At the bottom of Danes Road I paused to decide which way to go - I was thinking graph like, with the dip down into town and its granular uncertainties, the unappealing rise towards Stoke Hill and the hard-to-escape self-parodic grids of suburban roads. I recalled a conversation with Stephen about the private road beyond Taddyforde Gate and how I'd never been down there. I set off along the prison wall, the softness of the unfinished castle on my other side. Wild voices in a nearby street speeded my unsteady step. Stumbling past the Imperial and Thornlea I approached the Gate under a dread tunnel of tree roof and ivy - mundane when viewed from a car, on foot the passage on this night glowed green and slippery, silvery fishes of light squirming about in it. The world was beginning to liquefy, becoming part of my extended organism. But I was having to keep a part of me sharp so I didn't mesh with a car. Nothing coming and I ran across the wet road and through the dried blood sandstone Gate in which it is said is buried the body of one of the Kingdons (Iron Sam, I think) who gave Clifford his middle name.

There was a shapely noticeboard on the right: "Our vandal now entertains himself not by smashing the glass, but stealing the notices. There are some sad people about." This was the only notice. The sheet of wood to which it was attached rippled with dampness. A wave passed through me. I stumbled down the incline. A turning to the right and I thought I saw a kind of a dread place overgrown. It was at the end of a cold/cosy road among a ruin of shrubs. A boat named Cho Cho San. A house called The Chalet. I struggled through tall stems and slipped in the mud, leant against an ivy-scarred brick wall that was like the sucker-torn head of a Sperm Whale. The ground fell away, 40 feet straight down, a wire mesh fence wrapped somewhere inside a low wall of vegetation, but I could not quite see it, nor where exactly the ground gave way to emptiness. Be careful... On one side of me were ruins of garden furniture, then a stock of maybe twenty long sticks leant against an out building, a snap of cast iron guttering. I'm on a cluttered platform, out beyond the fence of furze there are long stems with heads full of seeds, and 40 feet below is the railway, the level crossing and the ends of the platforms of St David's Station; a burger van, doing quiet trade, is suddenly surrounded by two vanloads of police in yellow and black, fluorescent wasps cluttering. Once served, they stand, clumped, the groups not changing, for maybe half an hour as I watch unseen – the women with their hair pulled back. A city peaceful enough for the police to be redundant at 1.30am. Two trains cross – a sleeper and a freight train. I lean against the wall and the dampness spins around, the seeds swirl, I finger the ivy scars but I can't focus on them for long. One copper breaks away to speak to three lads sitting on a metal crash barrier – they slope off towards Exwick, the policeman pretending not to hear their impotent complaints. I stumble on something like a dog bowl. I can feel the vertigo kicking in. Sobering down a tube in the city. A pipette. Once stabbed in the leg with one of those, the cul-de-sac scar. Now, I'm hovering on a wound, an escarpment, a telescope, suspended over cops and burgers, a black and yellow calmness, their policed hair. I come away.

I went home. Past an edifice of chimney, like a meaty gravestone. Past the noticeboard, full of possibility. Back out under the Corpse-Gate.

I began the year seeking Z worlds with others. I ended my year's walking, thinking undersea, trying to plait ropes from water, to align fluid patterns of a walking consciousness with patterns in motion everywhere else. Would any of this even be substantial enough to register on the radar?

"Here I go again. Here I go... (pause)… again. Yeh!"   Tuung Good Arrows

Panography (Just The Gems)

The following 'biblio/filmo/discography', 'panography', 'reading/viewing list' or 'passport to virtual perambulation' is an incomprehensive, possibly incomprehensible one, chosen according to mythogeographical criteria from various reading lists in circulation among the walking cults.

Some inclusions are 'classics', familiar to anyone who knows the field superficially; these are perhaps unhelpful repetitions, but this is not an idiosyncratic list. If any of the entries is obscure, that was not a factor in its selection. Perhaps few of those who are familiar with psychogeography or aesthetic walking will have heard of Jon Downes, but his work is included here because of its exemplarily multiple layering – autobiographical, Fortean, crypto-zoological, historiographical, folklorist. Likewise, Gustav Meyrink. Deploying a wildly different, but perhaps even broader set of layers, Maureen Stone is included for her testing of a multiplicitous world against its walking. Susan Blackmore for the fabulous parabola described in her writings, from her early parapsychological experiments and their dead end, through memetics and Consciousness Studies to Zen. For its social and corporeal (almost anatomical) prolixity a 'cheap' horror movie, Higuchinsky's Uzumaki, exceeds in mytho-geographical force Tarkovsky's Stalker. So criteria are suitably, picturesquely, uneven: these are not the lists of 'renaissance' folk, though they have eclectic interests, but what characterises their lists is a resistance to the organic and their capacity to execute the corner of change.

Some otherwise useful sources (Solnit's Wanderlust perhaps outstanding) have been excluded for crimes against the dérive. Yes, it is borrowed without permission (isn't that the whole point of détournement?), no, it is not plagiarised flâneurie. (Mythogeography's problem with flâneurs is that they require the city and its crowds for their reveries and, yet, in every other respect, keep themselves aloof from them.) No place either for Perec's Species of Spaces, due to his lack of respect for the potency of nothingness.

So, these are just the gems. (Fine books and films mentioned in the texts above are not always repeated here.)

Mythogeography

www.mythogeography.com   (there you will find: this panography online with direct links to each 'gem'; a Starter Kit for drifters, a mythogeography archive of texts and performances; music to drift to; World Brains; how to get in touch; how to order the Economical or the Lovely editions of this book.)

Uzumaki (dir. Higuchinsky)
Black Woman Walking Maureen Stone
The Owlman & Others Jon Downes
The Rising of the Moon Jon Downes & Nigel Wright
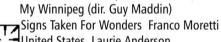TechGnosis Erik Davies
Outside Lies Magic John R. Stilgoe
The Cremaster Cycle Matthew Barney
The Parallax View Slavoj Žižek
Exploration Fawcett Col. P. H. Fawcett
In Search of the Light Susan Blackmore
The Meme Machine Susan Blackmore
Wisconsin Death Trip (dir. James Marsh)
My Winnipeg (dir. Guy Maddin)
Signs Taken For Wonders Franco Moretti
United States Laurie Anderson
The paintings of Kenny Scharf
The Collected Books of Charles Fort Charles Fort
The Invention of Hugo Carnet Brian Selznick
The Common Sense of the Exact Sciences William Kingdon Clifford
The Prehistory of The Mind Steven Mithen
The Extended Organism J. Scott Turner
Wax: The Discovery of Television by the Bees (dir. David Blair)
Tiny Colour Movies John Foxx
DW 8, DW 15, DW 3 Bernhard Lang
Alice In Sunderland Bryan Talbot

City of Women (dir. Federico Fellini)
A Mis-Guide To Anywhere Wrights & Sites
Marginalien Alan Halsey

Taxonomies

Codex Seraphianus Luigi Serafini
The Museum of Lost Wonder Jeff Hoke
Les Elemens Jean Féry Rebel
World Brain H. G. Wells
"Visions of Xanadu: Paul Otlet (1868-1944) and Hypertext," W. Boyd Rayward in Journal of the
American Society for Information Science vol. 45
The M5 Sights Guide Mike Jackson
An Anecdoted Topography of Chance Daniel Spoerri

Activism

"The public art we make of ourselves in the street… (is) either participatory or resistant."
off the map   hib & kika

Goat Island School Book 2
T.A.Z. Hakim Bey
The Situationist International: A User's Guide Simon Ford
The Fluxus Workbook
<yellow>Rhythms Eyal Weizman
Nato's Secret Armies Daniele Ganser
Mental Speed Bumps David Engwicht
The Yes Men (dir. Chris Smith, Dan Ollman & Sarah Price)
13 Experiments In Hope (dir. various)
Access All Areas: a user's guide to the art of urban exploration Ninjalicious
Visions of the City David Pinder
Exit Utopia: Architectural Provocations, 1956-76 (ed. Martin van Schaik & Otaker Máčel)
The J Street Project Susan Hiller
They Kay Dick
The Coming Insurrection The Invisible Committee (especially pages 97-102)
Paris Nous Appartient (dir. Jacques Rivette)
The Lonely Planet Guide To Experimental Travel Rachael Antony & Joel Henry
Souvenirs Michael Hughes
Dream Stephen Duncombe
Hollow Land Eyal Weizman

Tribulation 99 (dir. Chris Baldwin)
Spectres of the Spectrum (dir. Chris Baldwin)
The Posthuman Dada Guide Andrei Codrescu
Traité De Bave Et D'Éternité (dir. Isidore Isou)

Everyday

Journey To The Lower World Marcus Coates
Hello World: travels in virtuality Sue Thomas
Mundane Journeys: field guide to colour Kate Pocrass
Culture Is Everywhere Victor Margolin & Patty Carroll
Little People In The City: the street art of Slinkachu
The Wisdom of Crowds James Surowiecki
Perform Every Day Joshua Sofaer

Space

The Dreamer's Perambulator Raimi Gbadamosi
For Space Doreen Massey
Flatland Edwin A. Abbott
Projected Cities Stephen Barber
The Saragossa Manuscript (dir. Wojciech Has)
Snakes & Ladders Alan Moore & Tim Perkins
The Other Side Arthur Kubin
Manufactured Landscapes (dir. Jennifer Baichwal)
Last Year in Marienbad (dir. Alain Resnais)
The Man From London (dir. Béla Tarr)
A Snowglobe Christmas (dir. Ron Ranson, Jr)
Dark Skies Map Ordnance Survey
The Life of Space Maurice Maeterlinck
Ecstacity Nigel Coates

Place

Nadja André Breton
Paris Peasant Louis Aragon
Hidden City (dir. Stephen Poliakoff)

Place Tacita Dean & Jeremy Millar
Hue and Cry (dir. Charles Crichton)
The Stone Library Alyson Hallett
Séance at Hobs Lane Mount Vernon Arts Lab
The Highbury Working Alan Moore & Tim Perkins
Rodinsky's Room Rachel Lichtenstein & Iain Sinclair
18 Folgate Street Denis Severs
The City Formerly Known As Cambridge The Institute For Infinitely Small Things
The Village That Died For England Patrick Wright
The Alien World: The Complete Illustrated Guide Steven Eisler
An Exeter Mis-Guide Wrights & Sites
Chicago Adam Broomberg & Oliver Chanarin
Lights Out For The Territory Iain Sinclair
Roma (dir. Federico Fellini)
Akira (dir. Katsuhiro Otomo)
The Quiet Earth (dir. Geoff Murphy)
Essences of London (dir. Curious)
I, City Pavel Brycz
Destination Nowhere Roger Green
Come on feel the ILLINOISE Sufjan Stevens
Isolarian: A Different Oxford Journey James Attlee

Dérive

Guy Debord Andy Merrifield
Metromarxism Andy Merrifield
The Game of War Andrew Hussey
The Tribe Jean-Michel Mension
Occasional Sights – a London guidebook of missed opportunities and things that aren't always
there Anna Best
Drift: An Unguided Tour of Exeter (dir. Clive Austin)
The Theory of the Dérive Guy Debord
Robinson In Space (dir. Patrick Keiller)
MonsterHunter Jonathan Downes
A Formulary For A New Urbanism Gilles Ivain / Ivan Chtcheglov
The Brave One (dir. Neil Jordan)
June 8, 1968 (dir. Philippe Parreno)
Colquhoun's Peripatetic Randomiser Jim Colquhoun

Myth

The Zombie Survival Guide Max Brooks
The Air Loom Gang Mike Jay
How To Survive A Robot Uprising Daniel Wilson
Yokai Attack: The Japanese Monster Survival Guide Hiroko Yoda, Matt Alta & Tatsya Morino
Stalker (dir. Andrei Tarkovsky)
Maldoror Comte de Lautréamont (trans. Alexis Lykiard)
Axël Villiers De L'Isle-Adam
Captain Britain and MI:13 Paul Cornell & Leonard Kirk
Marvel Zombies (ignore the sequels) Robert Kirkman, Sean Phillips & Arthur Suydam
Father Ernetti's Chronovisor: The Creation and Disappearance of the World's First Time Machine
Peter Krassa
The Girard Reader René Girard
Dreams of the Rarebit Fiend Winsor McCay
Necronauts Gordon Rennie & Frazer Irving
Elmer McCurdy: The Life And Afterlife Of An American Outlaw Mark Svenvold
My Dinner With André (dir. Louis Malle)
Alphaville (dir. Jean-Luc Godard)
The Werckmeister Harmonies (dir. Béla Tarr)
Yella (dir. Christian Petzold)

Deep Water (dir. Louise Osmand & Jerry Rothwell)
Diary of an Amateur Photographer Graham Rawle
Strange Attractor Journals 1 – 3 ed. Mark Pilkington
Prehistoric London: Its Mounds and Circles E. O. Gordon
God In Us Anthony Freeman
The Hollywood History of the World George MacDonald Fraser
Uzumaki (vols. 1-3) Junji Ito (Unlike the movie version, in which an ecstatic eye is prised free
of its ruling organism, the manga Uzumaki is about an emergent pattern, a model for an
incremental Drift, a movement of sleeper cells that can spiral out of (anyone's) control. See The
Eye and the Cell, page 163 and Patterns of Patterns, page 174. It isn't time yet, but one day this
is all, thankfully, that need remain (if anything remains) of Mythogeography.)
Perséphone (dir. Luc de Heusch)
Metamorphoses Ovid (trans. Arthur Golding)

Walking

The Road To Damascus August Strindberg
You – The City Fiona Templeton
Walkscapes Francesco Careri
The Rings of Saturn W. G. Sebald
The Pedestrian Ray Bradbury
Pride and Prejudice With Zombies Jane Austen & Seth Grahame-Smith
The Walking Dead Robert Kirkman
Romantic Writing and Pedestrian Travel Robin Jarvis
Man On Wire (dir. James Marsh)
The London Adventure or The Art of Wandering Arthur Machen
Things Near and Far Arthur Machen
Bas Jan Ader: In Search of the Miraculous Jan Verwoert
Wild Pilgrimage Lynd Ward
Shank's Pony Morris Marples
Walking, Writing and Performance: Autobiographical Texts by Deirdre Heddon, Carl Lavery & Phil Smith (ed. Roberta Mock)
The Gentle Art of Walking Geoffrey Murray
The Gentle Art of Tramping Stephen Graham
The Walk: Notes On A Romantic Image Jeffrey C. Robinson
"There" by Phil Smith in Focus On Farmers (ed. Jennie Hayes)
"Inside The Darkness Outside" by Phil Smith in walkwalkwalk: stories from the Exeter archive
The Long Walk Stephen King
Monograph Janet Hand & Tim Brennan
Industrial Ruins Tim Edensor
Walk Don't Walk (dir. Thomas Struck)
Path Without Destination Satish Kumar

Stalking

Unrequited Love (dir. Chris Petit)
Unrequited Love Gregory Dart
Double Game Sophie Calle
Come This Way Jean Baudrillard
Confessions of An English Opium-Eater Thomas De Quincey
Following (dir. Christopher Nolan)
Politique des Zombies: L'Amérique selon George A. Romero (coordonné par Jean-Baptiste Thoret)

Nomadism

The Changes Trilogy Peter Dickinson

Neo-Symbolism

The Floating Islands Eugenio Barba
Petersburg Andrei Bely
The Order (dir. Matthew Barney)
World Without Words Michael Evamy
The Golem Gustav Meyrink
Absolute Wilson (dir. Katherina Otto)
Opium Geza Csáth
The Ghost Orchid – An Introduction to EVP

Performance

Theatre/Archaeology Mike Pearson & Michael Shanks
Perform Jens Hoffmann & Joan Jonas
Pranks 2 (ed. V. Vale)
Grapefruit Yoko Ono
Archaeology in Reverse Stephen Gill
Red Psalm (dir. Miklós Jancsó)
Tumbleweed In London (dir. Claire Blundell Jones & Ed Hartwell)
Seven Walks Francis Alÿs
The Mysteries of Harris Burdick (Portfolio Version) Chris Van Allsburg
Walking To Work Simon Whitehead
Guidebook: three manoeuvres Tim Brennan
Our Hitler: a film from Germany (dir. Hans-Jürgen Syberberg)
99 Ways To Tell a Story: Exercises in Style Matt Madden
Drama Queens Tim Etchells et al
The Travels Forced Entertainment

Patterns

Consciousness Susan Blackmore
Stripsody Cathy Berberian
House of Leaves Mark Z. Danielewski
Haunted Poe
The Phenomenon of Life Hans Jonas
Der Lauf Der Dinge (dir. Peter Fischli & David Weiss)
The paintings of Pam Longobardi
The Complex: How The Military Invades Our Everyday Lives Nick Turse
Dark City, Light City Michèle Roberts & Carol Robertson
The Self-Made Tapestry: pattern formation in nature Philip Ball
Atlas of the European Novel 1800-1900 Franco Moretti
Hypnerotomachia Poliphili: The Strife of Love in a Dream (trans. Joscelyn Godwin) (see The Real Sign of Four, Joscelyn Godwin)
Rhythms of Vision Lawrence Blair
The Byrom Collection and the Globe Theatre Mystery Joy Hancox